AF737915

The Foundations of Financial Management

The Foundations of Financial Management

D. Pitt Francis

BA MSc (Econ) ACCA

Senior Lecturer in Accounting and Finance, Middlesex Polytechnic

Pitman Publishing

First published 1973

Sir Isaac Pitman and Sons Ltd
Pitman House, Parker Street, Kingsway, London WC2B 5PB
PO Box 46038, Portal Street, Nairobi, Kenya

Sir Isaac Pitman (Aust) Pty Ltd
Pitman House, 158 Bouverie Street, Carlton, Victoria 3053, Australia

Pitman Publishing Company SA Ltd
PO Box 11231, Johannesburg, South Africa

Pitman Publishing Corporation
6 East 43rd Street, New York, NY 10017, USA

Sir Isaac Pitman (Canada) Ltd
495 Wellington Street West, Toronto 135, Canada

The Copp Clark Publishing Company
517 Wellington Street West, Toronto 135, Canada

© D Pitt Francis 1973

ISBN *Cased edition:* 0 273 31692 3
Paperback edition: 0 273 31702 4

This book may not be lent, re-sold, hired out or otherwise disposed of by way of trade in any form of binding or cover other than that in which it is published without the prior consent of the publishers.

Text set in 11/12 pt. Monotype Bembo, printed by letterpress,
and bound in Great Britain at The Pitman Press, Bath
G3 (B758/1049:46)

Preface

The Foundations of Financial Management is an attempt to present the basic concepts of financial management in a simple form. The reader is presumed to have no more than an elementary knowledge of economics and mathematics, but is nevertheless introduced to the kind of material which forms part of finance courses and examinations.

The book should be of direct help to Higher National Certificate and Higher National Diploma students; to University and CNAA undergraduates reading for BA degrees in Business Studies and in Accounting and Finance; to post-graduate management students and to scientists and engineers reading for short-term management accounting diplomas.

Students for professional accounting examinations and professional accountants will find the book of increasing help, because the examinations of the professional bodies are becoming more conceptual and less technical in nature, and the book should assist readers to think in terms of major issues which are so often clouded in some of the more traditional management accounting textbooks by masses of technical detail.

Although there has been every attempt to ensure originality in examples, illustrations and questions, I am nevertheless heavily indebted to the authors listed in the bibliographies and to some of my former tutors at the London School of Economics for some of the ideas which the book contains. I should also like to thank my colleagues Miss J. A. Eberhardt, MBA, CPA, and Messrs G. S. P. Gupta, ACMA, A. Hindmarch, MSc (Econ.), ACA, H. Mosert, FCA, and R. E. Nunns, MA, ACA, and my supervisor at The City University, Mr J. E. Lewis, MA, FCA, for their comments and observations, and my wife for her help.

Answers to the quantitative questions appear at the end of the book.

D. Pitt Francis
Hertford, April 1972

Contents

HOW THIS BOOK

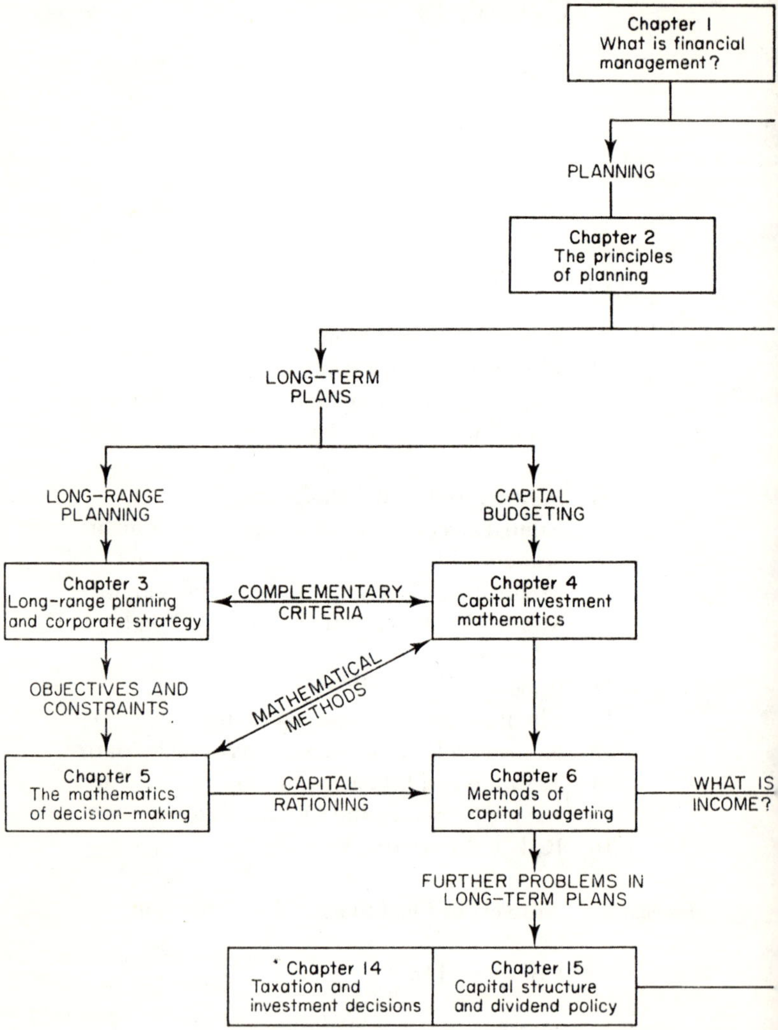

IS PLANNED

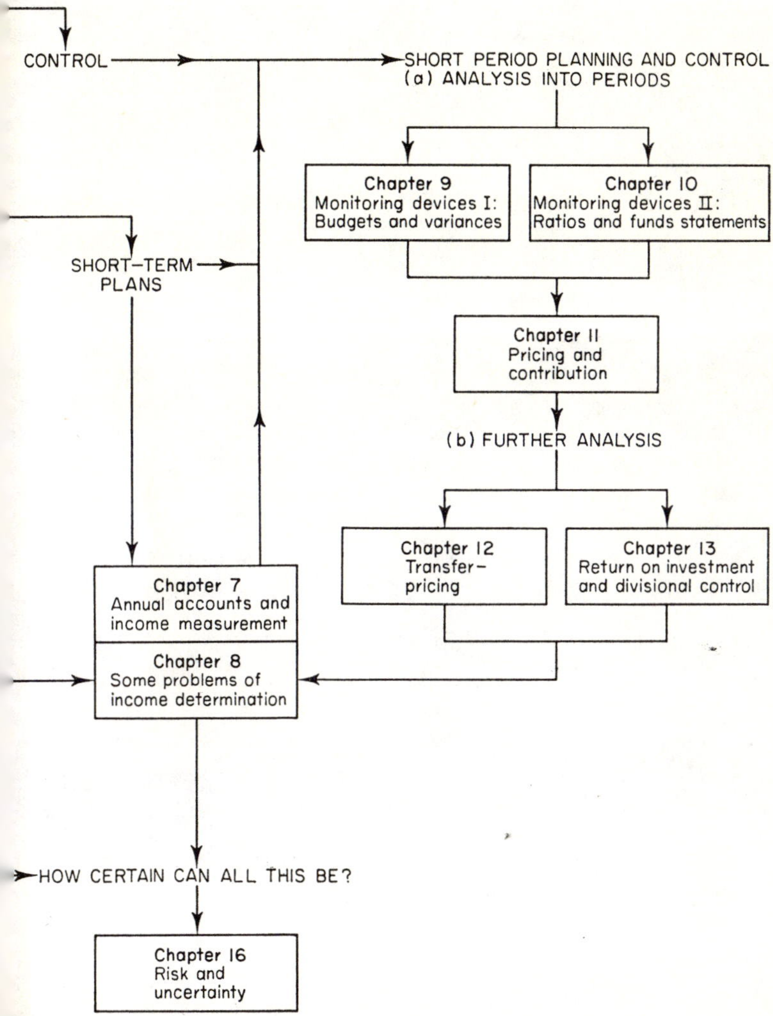
CONTROL
SHORT PERIOD PLANNING AND CONTROL
(a) ANALYSIS INTO PERIODS
Chapter 9
Monitoring devices I:
Budgets and variances
Chapter 10
Monitoring devices II:
Ratios and funds statements
SHORT-TERM PLANS
Chapter 11
Pricing and contribution
(b) FURTHER ANALYSIS
Chapter 12
Transfer-pricing
Chapter 13
Return on investment and divisional control
Chapter 7
Annual accounts and income measurement
Chapter 8
Some problems of income determination
HOW CERTAIN CAN ALL THIS BE?
Chapter 16
Risk and uncertainty

1 What is Financial Management?

Financial management is an integrated and composite subject. It welds together much of the material that is found in other subjects, such as accounting, economics, mathematics, systems analysis and behavioural science, and uses these other disciplines as its tools.

Less than a century ago accountants were not much more than advanced book-keepers who did little other than keep the financial records of businesses for the purpose of stewardship. Economists were political philosophers: they were people who studied the ends and means of governments, firms and individuals. They tried to discover rules which governed such behaviour, but such rules were not of much use in many practical situations for mathematical economics was in its infancy and there was no real attempt to apply the rules quantitatively.

It was not thought that advanced mathematics would be of much use to accountants, who merely needed to know how to add, subtract, multiply and divide. Far less was it ever imagined that there would be such acceleration in unheard-of branches of mathematics in less than a century and that many of these discoveries would be relevant to financial management. Behavioural science was in its infancy and there was nothing written upon systems analysis.

But our question remains unanswered, for to state that financial management is an integrated subject, which uses the other five subjects as its tools, does not help to define it. To define financial management involves examining its purpose rather than its methods and techniques. Financial management is the use of accounting knowledge, economic models, mathematical rules and aspects of systems analysis and behavioural science for the specific purpose of assisting management in its functions of financial planning and control.

The distinction between financial management and management accounting is a semantic one but the gap between the two meanings is rapidly closing, for financial management has the broader meaning of planning and control of all activities by financial means, whereas management accounting originally meant the internal management of finance in industry. Because many people think of management accounting as advanced cost accounting, and its widest meaning does not normally comprise the study of accounting principles, inflation and dividend policy, I have avoided using the term. To many people it will indicate no more than a branch of accounting, the specialism of "management accountants" as distinct from "public accountants". Instead I use the term "financial management" to indicate a synthesis of the five subjects which have been mentioned, applied more widely to planning and control both inside and outside the firm, and in which economist and mathematician play as great a part as accountant and manager do.

Planning

Note the recurrence of the terms "planning" and "control". Planning involves predetermining a course of action, for example, trying to decide the future growth, profit and investment of a business over a period. It involves formulating objectives in the light of available resources, that is, deciding what one's aims should be in the context of available means. It involves studying numerous courses of future action and the use of decision-making techniques to select the best alternative in relation to probable future financial outcomes.

The very facts that one has to deal with the future, and that the future is always uncertain must involve us in an examination of the mathematics of probability. It is also possible to build a mathematical "plan", called a "linear programme", in which objectives and constraints, that is, ends and means, can be quantified and the best feasible solution can be determined. So, in studying planning, we have already not only transgressed into economics, which is defined as the "social science which studies human behaviour as a relationship between *ends* and *means* that have alternative uses", we have also moved into the province of mathematics. The study of ends and objectives also requires introspection to discover what people really require. This involves the study of behavioural science.

Conversely, means, resources and the constraints upon resources must be considered. Accounting is the method of obtaining and recording information about resources. It provides us with methods of processing information about the cost and profitability of past resources. Thus we hope to learn from the mistakes of history and plan more effectively. It helps us to determine the real cost of present opportunities in terms of current resources. It has also a future usefulness, for it helps to measure the resources necessary for future projects and the probable outcomes of projects in terms of financial profit. Thus planning needs the services of mathematician, economist, behavioural scientist and accountant.

There can be little doubt about the need for planning. Even if the world were static and fashions, preferences and tastes did not change, large sums of money could still be wasted because of poor planning, and any decision which does not achieve satisfactory return or obtain the best value from a given set of resources comes into this category, for value does not depend upon outlay, upon past costs or upon bygone efforts as economists once thought. Bygones are forever bygones. It is possible to spend vast sums of money upon a supermarket or a factory on some desert island with few inhabitants. Cost would be high but value would be low. Projects, products, firms and companies can only be valuable if people demand them, and reasonably minded people will prefer purchases and investments which have high present and expected future benefits. They will tend to rank goods and investments in terms of present and future rather than in terms of the past.

In a dynamic world, that is to say, the kind of world where things continually change, there are even more important reasons for planning—

1. Fashions and tastes change and the planner has to anticipate such changes and to take appropriate action.
2. Technology is continually improving, and the planner must consider technological improvement from two aspects: it may assist his own production and help him to produce a more valuable product at smaller cost, or it may conversely render his means of production less efficient, his equipment obsolete and his labour force redundant.
3. The very change of technology may render his product useless and make it technologically obsolete.

Later we shall look more closely at the structure and method of planning. At this stage its importance is being stressed as the primary function of management and the precursor of control.

Control

Plans may be brilliantly conceived but are quite useless in themselves. Putting a plan into action involves publicity. It entails communicating it to persons responsible for implementing it, so that the appropriate action may be taken. The publicity stage is followed by the performance phase, and at this stage management can do little more than correctly motivate personnel responsible for performance. Performance is then reported, but reports are useless if they end up neatly filed away without any action being taken. Reporting must be followed by measurement, and measurement entails comparison. The original plan is available and the expected results have been quantified. We now have actual results and can study how they differ from intended results. Two things may have happened if there are significant differences. The original plan may have been unrealistic, either because it was over-ambitious and unfeasible, or perhaps because it was under-ambitious; and conversely something may be wrong with performance, and in this case reported results will help to isolate what is wrong with the implementation of the plan.

If comparison between actual and planned results leads us to suppose that the plan was deficient, the plan should be improved and a new planning cycle will commence. If there is something wrong with performance, there will be better attempts to communicate the plan to those responsible for carrying it into effect, and to motivate them to implement it. In either case, control is a cycle, consisting of communication, implementation, reporting and measurement. This cycle is often called a "feedback loop", and Professor Bromwich in a series of articles in the *Accountant* on "Standard Costing for Planning and Control" compared the control loop in financial management with the thermostat in a central heating system. Both do much the same thing. In one case a level of heat is predetermined; in the other case levels of profit and growth are planned. In both cases there are mechanisms to compare planned quantities with actual quantities produced, but the very essence of the comparison is that it should be useful. Significant negative differences should motivate the system to produce in the analogous case more heat, and in the case we are considering greater production, profit or growth as the case may be.

Control, like planning, is an integrated subject which draws its tools, rules and methods from various disciplines. The very concept of a control cycle or "feedback loop" comes from systems theory. The management accountant's budgets and forecasts are means of communicating quantified plans, showing targets in figures and depicting the ways in which such targets can be achieved. They are the first stage of the control cycle. The third stage is the reporting of actual performance, a function which has always been linked with the activities of cost and financial accountants. In the small weekly and monthly control cycles, the reports may take the form of miniature production, sales, income and results statements, whereas in the yearly cycle reports serve not only to provide higher internal management with a broader and more general picture of the way in which the company is moving, but some reports are published and act as a means of communicating the company's results not merely to the original planners, but to the public generally, so that potential investors, customers and the Government may watch the company's progress. Manufacturing and trading accounts are internal statements of performance; that is to say, the management accountant may be able to compare them with planned production and planned sales and find how the actual performance of the company over the year has differed from the plan, both in absolute terms, expressed as an arithmetical difference between two figures—for example planned sales less actual sales—or in terms of ratios and proportions. Profit and loss accounts and balance sheets, unlike manufacturing and trading accounts, are external statements of performance, that is, statements published to be read externally, in addition to being used and read by the management of the company. Although there are many reasons for publication, such as Government legislation, one of the major functions of publication of these accounts is to act as monitoring devices to assist investors and potential investors to exercise control over the company. In practice, of course, the individual shareholder has little "say" in running his company, but he can, at least, sell his shares if performance is mediocre or, on occasions, invest more money if the concern is profitable. A balance sheet is an accountant's attempt to measure the worth of the company, breaking down its value into the individual values of its assets such as buildings, machinery, stock-in-trade and debtors, less any accounts which may be payable to other companies; whereas the profit and loss account is simply a statement of the company's profit and how it has been employed, distributed or ploughed back into its business. Because profit is not identical with cash, some companies also publish funds flow statements, which indicate sources and applications of the company's cash and other funds.

Of course, it may be argued that external readers of published accounts cannot effectively measure results because they have no criterion against which to measure them. They do not know how much profit was planned, what level of production or turnover was budgeted, and how much growth internal management intended to achieve. But in their case this is unnecessary for they can measure the company's performance against their own standards of what the company ought to have achieved. They can look at the balance sheets and profit and loss accounts of comparable companies and compare results and they can compare the company's present performance with its previous performance. For this reason it is a legal requirement that all published sets of final accounts should show comparative figures for previous years. So even in the external reporting of companies' affairs to the general public, there are aspects of the same cycle, of planning, decision-making and control.

Mathematical tools are particularly helpful in the measurement stage of reporting performance. The accountant tries to measure actual performance against the yardstick of planned performance by means of absolute differences (variances) and by means of ratios. But actual and percentage differences may not be sufficiently significant to initiate action to find out what has gone wrong. The study of the mathematical concepts of variance and standard deviation is very helpful in investigating variances and percentage differences, and in particular the cost of investigating variances must be compared with the benefit which the investigation will provide. Similarly the mathematical tool of linear regression can be useful in helping us decide which of our costs were fixed and which varied with production, so as to measure the level of production at which production is most efficient.

Behavioural scientists contribute a means of bridging the gap between stages one and three of the control cycle. The accountant can help to communicate plans in the form of budgets, and accountants and mathematicians will assist in the third and fourth stages, in reporting and measurement of performance, but the second stage is performance itself, and in particular the study of how plans may best be communicated and performance motivated. The economist also studies human behaviour, but his contribution to financial control is of a more global character, particularly in the study of variable and marginal costs and in the field of pricing.

Control, like planning, is a structure which rests on a number of pillars, and, as we have seen, accounting, mathematics, economics, behavioural science and systems theory form a complete foundation for the superstructure of control study.

Capital investment theory

Control leads to further planning, and further experience in implementing plans should lead to more effective control. The mathematics of evaluation in the feedback stage of control is therefore not entirely unrelated to the mathematics of decision-making for more effective planning. In this context capital investment theory is also helpful. This is an application of the mathematics of compound interest to evaluate whether any longer-term project is sufficiently profitable to merit investment, taking into consideration both outlay and the "present value" of anticipated future profits, returns or benefits. Because most people prefer to have money now than to have it at some future time, the mathematics of compound interest must be studied. Yet capital investment theory, like all other aspects of planning and control, has an interdisciplinary history. It was originally a mathematical tool, subsequently entered into economic thought, was later used by actuaries in the calculation of life assurance risks, and has only in relatively recent years been used by accountants.

Summary

What we have been saying in this chapter can be expressed in the following way:

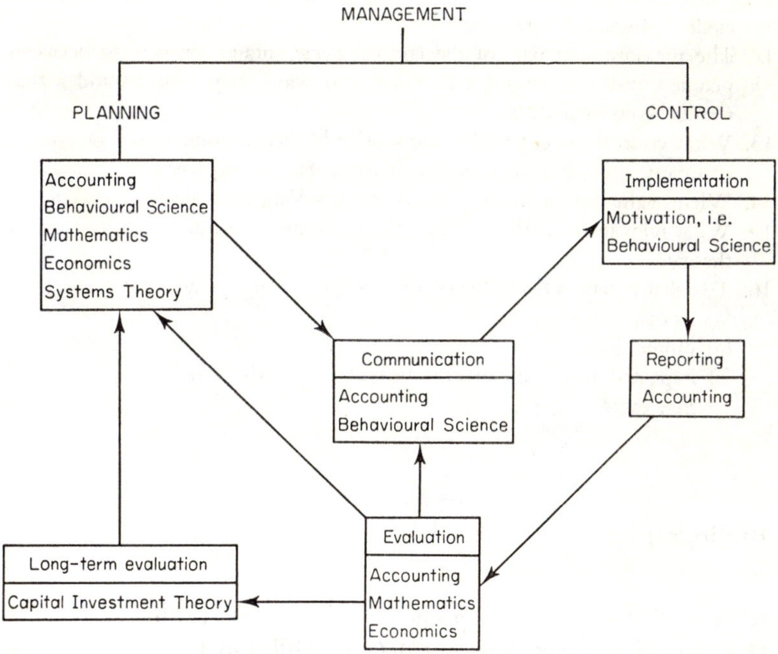

Fig 1.1

Questions

1. Why is financial management "an integrated and composite subject"?
2. Into what two functions is management divided?
3. What is a plan?
4. What disciplines are helpful in the study of financial planning?
5. How is planning related to decision-making?
6. The planner is faced with objectives and constraints, with ends and means. What name is given to a mathematical model, constructed to solve the problem of best achieving objectives with given means and constraints?
7. Discuss reasons for planning in—
   (*a*) a static environment;
   (*b*) a dynamic environment.
8. State the four constituent parts of the control cycle.
9. How does management accounting assist in the communicating of plans to lower-level management and to operatives?
10. What discipline is most useful to assist management in the implementation of plans?
11. "Cost and financial accountants assist in the reporting stage of the control cycle." Discuss this statement.
12. The measurement part of the control cycle entails comparison between planned and actual results. In what two ways may planned and actual results be compared?
13. What control do external readers of published accounts exercise over a company and with what may such accounts be compared?
14. What evaluation techniques can be used in long-term decision-making?
15. What relevance has the mathematics of compound interest to investment theory?
16. To what extent is the value of an article or project related to—
    (*a*) its original cost;
    (*b*) public demand;
    (*c*) expected future income or benefit which the article or project will generate?

Bibliography

R. Ackoff, *A Concept of Corporate Planning* (Wiley, 1970)
H. I. Ansoff, *Corporate Strategy* (McGraw-Hill, 1965)

C. P. Bonini (ed.), *Management Controls: New Directions in Basic Research* (McGraw-Hill, 1964)
M. Bromwich, "Standard Costing for Planning and Control", *Accountant*, April/May 1969
B. V. Carsberg & H. C. Edey (eds.), *Modern Financial Management* (Penguin, 1969)
D. W. Ewing, *The Practice of Planning* (Harper & Row, 1968)
Y. Ijiri, *Management Goals and Accounting for Control* (North Holland, 1965)
A. A. Robichek (ed.), *Financial Research and Management Decisions* (Wiley, 1967)
J. Sizer, *An Insight into Management Accounting* (Penguin, 1970)

2 The Principles of Planning

The word "plan" may have two different meanings. To some people a plan may be nothing more than a sketch-map, an abstract from a much more complete map, with a particular aspect of the area's geography being detailed. A balance sheet could be regarded as a "plan" of a business, in the sense that one does not have to tour all the factories and branches of a business to find out what the business is worth, for the balance sheet should be prepared in such a way as to demonstrate not only its total value, but also the values of the various categories, such as property, machinery, goods, debts and cash, into which its wealth is divided. If these categories have a positive value they are called "assets" and the balance sheet could be described as a systematic plan of these assets viewed from one aspect, that of how much they are worth, in the same way that a plan of an underground railway is a systematic arrangement of stations viewed not necessarily from an accurate geographical standpoint but purely from the aspect of their relationship with each other from a travel standpoint. Those who wish to examine this aspect of plans and balance sheets, purely as means of communicating specialized information may like to read the chapter upon "Surrogates and Principals" in Yuji Ijiri's *Foundations of Accounting Measurement*.

In the present book "plans" and "planning" have more specialized meanings. The purpose of preparing a plan of an underground railway is to prescribe a course of future action. The purpose of preparing a plan of a house is to prescribe future action in building it. To take the underground railway example a little further, upon London Underground there are two kinds of plans, a general plan which appears at most stations, and the plans of particular lines which appear upon the trains. If a traveller is using several lines to travel from, say, Upminster to Cockfosters, the line plans can be regarded as short-term plans to cover a particular stage of the journey and the general plan can be regarded as a long-term route to get to the destination in mind. There may be many ways of travelling to the destination but the traveller obviously wishes to do so in the shortest possible time. He is therefore said to have an objective or end in view, and he also has means which he is constrained to use, for he may be restricted to travelling upon London Underground.

Planning method

A plan is a predetermined course of action and is constructed in stages. We may well list the stages of planning in the following order—

(*a*) definition of objectives
(*b*) listing and evaluating resources and constraints
(*c*) analysis of stages and operations necessary
(*d*) synthesis of possible plans
(*e*) evaluation of alternatives
(*f*) choice of the most satisfactory plan
(*g*) implementation

Defining objectives The planner must first know what he wants. In the case of the traveller from Upminster to Cockfosters it was perhaps unnecessary for him first to sit down and decide what he wished to do. He may have been a commuter who habitually travelled upon that particular route. Even if the individual has no habitual need and the particular journey is an unusual one, this primary introspective stage may still be a short one for most people seem to know what they want at a particular point of time. This is not true of companies or of groups of people however, for companies only have objectives if their policy-makers are unanimous about what those objectives should be and this is rarely so. Although economists at one time regarded the maximization of profit as the principal objective of every business, this assumption has been questioned in recent years. Managers may prefer to maximize their sales so that they can maximize their income from the company and busy executives may wish to maximize their free time, but even the serious-minded policy-makers who have the company's interests entirely at heart may differ as to whether they think the company should maximize long-term growth in the company's assets or try to obtain the greatest amount of income in the short run. The matter will be studied in detail later, but it should already be apparent that companies will define objectives in different ways.

Means, resources and constraints All the factors which a business has at its disposal are limited and it is necessary to use these to the best advantage. If we assume that the passenger in our example has already purchased a London Transport ticket and boarded a District Line train at Upminster and has spent all his money, he is committed to a course of action in which he is constrained to travel by London Transport trains only, and in which the resources at his disposal are the services they provide—although he may have travelled to his destination more quickly by booking to the nearest British Rail station and using the Underground only in Central London if he had thought of it earlier.

A company's resources are similarly limited. The accountant would define these as the assets which the company possesses, but some resources cannot be adequately valued by accountants and are categorized under the general term "goodwill" on the company's balance sheet, yet they are resources which planners should take into account. A company has borrowing opportunities, but cannot borrow unlimited funds. Both physical and capital resources are rationed and skilled labour is at a premium. The very cohesiveness of the management and the labour force may in itself be a resource or a constraint, depending upon its quality. There are also legal, social, political and time constraints.

Analysis of operations Plans must be analysed into operations and stages so that they can be pieced together in the best possible way. The committed passenger must decide how much of his journey must be travelled on District, Metropolitan and Piccadilly lines, and in a similar way the company's long-term plan must be subdivided into a number of short-term plans. Capital expenditure is a long-term matter, and once resources are committed the company will find it difficult to make an alternative decision. However, even when its capital has been spent upon property, machinery and equipment there is still room for flexibility in short-term planning, and to do this effectively the company should prepare short-term budgets. It can prepare annual targets for production and selling. It can estimate how much should be spent upon administration. If production requires several processes a separate plan or budget is necessary for each process. If selling is carried out in a number of areas it may prepare budgets for each branch.

Thus the company's analysis of operations is more detailed than that of the simple passenger illustration for it is not only divided on a time basis into a number of shorter-term cycles, such as annual budgets, but it is divided functionally into categories of activity, and even one activity such as production may require separate plans or budgets for each process, and the costs and revenues of operations may also be analysed upon a geographical basis.

Synthesis of operations From the smaller and specialized plans or budgets a master budget is prepared for each year and tentative budgets may be prepared for a number of years ahead. If the long-term plan now looks inadequate the miniature budgets may be put together in other ways, for the company's policy-makers continually try to allocate capital to resources and the optimum "mix" of these resources is not always initially apparent. Several alternatives will appear in the initial planning stage and the problem will be that of evaluating each alternative and selecting that which appears to be the best, but even when the cycle has started selection may not be absolute, for although alternatives have been eliminated there should still be an element of flexibility. In long-term plans this could take the form of an escape mechanism for making the best use of all the firm's resources if the initial plan should fail, and in short-term budgets it takes the form of diversifying production (that is, of producing several types of product) and of flexible budgeting.

Evaluation of alternatives This is the critical stage of the planning process. The company has several long-term plans and wishes to select that which appears to be best. How can its policy-makers decide between them? Economic theory and mathematics have provided us with a discounted cash flow technique, which can be used as a means of evaluating each plan from the standpoint of its estimated future benefit to the company expressed in present terms upon a realistic compound interest basis, and from the standpoint of present and future cost.

In the short-term cycle we may have problems of allocating physical resources and deciding which plan achieves our objective in terms of a number of different categories of resources in varying amounts. Mathematical model building can assist us in this task, and such model building has been extended in recent years to solve many of a company's other problems: capital rationing in the long period, allocation of resources between divisions and even asset valuation and allocation.

Choice and implementation We deal with the two final stages in the planning process together for we have already said that choice should still leave an element of flexibility. Capital commitment often amounts to burning bridges. Indeed the company which has purchased both land and pipeline materials for the construction of a large pipeline across a stretch of desert could hardly afterwards plan to do otherwise without incurring considerable loss, although it may be able to sell its pipeline equipment. It could hardly decide to grow vegetables on the land which it had purchased without employing an entirely different kind of scientific labour force and spending large sums on differently orientated research and development, although it may decide to cut its losses and use its oil pipeline for irrigation purposes. Short-term planning is more flexible and the special branch of short-term planning called flexible budgeting will be discussed later.

Implementation is only part of the control cycle, and control is not itself part of planning, but the very act of implementation necessitates control. Plans require monitoring devices so that activities can be measured, either to discover whether they conform to the plan and produce greater conformity, or so that flexible plans may be revised. Budgets are monitoring devices. When actual accounts are prepared variances between budgeted and actual figures under each heading provide us with "feedback" to indicate to what extent the plan has been carried out.

At this stage we can consider in more detail the analogy of a thermostat. Both the article by Professor Bromwich listed in the bibliography to Chapter 1 and the reading by G. S. Hardern on "Planning and Control" in Langley's *Introduction to Accounting for Business Studies* use the analogy. In a heating device a thermostat is employed to keep temperature at a given level. It compares the actual level of temperature with that planned and if the actual temperature is too low it allows the supply of fuel to continue until the desired temperature is reached. If the temperature is too high the fuel supply is switched off or reduced. The thermostat is an evaluation device similar to variance analysis in planning, and as the "variances" produced by a thermostat are feedback devices to assist in maintaining a general level of temperature so variances between budgeted and actual accounts act as a feedback device to help maintain financial plans.

The analogy continues. As it is sometimes necessary to alter a planned level of temperature because of changed environment such as the weather, so it is frequently necessary for the company to alter its planned budget, whether of expected profit, output or sales, because of the changed economic environment in which it operates. Figure 2.1 illustrates the analogy between a budgetary control system and the thermostat in a central heating system.

It will be clear that the feedback loop is only another way of looking at the control cycle of the previous chapter. In that chapter however we analysed the cycle into its constituent parts. In the present chapter the purpose of the cycle has been examined, and it has become clear

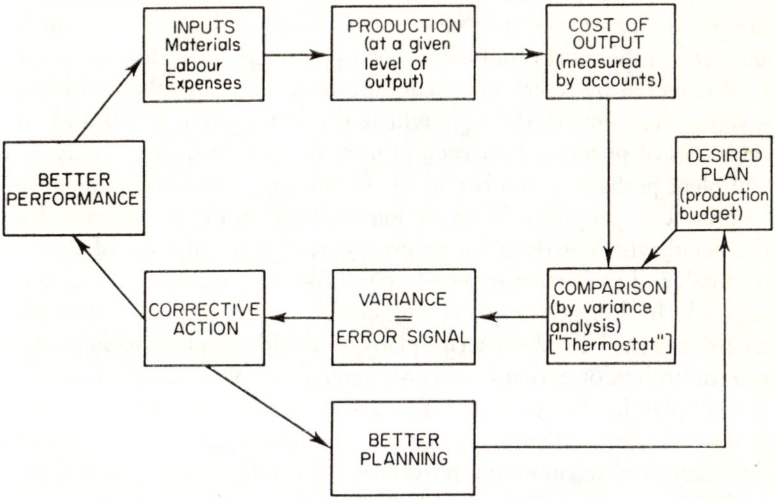

Fig 2.1 The feedback loop illustrated by a production budget

that it exists not only as an aid to more effective control but as a teaching device to the planners themselves to assist them in more effective planning.

Summary

A plan may be one of a number of things, ranging from sketch-maps to accountant's budgets. The word is generally used for something which illustrates the relationship between a set of items for a specific purpose. The balance sheet of a company is a bird's-eye view of its wealth from a financial viewpoint, and analysed into categories. In this book, however, the word "plan" has a more specific meaning. It is a predetermined course of action. Budgets are financial plans expressed in financial terms.

Preparation of plans involves decision as to what one's objectives are, what aims or ends one has in mind. In the case of individuals this is relatively easy but companies may find it more difficult to express them accurately because of differences of opinion among policy-makers. The company's planners must also look at its resources, whether financial, material or human, and the constraints upon these resources. There are social, legal, political, moral and time constraints.

The plan must be built up from a number of shorter or smaller plans. Long-term plans can only be constructed if we know what can be achieved in the short run. Income for a period is similar, for it can only be discovered by reference to sales, production and to the number of geographical outlets through which the company can sell and the capacities of plant used for each process and product. Once analysis is complete perhaps a number of plans can be constructed which will help the company to achieve its objectives given the resources and all the detail which analysis has made apparent, but only one of these is optimal, and evaluation is necessary in order that the best plan may be selected. In long-term plans this could require capital investment techniques and in short-term plans it could require mathematical programming, or perhaps even computer simulation models. Once the correct plan has been selected it is ready for implementation. Control is simply regulated implementation. Budgets communicate plans to operatives and accounting reports feed information about performance back to management. Evaluation compares two alternatives, and in much the same way as a thermostat indicates a temperature variance so that more or less fuel may be fed into the heating unit in order to increase or decrease heat, so accounting variances should help management to bring performance nearer to the planned level of output.

However, setting a thermostat is in itself an educational experience. Different temperatures are needed for different environments. In a similar way, all plans should allow room for modification, and variances help the planner to become more accurate in future planning cycles.

Questions

1. In what sense may a balance sheet be described as a "financial plan" of a company?
2. How would you define "plan" in the sense in which it is used by management?

3. What are the seven constituent stages in planning method?
4. Why is it often difficult for a company to decide its objectives?
5. Would you say that a "balance sheet" lists all the resources of a company? If not, what resources cannot be listed on the normal financial balance sheet?
6. What is the relationship between resources and constraints?
7. In what ways may a company's plans be analysed?
8. What evaluation techniques may be used to choose between alternative plans in the long run, and to decide upon optimum strategies in the short run?
9. What comparison is there between thermostatic control and variance analysis?
10. A variance between actual performance and planned performance need not always mean that performance is at fault. What else may it mean?

Bibliography

All the books listed in the first chapter are relevant with the following additions:

H. I. Ansoff (ed.), *Business Strategy* (Penguin, 1969)

F. E. Emery (ed.), *Systems Thinking* (Penguin, 1969)

Y. Ijiri, *The Foundations of Accounting Measurement* (Prentice-Hall, 1967)

R. A. Johnson *et al.*, *The Theory and Management of Systems* (McGraw-Hill, 1963)

J. G. March & H. A. Simon, *Organizations* (New York: Wiley; London: Chapman & Hall 1958)

3 Long-range Planning and Corporate Strategy

Previous chapters have stated that management is a matter of planning and control and have examined the interrelationships between the two. We were also able to analyse the stages necessary in the planning process and the way in which the control cycle should provide a "feedback loop" for management, not only in order to improve performance but also to achieve a better standard of planning.

We have also analysed planning into two types, long-term and short-term, and would assume that the company's policy-makers must have some idea about what they wish to achieve in the long term before they are able to make detailed plans in respect of the short term. Obviously a long-term plan can only be regarded as reasonable if the benefits which the company will achieve, expressed in financial terms, are higher than the costs or outlay. This is the essential rule of capital investment theory. Very few people wish to waste money or give it away for its own sake. They will, of course, give to charitable organizations, but this is because they have a feeling that it will be usefully employed by them.

Long-range investment is however a more complicated subject than simply discovering whether total cost is less or more than total benefit, expressed in terms of income or revenue, for time itself, as we stated earlier, is a constraint. People have limited lives and companies do not last for ever. Because of this we tend to value the prospect of receiving a pound today as greater and more relevant to our present situation than the prospect of receiving a pound in ten years' time. Economists call this concept "time preference", mathematicians would express it in terms of compound interest formulae and accountants think of it in terms of "discounting" future benefits. It simply means that any future income which we may expect from any plan or project must be "discounted" or scaled down to allow for the inconvenience in terms of the time which we shall have to wait for it, or conversely to allow for the cost of borrowing capital now, because other people who lend to us have the inconvenience of not being able to use their capital for other things.

So it seems that, if a company simply chooses the plan or project which has the highest present value in terms of future benefits and present or future costs, and decides to produce those products which have the highest present value measured in terms of future benefits to customers, it will be successful. But the position is not as simple as this, for people tend to differ in their rates of time preference, and even as

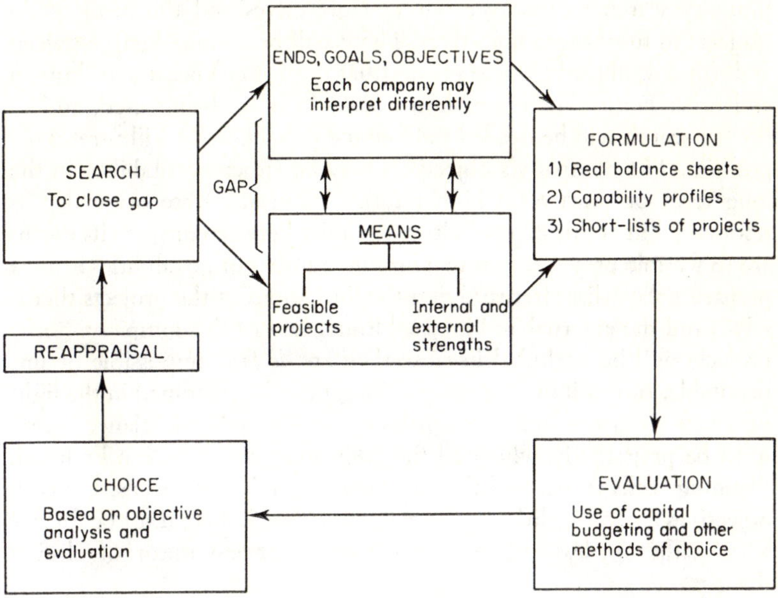

Fig 3.1 The problem-solving antecedents to capital budgeting

individuals they change continually. Sometimes they are highly conscious of the present and at other times they tend to "live" in the future. If individuals change frequently in their attitude to time and if they differ from each other in respect of such attitudes, there will be no exact agreement between a company's directors whether to plan for immediate profit or for long-term growth and survival, for one director may be about to retire and another may have thirty years' future career with the company at stake. Shareholders will differ similarly in their plans for the future and their personal intentions.

Another reason for difficulty in applying the capital investment rule is that no one has a self-made list of profitable projects. It would take infinite time to list every available project and, even while this was being done, the world, the environment and the very things which were the subject of evaluation would be continually changing. Therefore, even if we can decide on a uniform rate of "interest" to allow for the fact of time preference, we must have a decision rule to "short-list" or screen those projects from which ultimate choice can be made.

This involves correct perception of the problem and adequate preliminary search to discover our real objectives and the most likely projects to fulfil those objectives. There will be an initial gap between ends (that is, objectives) and means (that is, projects) because of human and other constraints upon the means which are being used, and so further search will be needed to close the gap. Figure 3.1 illustrates the position. The company's objectives may be either profitability in the long term or short-term high returns. Its means were originally its resources, but at this stage of ultimate choice between projects its means are its feasible projects. From an infinite number of possibilities it must prepare a short-list after studying the limitations of the projects themselves and the external and internal limitations of the company. Some projects will be excluded because they are *de facto* impossible or unprofitable. Impossibility or unfeasibility, must be examined in the light of given resources and so a capability profile or "real balance sheet" must be prepared in which all the company's resources can be listed. Planning seeks to narrow the gap between ends and means, between objectives and capabilities. If the gap is not closed, there must be further search either for less ambitious objectives or for new means of closing the gap.

Long-range planning method

Long-range planning is not entirely new, for it must have been used to construct some of the masterpieces of the ancient world. But the scale and extent of long-range planning in modern times is unique. This is because of the rapid acceleration of technological change, in which standing still is the equivalent of moving backwards in economic relativity. People are now more ambitious than ever before and tastes and requirements are multiplying. If a company fails to satisfy its customers' changed requirements its competitors will soon do so. But the very act of satisfying requirements itself leads to other changes of taste and to reduced demand for previous requirements. Rises and falls of demand for each product must be anticipated and the correct timing in the changes of taste foreseen. Further, computer technology has made projects of a hitherto unknown scale possible, but greater projects need longer lead-times and greater capital outlay over a longer period.

Yet, paradoxically, although we now need more time than ever to accomplish worth-while projects, the present dynamic environment assists innovation, and so it is possible that a competitor's discovery will make the project obsolete before it has even left the planning stage.

The solution to this dilemma is not to abandon long-range planning and live entirely for the present, but to refine planning methods so that, even if long-range plans become less profitable than imagined, we shall not lose out entirely. This demands flexibility, both between present and future and between one project and another. It means not putting all eggs into one basket, so that some capital is perhaps committed to a different plan or set of plans, and resources are used which can be diverted to other plans if the major plan fails. Thus we are not entirely committed and can frequently reassess the firm's relationship with its environment in the ever-changing present.

Analysing objectives

Before searching the environment for feasible and profitable projects we must introspectively search ourselves for our real objectives. Economists say that the company's basic objective is to maximize its profit, but short-sighted and long-sighted policy-makers define "maximizing profit" differently. Sometimes return on investment is regarded as a criterion of profitability, so that the project having the highest financial rate of return on net assets (however valued) is regarded as the most profitable, but not all agree. Someone shortly to retire to the Bahamas may not be so interested in the return which his company will make on its investment after his retirement, but would have a high discount preference because of his limited future, and would prefer maximizing present value of the investment to maximizing a rate of return. Both these definitions of profitability are only broad criteria for assessing projects in the medium or long term, for many projects which in theory have a high net present value in terms of discounted future benefits and which have a good potential rate of return on investment would still be impracticable for other reasons.

Figure 3.2 exhibits a hierarchy of objectives. A company competes for both capital and customers. Its external strength is marked by its stability, by growth of sales, market share, market scope and earnings, and also by growth of the range of its available products. Instability of sales could be fatal because periodic shortages of revenue will lead to unstable fluctuations of working capital and would therefore adversely affect production, lead to longer waiting periods and so induce loyal customers to go elsewhere for products.

Therefore, growth and stability indicate external strength in the company's ability to stand competition. But externally strong companies may be internally diseased. Compare the case of a strong man who suffers from a weak heart. Even a healthy individual can die from an "external" accident and, similarly, healthy companies can be ruined by external environmental mishaps. For example, a postal strike can kill a mail-order company. Despite the possibility of corporate "death" at any time, resulting from strikes, war, weather or other environmental mishaps it is still prudent management for a company's policy-makers to ensure that it is internally strong. The three criteria of health are—

(i) physical assets;
(ii) working capital;
(iii) human resources.

It may be a good exercise to compare a company with an individual in this respect. The body's tissues deteriorate. The company's physical assets are its tissues. If they are not periodically replaced they will be functionally starved. The very source of such replacement and rejuvenation is the circulation of money, the life-blood of business, and as individuals die from poor circulation so companies can cease to exist if they lack working capital. A tactically useless person cannot of himself survive in his environment, and company survival must in the same way be a function of the managerial and technological skills of its directors and employees.

All three are important. It is difficult to express skills in a company's balance sheet because in a free labour market skilled personnel can leave the company or strike. The nearest approach to showing skills on a conventional balance sheet is to show training, research and development costs as an "asset" on the balance sheet instead of writing them off as an annual cost to the company. But the financial balance sheet does exhibit the other two criteria of health, physical assets and working

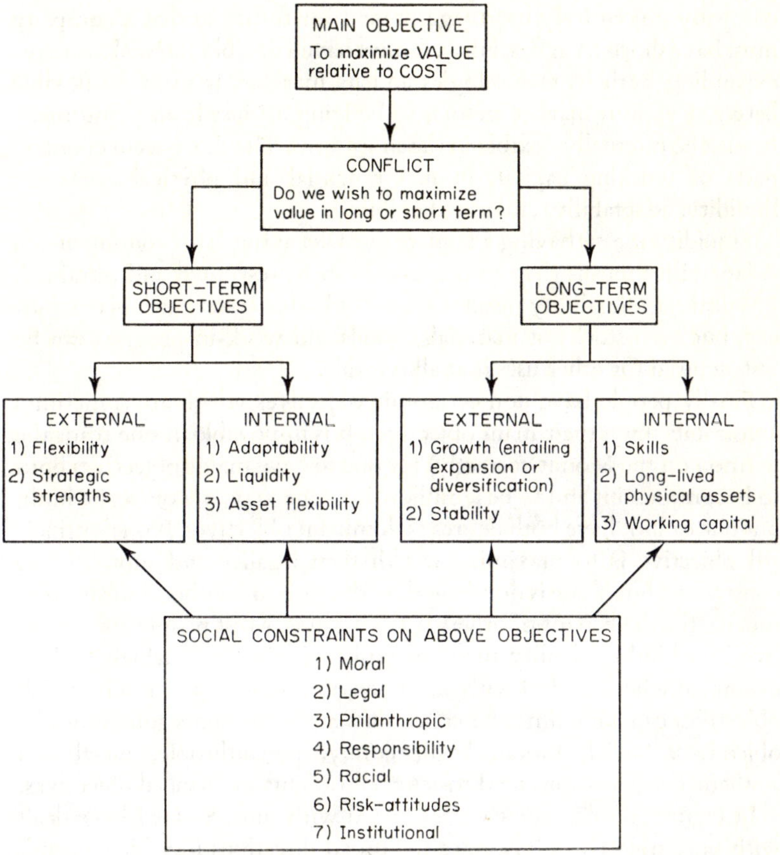

Fig 3.2 Hierarchical analysis of objectives

capital, and in the short term it may be possible both to buy assets out of working capital and to mortgage assets for working capital. It may even be possible to obtain physical assets from a leasing company, provided that funds can be guaranteed to pay for future rentals. Yet, in the long term both physical assets and working capital must be satisfactory if the company is to be healthy.

This analysis of the company's major objective to maximize value implies that it must have worth-while projects and behave properly in its environment, demonstrating stability and growth and having healthy physical assets, working capital and human potential. However, no company can entirely mortgage present for future so that a company must have short-term flexibility. It must have a flexible external strategy, expanding both its technologies and its markets. It must be flexible between various market sectors, so hedging against losing customers. It must be internally flexible in the short term. The short-term counterparts of working capital, human potential and physical assets are liquidity, adaptability and asset flexibility.

Liquidity means having adequate short-term funds for contingencies. Adaptability means that human assets can be re-routed and retrained. Physical asset flexibility means that not only fixed assets such as machinery, but even stocks of materials, goods and work-in-progress can be restructured for other uses if at all possible.

Finally people have non-economic objectives which are sometimes constraints upon their main objectives. It is impossible (if one reads the Sermon on the Mount correctly) for one to have major objectives both to become a saint and to be a millionaire. One may, of course, be both, but one cannot have both desires as dominant objectives. If one's principal objective is to maximize wealth then legality and morality are constraints, but if one is dominated by the path to sainthood the need to survive for the benefit of others is a constraint. Most people attempt to live in a kind of duality theorem position, a position which will be examined when we deal with linear programming, a position in which objectives can sometimes be constraints and constraints sometimes be objectives. Social, moral, legal, family, philanthropic, racial and aesthetic considerations tend to act as constraints to financial objectives.

In Figure 3.2 objectives are associated with ends. So far I have dealt with pure objectives. They are the broad directions in which a firm's constituents wish to travel. They may wish to maximize (make greater), optimize (make better) or simply "satisfice"[1] (perform satisfactorily) either in economic accomplishment or in any mixture of qualities such as flexibility and growth. But objectives are not ends. An objective is the direction in which someone wishes to travel, but an end or goal is the destination to which he wishes to travel. When planners talk of

[1] *See* R. L. Ackoff, *A Concept of Corporate Planning*, p. 70.

modifying objectives to suit means or improving means to attain objectives, they often think of goals or ends rather than the directions to those goals. Closing the gap between ends and means is the basic problem of planning.

Analysing means

Corporate planning philosophy says that, although it is easier to close the gap between ends and means by restricting ends and being satisfied with mediocre goals, it is always better to improve the means of attaining ends. Both are usually revised, but it is far more satisfying to have always the highest feasible goals. Only unfeasible goals should be excluded completely, and all potential resources should be correctly listed and analysed in a "real balance sheet". This term means something a little different from the term "balance sheet". It is not just a list of those assets of a company which are immediately recognized as being valuable in financial terms, but includes other things of potential value such as the company's skills, the qualities of its personnel and its borrowing opportunities, items which are normally excluded from the financial balance sheet because they cannot be adequately valued. Internal appraisal of the company not only means making sure of having adequate human, physical and financial resources but seeing that they are optimally employed. Better methods, organizational changes and creation of new divisions may all affect the functioning of human, financial and physical assets in an integrated unit, and so add value to the firm as a total unit. There is also "synergy" defined by Ansoff in *Corporate Strategy* as the "$2 + 2 = 5$" effect of jointness such that the value of a whole operation is greater than the sum of its parts. A company should diversify in fields where it can employ existing managerial, marketing and manufacturing skills and use its past fund of research and development in the best possible way.

So a company may be able to use existing cooker sales personnel to sell radio sets, and an ice-cream company may use its slack resources to provide hot meals in the winter. There is usually good synergy between similar industries but synergy between consumer and construction industries is often negative. Synergy often explains diversification and merger. It is not only the question of the whole operation not being equal to the sum of its parts in value, but frequently a matter of using unused capacity. Just as warehouse space can be sublet and computer time can be sold, so there are unused capacities in management, research, manufacturing and marketing, and synergy involves using these latent assets for additional purposes.

After internal appraisal of the structure of its resources, the company should conduct external appraisal of the means of using such resources. In its struggle to continue to adapt itself to its environment the company will deteriorate in performance if it does not conduct such an appraisal, and study new markets for existing products, new products for existing markets and new products for new markets. In each of these three fields its capacities and strengths must be re-examined *vis-à-vis* the market generally and competitors. What is the inherent potential of each of these fields of activity to the company? To what extent do diversification, expansion and both of these in combination help the company's policy-makers to maximize value and to achieve stability and flexibility? To what extent can the company benefit by altering its strategy? The answers to these questions are listed in an inherent potential profile, which shows how each field of activity will benefit the company.

The inherent potential profile indicates the ends which can be achieved by entering a field of activity. In contrast a capability profile must also be drawn up which lists the means or capabilities which are demanded of the company before it can enter the particular field. Planners can now look at each field in turn and isolate the field which has an inherent potential profile most akin to its own objectives, ends and goals, and a capability profile most akin to its own resources, capabilities and means, and thus discover the field of activity most likely to close the gap between ends and means.

These comparisons are easier for the planners if comparative profiles are constructed for each field. Comparative profiles are similar to "variances" in the search process. The comparative objective profile will show the difference between the company's objectives and those which can be attained in the particular field of activity being considered. On the other hand, the comparative capability profile shows the difference between the company's resources and those required for the particular field of activity. Figure 3.3 shows the strategy for closing the gap between ends and means in each field of activity. This is a continual process in an ever-changing environment against which the company's planners will be continually battling, for competitors, suppliers, investors and customers are always changing, as indeed is the company itself. If it has grown it may be better able to take a project which it refused at a previous decision-point or even choose other projects because it has developed latent capacities which can now be used in new fields of activity. So, at each reappraisal, planners must test for latent capacity and for synergy, and they must ask whether

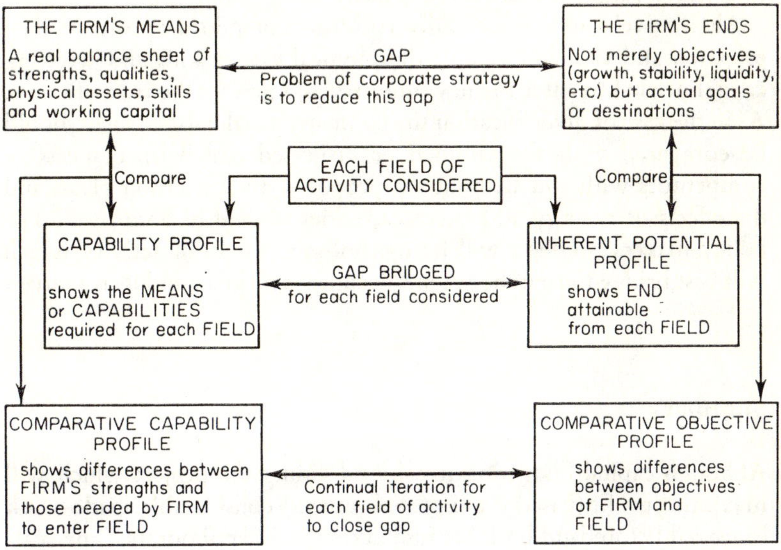

Fig 3.3 Iterative strategy to close gap between ends and means

existing resources contain useful synergy to enter new fields of activity and whether new possible projects would contain useful synergy in relation to each other.

Testing opportunities

Two major fields of activity are expansion and diversification. In each case the company should compare its own strengths with those required by the field of activity, in respect of both its customers and its competitors. In the case of expansion this would involve preparation of a mission profile where new markets and new but similar products are listed, the company's share of the market compared with its desired share and in which new risks of expansion can be calculated. The real balance sheet of the company should be prepared and compared with projected real balance sheets of its competitors and the effect of expansion predicted. Lastly, we should again test for synergy. Has the company latent capacities in research, marketing, manufacturing or administration which can be utilized if it expands?

Alternatively, in the case of diversification an industry profile will be prepared and this will exhibit the physical assets, skills and working capital needed to enter the new industry and predict the risks of entry. As in the case of diversification the company's real balance sheet should be compared with the assumed or projected real balance sheets of competitors with and without the proposed diversification plans, and the effects of synergy and latent capacities studied in both cases. The policy-makers' strategy will be to choose the field of activity which will best bridge the gap between the company's goals and its resources.

Summary

Although capital budgeting involves deciding the project which will maximize profit (based on expected returns) considerable spade-work is needed beforehand both because investors differ about the time-scale in which they desire returns and because there is no self-made list of projects. Each possible project's feasibility must be studied and a short-list prepared. Long-range planning is desirable not only because projects are longer and larger than ever before but because of the objectives of growth and stability, and the flexibility objective acts as a constraint upon the rigidity of such plans. Thus, long-term internal strength of physical assets, skills and working capital and external stability and growth on the one hand must be balanced with flexibility and quick profit on the other hand. Further there is a social need to consider non-economic objectives.

Resources must be considered and a real balance sheet prepared. Internal appraisal will pinpoint the strength of human, physical and monetary assets and external appraisal involves studying how the company may best use these real assets. Fields of activity, such as expansion and diversification, must be studied for the objectives which each will satisfy, and for the resources which are required for entry to each field. Planners should study the market profile if they want expansion, listing the requirements and risks of expansion, so comparing the firm's real balance sheet with those of competitors and investigating potential synergy. If they want diversification planners should study the industry profile, listing the requirements, risks and costs of diversification or entering a new industry. The company's real balance sheet should be compared with those of competitors and synergy tested. Thus the resources needed to enter each field of activity are weighed against the ends which can be achieved from entering the field and planners will choose the field of activity with the greatest inherent potential for satisfying the company's own objectives and which requires those capabilities, qualities and strengths most akin to its own capabilities, qualities and strengths. Continual revision ensures that the company best uses its resources, but choice of field of activity sets the pace for choosing feasible projects.

Questions

1. What groundwork is necessary before capital budgeting techniques can be applied?
2. What is the fundamental rule of capital investment theory?
3. Why does the time-scale complicate cost and benefit decisions in the long run?
4. What is "time-preference"? State how you think it is related to the mathematical concept of compound interest and to the accounting concept of "discounting"?
5. Why has long-range planning developed in recent years?
6. Why does maximizing value mean different things to different people?
7. Construct a hierarchy of objectives.
8. What objectives are most important (*a*) in the long term and (*b*) in the short term?
9. How do objectives differ from constraints?
10. What is the difference between an objective and a goal?
11. How may objectives become constraints and constraints objectives?
12. What are the three criteria of a company's internal health? What analogy can be drawn between criteria of corporate health and criteria of human health?
13. List some social constraints which all companies should satisfy.
14. What are fields of activity?

15. Discuss the way in which inherent potential profiles and capability profiles feature in decisions about fields of activity.
16. What are comparative objective profiles and comparative capability profiles? How can they be regarded as "variances"?
17. Discuss the meaning of synergy.
18. What sort of synergy should be desired in diversification and expansion decisions?
19. What do you understand by (*a*) real balance sheet, (*b*) mission profile, and (*c*) industry profile?
20. Synergy can be regarded as the use of latent capacities in marketing, administration, manufacturing and research. Discuss the concepts of synergy and unused capacity and compare them.

Bibliography

Most of the books mentioned in the bibliographies of Chapters 1 and 2 are relevant in connection with this chapter, in particular—

R. Ackoff, *A Concept of Corporate Planning* (Wiley, 1970)
H. I. Ansoff (ed.), *Business Strategy* (Penguin, 1969)
H. I. Ansoff, *Corporate Strategy* (McGraw-Hill, 1965)
H. I. Ansoff, "Quasi-analytical Approach" in Carsberg & Edey (eds.), *Modern Financial Management* (Penguin, 1969)
D. W. Ewing (ed.), *Long-range Planning for Management* (Harper & Row, 1964)
D. W. Ewing, *The Practice of Planning* (Harper & Row, 1968)
J. Sizer, *An Insight into Management Accounting* (Penguin, 1970)

4 Capital Investment Mathematics

In the previous chapters the major implications of planning have been stated, and two principles have emerged. It has been shown that the purpose of planning is to make the best use of resources to achieve stated objectives and that no plan should be countenanced if its costs (expressed in terms of resources) are greater than the benefits which the plan or project is likely to produce in the future. It was indicated that the matter of discovering whether a plan had positive or negative value in terms of costs and benefits is a little more complicated than it would seem. One has to do more than discover the total cost and total benefit of a project and subtract costs from benefits, because time is itself a resource, and for this reason it is preferable to have £100 today than to have a valid promise of £100 in ten years' time. Economists call this the principle of time preference, and it is, of course, the reason why people expect interest upon their savings and anticipate having to pay interest upon mortgages. To economists and investment specialists the cost of capital is the "interest rate" at which one expects to borrow capital, and management accountants view the time pattern of investment in reverse. They think of "discounting" future benefits or income, that is, of deciding the present value of those benefits, after allowing for the fact of time preference or for the cost of capital.

Before it is possible to study capital investment theory, therefore, it is essential to understand the mathematics of compound interest, and in this chapter we shall illustrate six compound interest concepts, for which six different tables appear in some textbooks. We shall take a simple example and a short period of four years for our illustration, but unlike many expositions of the subject, the present illustration will use the very high rate of 40 per cent for the following reasons—

(i) it makes for good graphical presentation of the differences between the concepts;
(ii) there will be less likelihood of confusing the actual factors than if lower rates are used;

(iii) people expect very high rates of return from good investments; and
(iv) many of the rates normally used in exposition are unrealistic in view of inflation.

The concepts are—

(*a*) the compounded value of a single payment after n years at $r\%$, $(1 + r)^n$;
(*b*) the total value of a sinking fund after investing £1 per annum for n years ar $r\%$, s_n;
(*c*) the sum which has to be invested per annum for n years at $r\%$ to provide a total of £1 at the end of the nth year, $s_n{}^{-1}$;
(*d*) the present value of a future payment of £1 in n years' time at $r\%$, v_n;
(*e*) the present value of a sum which when invested at $r\%$ will provide equal payments of £1 per annum every year for n years, a_n;
(*f*) the annuity or equal sum per annum which £1 will provide if invested at $r\%$, to be payable over n years, $a_n{}^{-1}$.

(a) The compounded value of a single payment after *n* years at *r*%

(i) The principle This is clearly $(1 + r)^n$ where r is the rate of interest and n is the number of years. Figure 4.1 illustrates how £1 grows at 40 per cent interest to become £3·84 after four years. At year 0 (i.e. the beginning of the first year when the money is invested) it is £1, mathematically £$(1 + r)^0$. After one year it becomes £1·40, or £$(1 + r)^1$. After two years it becomes £1·96, or £$(1 + r)^2$. In three years it becomes £2·74, or £$(1 + r)^3$ and at the end of the fourth year £3·84, or £$(1 + r)^4$.

(ii) Application Using this concept in decision-making, if our time preference rate really were as high as 40 per cent and we had to choose between spending £1 today and £4 in exactly four years' time we should choose to spend £1 today. But we should choose to receive £1 today rather than £3 in exactly four years' time because our £1 could be invested to become £3·84 then.

(b) The total value of a sinking fund after *n* years

(i) The principle If £1 is invested now, £1 in a year's time, £1 after a second year etc., for *n* years, at the end of the *n*th year the value of the total investment would be £$(1 + r)^0$ + £$(1 + r)^1$ . . . £$(1 + r)^n$

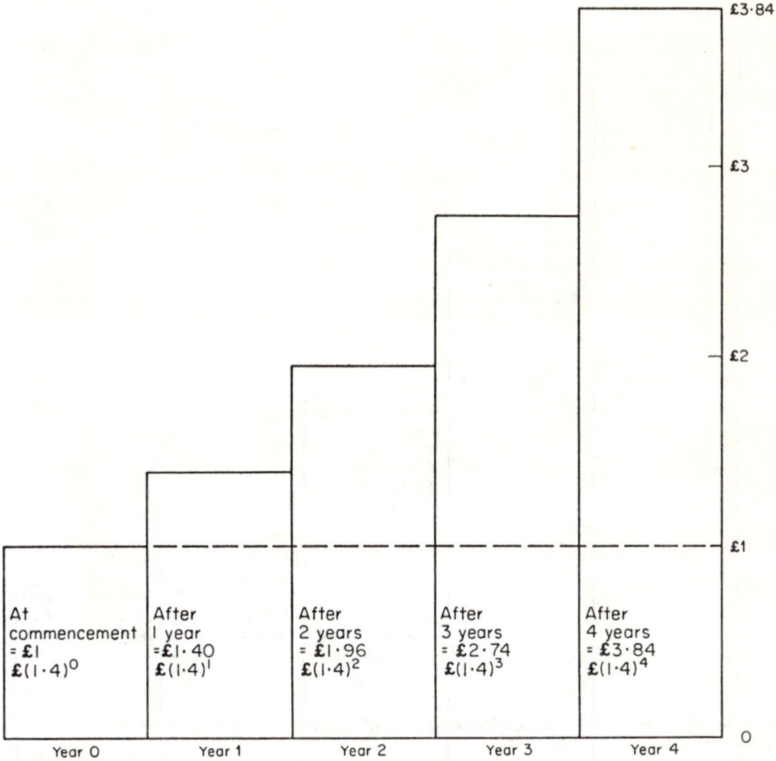

Fig 4.1 The growth of £1 at 40 per cent interest over a period of four years

This is because at the end of the period the first investment would have been invested for *n* years, the second pound would have been invested for *n* — 1 years, etc., down to the final pound which would only just have been invested. Figure 4.2 illustrates graphically how a sinking fund is compounded. In mathematical symbols it is expressed $\sum_{j=0}^{n} (1 + r)^n$ and in some compound interest tables it is s_n.

Figure 4.2 shows how, by adding the "bars" in our diagram, we can calculate the ultimate sum to which a sinking fund of five annual investments of £1 per annum would accumulate at the end of the fourth year—or the beginning of the fifth year. By adding in the reverse direction, from left to right, we can construct a table of sinking fund

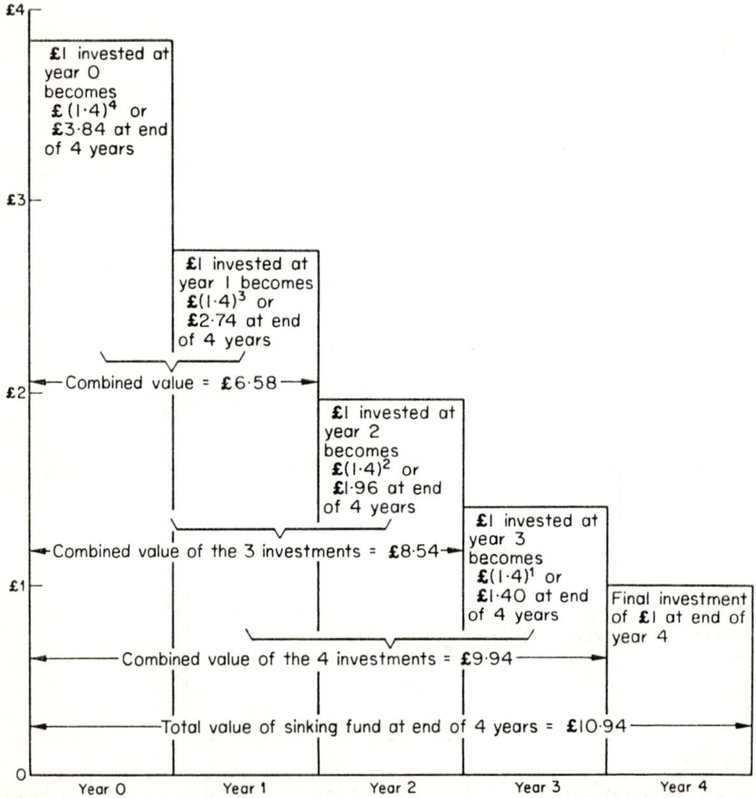

Fig 4.2 The growth of a sinking fund—regular investments of £1 at 40 per cent interest

accumulations at the beginning of years 1, 2, 3, etc. It is an important fact that sinking fund tables s_n show the position of the sinking fund at the *beginning* of the year in question. Hence £10·94 would appear in the 40 per cent table under year 5, not year 4.

To illustrate—

Year n	$(1 + r)^n$	s_n
1	1·40	1·00
2	1·96	2·40
3	2·74	4·36
4	3·84	7·10
5	5·38	10·94

Table 1 Construction of table of sinking fund values

(ii) Application Of what use is this kind of table? Suppose that we can invest back £1m into reserves each year and place them in a fund to earn interest at 10 per cent per annum. We may schedule a redevelopment project to take place after ten years, and may wish to know how much will be available for new factory buildings in the tenth year. This type of table is used to calculate how much will be available.

(c) The sum which has to be invested annually to provide £1 after *n* years

(i) The principle More often we shall be told the estimated amount needed after n years, for example for factory development, and not asked "How much will our annual investment generate after ten years?" but "How much must we invest every year to obtain this sum required in ten years' time?". We could, of course, use the above type of table and divide by the factor instead of multiplying by it, but would find this time-consuming. It is easier to multiply than to divide.

Suppose we wished to calculate the amount to be invested annually to obtain £1,000 at the beginning of the fifth year. We could use Table 1 and divide £1,000 by 10·94, but it would be better if we could consult a table showing the reciprocal of £10·94, and multiply this reciprocal figure by £1,000. Such tables are constructed by dividing 1 by the s_n factor concerned. To find how much has to be reinvested annually for n years at r per cent to provide a specified sum after n years, we then multiply by the reciprocal factor, s_n^{-1}. These converted tables are easily constructed as Table 2 illustrates.

Year n	s_n	$1/s_n$ or s_n^{-1}	s_n^{-1} (converted)
1	1·00	$\frac{1{\cdot}00}{1{\cdot}00}$	1·00
2	2·40	$\frac{1{\cdot}00}{2{\cdot}40}$	0·417
3	4·36	$\frac{1{\cdot}00}{4{\cdot}36}$	0·229
4	7·10	$\frac{1{\cdot}00}{7{\cdot}10}$	0·141
5	10·94	$\frac{1{\cdot}00}{10{\cdot}94}$	0·091

Table 2 Calculation of reciprocal sinking fund values

(ii) Application This table is valuable. If we need to replace machinery in four years' time, and assume our fabulous interest rate of 40 per cent, how much shall we invest per year, commencing now and ending with a fifth payment at the end of the fourth year? Assume that the machine will cost £5,000. The table shows that an investment of £455 per year (£5,000 × 0·091) is all that is required. In real life interest rates, of course, are not so high but the fact is well illustrated. These tables are the type that building societies and insurance companies employ to illustrate the "fabulous"(?) effect of regular persistent saving. They are invaluable to companies in solving the problem of machine depreciation and replacement.

(d) The present value of £1 in *n* years' time

(i) The principle This concept is the very foundation of the discounted cash flow method of investment appraisal. I suggested earlier that value of an investment is related to the expected future stream of benefits from it taking into account a compound interest factor. For illustration, let our interest factor remain 40 per cent. The present value of £1 receivable at the end of n years, commonly styled v_n in actuaries' and accountants' tables is simply the reciprocal of $(1 + r)^n$.

(ii) Application If an investment does not yield a constant income for each year, but provides an extra £1,000 income at the end of year 1 and £1,500 income at the end of year 2, the present value of the investment is calculated by taking the extra income receivable from the project in each successive year and multiplying it by the appropriate

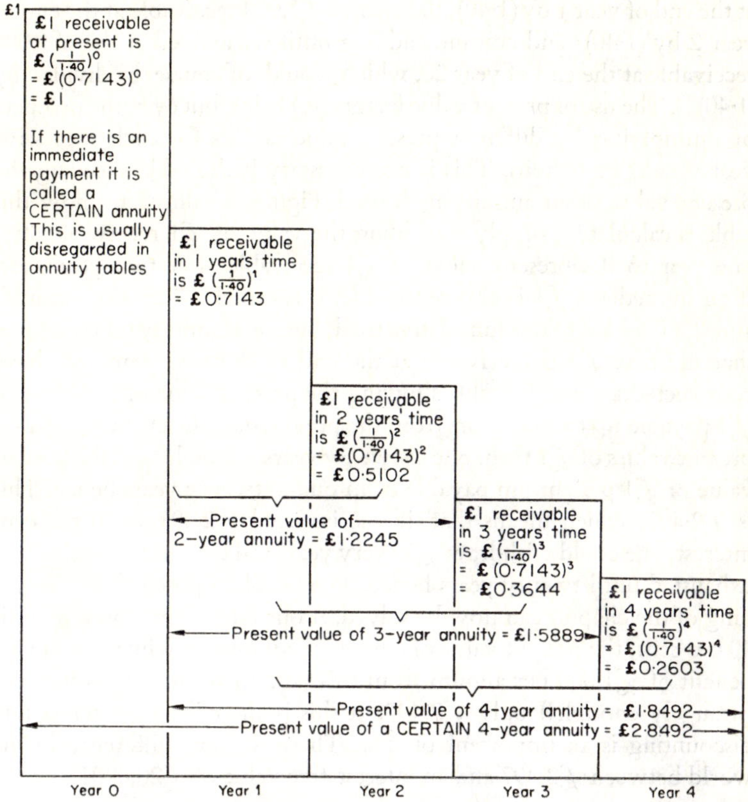

Fig 4.3 The present value of £1 receivable after *n* years at 40 per cent interest—illustrating accumulation of annuity values

present value factor, the £1,000 in year 1 by v_1, the £1,500 in year 2 by v_2. In our case, the £714·3 (present value of year 1 income—see Figure 4.3) would be added to the £765·3 (present value of £1,500 in year 2), and so on until the total present value of the investment would have been calculated.

(e) The present value of an annuity

What is the present value of a machine which yields a constant £1,000 per annum extra income for the next twenty years? Assume there is no immediate "income" of £1,000 as soon as the first year commences. To discover such a present value, we could divide the £1,000 receivable at the end of year 1 by (1·40), the second £1,000 receivable at the end of year 2 by $(1{\cdot}40)^2$ and continue adding until we arrived at the £1,000 receivable at the end of year 20, which would, of course, be divided by $(1{\cdot}40)^{20}$. The use of present value factors (v_n) helps, but even the prospect of multiplying by different present value factors for each successive year would be tedious. This is not necessary if the table showing the present value of an annuity a_n is used. Figure 4.3 illustrates how this table is calculated, simply by adding the value of £1 receivable after one year to the present value of £1 receivable after two years, etc. If an immediate £1 is also receivable, it is called a "certain annuity" and £1 is added to the cumulative total, but most annuity tables assume that the first £1 is receivable at the end of the first year. We have constructed an annuity table showing the present value of annuities of £1 payable up to four years from the present date, but by aggregating present values of £1 from one to twenty years we could find the present value of £1 per annum payable from one to twenty years hence. This is £2·497, which means that, if one invested £2·497 at 40 per cent interest, one could withdraw £1 every year, and the fund would not be exhausted until twenty years hence. The problem posed at the beginning of the chapter can now be solved. If our rate of time preference is 40 per cent, the present value of a piece of equipment which provides a benefit of £1,000 per annum from this year to twenty years hence is (strangely enough!) only £2,497. If this is the effective interest rate discounting is an important process. There is every difference in the world between £2,497 and an interest-free value of £20,000!

(f) The annuity payable from a present investment Sometimes it is helpful to know the reciprocal of the above, that is the amount payable per annum which a present investment will provide. If £1,000 is invested now, how much could be withdrawn at the end of every year for twenty years without exhausting the fund? From the last paragraph, this is clearly £1,000/2·497 or about £400·5, which means that, if £1,000 is invested at 40 per cent interest, I can withdraw £400·5 every year for twenty years and the fund will be exhausted in about twenty years' time. This inverted annuity value, a_n^{-1} is simply the reciprocal of a_n.

Year n	a_n	$1/a_n$ or a_n^{-1}	a_n^{-1} (converted)
1	0·7143	$\frac{1\cdot0000}{0\cdot7143}$	1·400
2	1·2245	$\frac{1\cdot0000}{1\cdot2245}$	0·817
3	1·5889	$\frac{1\cdot0000}{1\cdot5889}$	0·629
4	1·8492	$\frac{1\cdot0000}{1\cdot8492}$	0·541
5	2·0352	$\frac{1\cdot0000}{2\cdot0352}$	0·491

Table 3 Calculation of annuities which a present investment of £1 will provide

Summary and comparison of the concepts

A high rate of interest was deliberately chosen for better graphical presentation, and because the differences between the six concepts are easier to illustrate. The differences for low rates are less marked. The 40 per cent table which we have constructed appears below. Once the differences between the six concepts are appreciated it is easy to use the tables at the end of the book.

Year	$(1+r)^n$	s_n	s_n^{-1}	v_n	a_n	a_n^{-1}
1	1·40	1·00	1·000	0·7143	0·7143	1·400
2	1·96	2·40	0·417	0·5102	1·2245	0·817
3	2·74	4·36	0·229	0·3644	1·5889	0·629
4	3·84	7·10	0·141	0·2603	1·8492	0·541
5	5·38	10·94	0·091	0·1860	2·0352	0·491

Table 4 Compound Interest Tables—40 per cent

Questions

1. At a capital cost of 10 per cent calculate which you would prefer to receive in payment for a house—
   (*a*) £5,000 now
   (*b*) Annual rent of £500 for fifteen years commencing now, but with no payment at the end of the fifteenth year, the house being fit for demolition then and having no residual value
   (*c*) £7,000 in three years' time
2. Howard expects to receive the following amounts of income at the end of each of the next four years—

	£
1	400
2	260
3	540
4	635

   How much is all this worth in terms of present value if his rate of time preference is 9 per cent, and these amounts are discounted at that rate?
3. Marsh receives a Christmas bonus from his employer amounting to £100 per year and he decides to invest it over six years for the purchase of a motor-car. He puts the money in a bank who offer 5 per cent interest, arguing that his £600 instalments at 5 per cent will accrue another £30 interest and so enable him to purchase the car at £630. Is he right in his calculations? What is the basis of his supposition? (Ignore tax.)
4. What is the present value of a single sum of £1,000 receivable in ten years' time at 9 per cent per annum discount?

Bibliography

W. J. Baumol, *Economic Theory and Operations Analysis* (Prentice-Hall, 1965)

H. Bierman & S. Smidt, *The Capital Budgeting Decision* (Collier-Macmillan, 1968)

I. Fisher, *The Theory of Interest* (New York, 1930)

A. J. Grant, *Accounting Made Simple* (W. H. Allen, 1970)

J. G. Kemeny *et al.*, *Finite Mathematics with Business Applications* (Prentice-Hall, 1962)
J. T. S. Porterfield, *Investment Decisions and Capital Costs* (Prentice-Hall, 1965)
E. Solomon, "The Arithmetic of Capital Budgeting Decisions", *Journal of Business*, Vol. 29, 1956

5 The Mathematics of Decision-making

At the beginning of the previous chapter I stated two principles which had emerged from the preliminary discussion of planning. They were that the purpose of planning is to make the best uses of resources to achieve stated objectives and that no planning is feasible if its total costs are greater than its total benefits. The first principle is a statement of purpose while the second is a "golden rule" which must always be applied if planning is to be useful at all. The previous chapter discussed the implications of this rule and showed that it was often complicated by a time preference factor, by the fact that time is a constraint and a resource, and that it is more satisfying to achieve ends in the short run than in the long run.

In this chapter we can return to the first major principle, to the statement of the purpose of planning. In Chapter 3 we viewed the planning problem from the strategic and economic aspects, and we interpreted *ends* as goals or targets and *means* as the resources of whatsoever kind which were available in the achievement of such targets. As in the case of the earlier example of feedback systems and standard costing there exists an inevitable gap between what we have and what we want and the purpose of search technique is to narrow and possibly close the strategic gap.

Mathematical programming is a different approach to a similar problem. Instead of defining our ends as targets or goals, we now define them as objectives, as the direction in which we are going. As stated in Chapter 3 (page 24), we may desire to maximize, optimize or "satisfice". Often optimizing and maximizing amount to the same thing, but not necessarily so, for maximizing the use of plant may mean over-using it and maximizing production may mean straining storage capacity with a product which cannot be sold. In the mathematical model, means are resources as previously, but because they are limited in quantity, they are shown as constraints. If we had the problem of maximizing production of one type of product with one set of resources we would simply use the resources until they were exhausted, but mathematical programming helps us decide how much of our resources will be spent upon each form of production. Programmes may be either (*a*) linear, or (*b*) non-linear.

(a) Linear programming

The term "programming" may be misleading, for it may suggest computer programming. In fact, mathematical programming is a method of solving a kind of problem involving one objective and a number of constraints. Assume that a firm uses two restricted inputs, sugar and labour, in the manufacture of syrup and cough-linctus, that every batch of syrup produced and sold adds £2 to the firm's profits and every batch of bottles of cough-mixture produced and sold adds £3 to the firm's profits. There are only 140 units of sugar, of which 7 units are needed for 1 unit of syrup but only 2 for 1 unit of linctus. There are only 100 units of labour, of which 2 units are needed for 1 unit of syrup, but 5 units for making 1 unit of cough-linctus. We can formulate the problem by letting a and b be the quantities of syrup and cough-linctus respectively—

Objective:	Maximize	$2a + 3b$
Constraints:	Subject to	$7a + 2b \leqslant 140$ (sugar units)
		$2a + 5b \leqslant 100$ (labour units)

Our solution must not be negative so: $a,b \geqslant 0$ (non-negativity). (The sign $\leqslant$ means "less than or equal to" and $\geqslant$ means "greater than or equal to".)

Graphical solution In Figure 5.1 units of syrup are shown on the vertical axis and units of cough-linctus on the horizontal axis. If all sugar was used for syrup production we could make 20 units of syrup, but if all sugar was used to produce cough-mixture we could make 70 units of cough-mixture. The "sugar constraint" line on the graph is a locus of combinations of production points at which all sugar is exhausted. Feasible production must be under this line. Similarly, if we used all labour on syrup production we could produce 50 units of syrup, but if we used all labour on cough-linctus production we could only produce 20 units of cough-mixture. The "labour constraint" line is a locus of combinations of output at which all labour is exhausted. Taking into account non-negativity, the feasible area (that where production is possible) is now the area bounded by the shaded lines in our graph, *OYXZ*.

You may now guess that the best combination is at *X* where the lines intersect, but you could be wrong. Much depends on the objective function. If there were no profit from cough-mixture in any one year we should produce at *Y*. To be sure that *X* is the optimal point at which to produce, we must draw upon the graph *isoprofit* lines. Any line parallel to that drawn on our graph falls into this category. The gradient

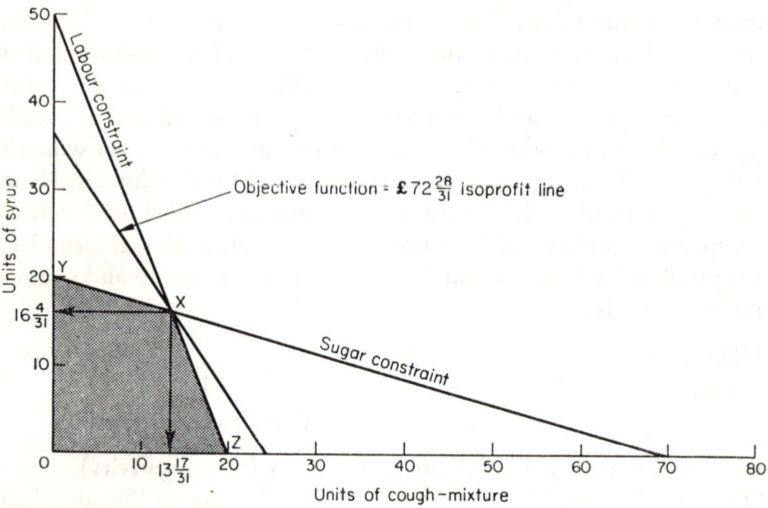

Fig 5.1 Graphical solution of a linear programming model

must be such that 3 units of syrup have to be produced for every 2 units of cough-mixture because cough-mixture is 1·5 times more profitable than syrup. The highest point of tangency between an isoprofit line and the feasible area is indeed at *X* where nearly £73 profit can be earned. To make this profit by producing only syrup we should have to produce over 36 units of syrup earning £2 per unit. To make this profit by producing only cough-linctus we should have to produce over 24 units of cough mixture at £3 per unit. As you can see, the isoprofit line which is tangential to the feasible area at its highest point is that which connects $36\frac{14}{31}$ on the syrup axis and $24\frac{9}{31}$ on the cough-mixture axis. It is only possible to make this profit £$72\frac{28}{31}$ at *X*, and *X* is therefore the point of optimum feasible output.

The simplex method We can draw graphs where there are one objective function and two constraints. If there are three constraints and three possible products we need a three-dimensional graph. If constraints and products are more numerous then solution by graphs is impossible. The simplex method is a means of solving linear programmes by logical iteration (trial and error). Because of linearity on a two-dimensional graph, the solution lies at one of the corners (except in the odd case where one of the constraints is parallel to the objective function, so that the optimal solution lies anywhere along that constraint). On a two-dimensional graph we can usually tell at a glance the optimal corner.

Once it is realized that the solution usually lies at a corner, it may be assumed that in a "graph" drawn in *n* dimensions the solution would be at one of the "corners". The simplex method starts at corner O and progresses upwards, comparing one "corner position" with another until the optimum is reached. If one corner is better than those previously tried, it is compared with the untried corners, and as soon as further comparison reduces profit optimality is reached. So only some of the feasible solutions need be examined, and the method ensures that each successive "corner" examined is more profitable than those previously examined.

We start at point O and create two dummy activities which will use up the waste resources of sugar or labour, so that our constraints can be expressed as equations. Let the dummy activities be *S* and *T*, and profit be *P*.

$$P = 0 + 2a + 3b$$
$$S = 140 - 7a - 2b$$
$$T = 100 - 2a - 5b$$

These three equations are at corner O, where nothing is produced, so *a* and *b* are 0, there is no profit (*P*) and there are respectively 140 and 100 slack units of sugar and labour. Let us put this in matrix form.

		A	*B*
P	0	2	3
S	140	−7	−2
T	100	−2	−5

The next best corner is at Z. We get there graphically by moving along the more profitable horizontal axis to reach corner Z and checking the profit P with that at the corner vertically above O (Y on our diagram) to see which is preferable. To get there mathematically one transforms the above matrix observing the rules—

1. Choose a pivot element, the element which diverts the greatest amount of resources from the slack activities. It is the lowest element in the most profitable column. The column is B so the pivot element is —5.
2. Substitute the reciprocal of the pivot element in its place ($-\frac{1}{5}$).
3. For all other elements in the same row as the pivot element, change the sign and divide by the pivot element.
4. For all other elements in the same column as the pivot element, do not change the sign but divide by the pivot element.
5. For all other elements, substitute new elements by applying the formula—

   New element = Old element — (product of the other two "corner" elements, divided by the pivot element).

The first transformation illustrated below shows the position at Z, at "20" on the horizontal axis—

		A	T
P	60	$\frac{4}{5}$	$-\frac{3}{5}$
S	100	$-\frac{31}{5}$	$\frac{2}{5}$
B	20	$-\frac{2}{5}$	$-\frac{1}{5}$

Having reached Z where 20 units of cough linctus are produced earning £3 per unit making a total profit of £60, now we move up the oblique line to X by a second transformation adopting the same rules except that now our pivot element is $-\frac{31}{5}$ which we transform to $-\frac{5}{31}$

		S	T
P	$72\frac{28}{31}$	$-\frac{4}{31}$	$-\frac{17}{31}$
A	$16\frac{4}{31}$	$-\frac{5}{31}$	$-\frac{2}{31}$
B	$13\frac{17}{31}$	$\frac{2}{31}$	$-\frac{7}{31}$

The second transformation brings us to X on the graph where we make £$72\frac{28}{31}$ profit from the production and sale of $16\frac{4}{31}$ units of syrup at £2 per unit (£$32\frac{8}{31}$) and $13\frac{17}{31}$ units of cough mixture at £3 per unit (£$40\frac{20}{31}$). This agrees with the graphical solution.

The dual problem Sugar and labour are limited resources so their "value" depends on the profit which can be made from the products. These scarce resources would be bought only if profit could be made by selling the products. The additional price we would be prepared to pay for sugar and labour given the above constraints and levels of profit is calculated by means of a minimization model which looks very much like our original problem turned sideways. Let M and L be the cost per unit of sugar and labour.

Objective: minimize cost. Minimize $140M + 100L$

Constraints: Subject to $2M + 5L \geqslant 3$ (cough-mixtures).

$7M + 2L \geqslant 2$ (syrup).

$M, L \geqslant 0$ (non-negativity).

By solving this problem one obtains the solution matrix of the previous problem turned sideways in much the same way, so that the figures $+\frac{4}{31}$ and $+\frac{17}{31}$ now appear in the first column as values of M and L respectively. These dual values represent the contribution which each unit of the factor makes towards profit, given the scarcity of resources and the level of profit. They indicate how much it is worth paying for the scarce factors in excess of their market price in order to continue making a profit. The proof of our solution is—

$$140\left(\tfrac{4}{31}\right) + 100\left(\tfrac{17}{31}\right) = 72\tfrac{28}{31}$$
$$2\left(\tfrac{4}{31}\right) + 5\left(\tfrac{17}{31}\right) = 3$$
$$7\left(\tfrac{4}{31}\right) + 2\left(\tfrac{17}{31}\right) = 2$$

We have examined one use of linear programming. Later we shall discuss its value in solving capital budgeting problems in a capital rationing situation and in divisional control.

(b) Non-linear programming

As we shall see later, linear programming is rather too simple to explain decision-making fully in real life, for the profit per unit is not as uniform as it would seem. Demand for a product tends to restrict the number of units which can be placed on the market and the profit which can be made, so that the objective function may be influenced by other factors apart from supply, and the ratio between the profits-per-unit of different products may suddenly vary. The "constraint" boundaries in the programming diagrams of the category of Figure 5.1 may be curves, not straight lines, and make solution far more difficult.

This fact could be illustrated with some of the concave and convex curves which the economists use in order to illustrate that there would, for example, in the case illustrated earlier in the chapter, be an optimum amount of syrup or of cough-linctus which could be produced from the resources, quite apart from the profitability of either of these items. If we were to substitute concave or convex curves for the constraint lines in Figure 5.1, and if the objective function altered in angle for varying amounts of each of the products, the programme would become far more complicated. But real-life diagrams are not linear, that is, their functions are not straight lines. It does not need an economist to convince factory managers that if, say, the syrup production department were entrusted with very large stocks of sugar because it appeared to be the more profitable, disproportionately larger quantities would be wasted or would tend to disappear.

Non-linear programmes are better solved by computer. From experience data can be prepared and analysed by using advanced techniques, so that the computer can be employed to define the curve most appropriate to the constraint and confine itself to the area bounded by such constraints in providing a solution.

In much the same way, the computer can be employed to solve programmes which are constrained, not by curves nor by straight lines, but by steps. Integer programming is needed when we are concerned about the number of whole units of each product that will best satisfy the conditions. In the example, it matters very little that the optimum solution is $16\frac{4}{31}$ units of syrup and $13\frac{17}{31}$ units of cough-mixture, instead of 16 and 13 respectively because we are presumably dealing with small units, but it would matter a great deal if the units were ocean-going liners. Integer programming employs the "integer mode" in computer programming so that the constraints have each a kind of step pattern, and the solution will always be in whole numbers.

Computers often use iterative processes (calculated guesswork) in providing solutions because they can perform a very large number of calculations at high speed. For this reason it is often possible to build a complete model of the firm in a computer and provide even more exact answers. It is, however, in most cases simpler to use linear models to get approximate solutions, and as they provide the best means of illustration, we shall be using this kind of model in the rest of the book.

Summary

Instead of regarding ends as goals, and means as the resources required for attaining such goals, and calculating the gap, we may instead consider our ends to be broad objectives, such as maximizing profit or minimizing cost and mathematically quantify resources to discover which combination of them is best in achieving the particular objective upon which we have decided.

The best method of illustration is the use of a simple graph with one objective function and two resources as in Figure 5.1, where the hatched area is feasible, and the point *X* is optimal. Because it is difficult to draw graphs in more than two dimensions a method of programming, known as the simplex method, is utilized to provide optimum solutions. The easier kind of programming problem can be solved manually, but high-speed computers are necessary in cases where there are many constraints.

Constraints may not always be straight lines, and computers can often be employed to discover the best type of curve to use in the solution of the more complex type of programme. Similarly, programmes can be written in integer in cases where there are large units involved and an optimum solution is required in whole numbers. Often a complete model of a given company can be built in a computer and even more exact solutions provided, but the cost of doing so is high. The simple linear programme in two dimensions is quite adequate for illustrating the uses of programming, and we shall be confined to this kind of programme in the rest of the book.

Questions

1. Model M makes £5 per unit profit and model N makes £3 per unit profit. Model M requires 7 material units and 1 hour labour and Model N requires 1 material unit and 3 hours labour. Total materials available are 700 units and total available labour is 300 hours. Formulate the problem as a linear programme.
2. Solve the above problem using (*a*) graphical method and (*b*) the simplex method.
3. Write the dual programme which corresponds to the above maximization programme.

4. Calculate the shadow costs (opportunity costs) of (*a*) a material unit and (*b*) a labour hour.
5. What is a non-linear programme?
6. Discuss the reasons for integer programming. In what industries is integer programming needed?
7. What is the reason for using simple linear programmes if the more complex programmes provide more exact results?

Bibliography

M. Alexis & C. Z. Wilson (eds.), *Organizational Decision Making* (Prentice-Hall, 1967)

W. J. Baumol, *Economic Theory and Operations Analysis* (Prentice-Hall, 1965)

B. V. Carsberg, *An Introduction to Mathematical Programming for Accountants* (Allen & Unwin, 1969)

J. G. Kemeny *et al.*, *Finite Mathematics with Business Applications* (Prentice-Hall, 1962)

J. Sizer, *An Insight into Management Accounting* (Penguin, 1970)

D. Solomons (ed.), *Studies in Cost Analysis* (Sweet & Maxwell, 1968) (articles by Demski and Samuels)

H. Thomas, *Decision Theory and the Manager* (Pitman, 1972)

6 Methods of Capital Budgeting

We are now in a position to combine some of the principles which were considered in Chapters 3, 4 and 5 and to see how they should be applied in choosing between alternative plans or projects which are likely to be beneficial in the long run. Planning at all levels is a matter of trying to close the gap between what we have and what we want. In the lower levels of control the gap may take the form of a variance between actual performance and expected performance, but in the higher levels of planning the gap exists either because targets (or goals) are too high or because resources are not being fully used, or perhaps for both reasons. It is sufficient to move in the direction of our goals, but to set a standard which is feasible. To use Figure 5.1, this means that, instead of moving to some vague unfeasible target in the top right-hand corner of the diagram, we decide instead to move to X and set X as our target. Note, however, that before we could even set X as our target it was necessary to make up our minds as to what to maximize. If either a or b had been unprofitable the position would have been different.

In the short-term product problem it was easy to decide upon the objective function, to maximize $2a + 3b$. Long-term problems are complicated by the time factor. Chapter 4 showed how it was possible to allow for the time factor by using a "discount rate" or rate of time preference, but this goes only a small way to solving the problem of how to account for the time factor in planning. Much depends upon what we decide to maximize. If all the money in the world could be borrowed at a uniform rate by everybody it would be a simple matter to discount all the costs and benefits of each project at the standard rate of interest, and find out which had the highest "net present value" (that is, the present value of total benefits less the present value of total costs). But do we really wish to maximize our present worth? Further, there is no uniform discount rate. Some think that it is better to try to discover which project has the highest inherent profitability expressed as a rate of interest, while others would try to discover the profitability of the project expressed as a ratio between costs and benefits after a given (sometimes arbitrary) cost of capital rate is taken into account.

For this reason five widely used methods of capital budgeting will be considered:

(i) payback;
(ii) internal rate of return;
(iii) net present value;
(iv) net terminal value; and
(v) adjusted value-cost ratio.

Then problems of capital rationing are outlined.

Payback

This means calculating the length of time it takes to recover the cost of an investment, disregarding interest rates. If an extra £600 income per year can be earned by spending £6,000 on a new machinc, payback period will be ten years. Compare this with another project demanding an outlay of £6,000 but yielding an annual benefit of £500 per year. The second project has a payback period of twelve years, and so the first project appears better. But quite apart from compound interest considerations the valuation formula in Chapter 1 assumes that value depends on all expected costs and benefits from a project, not merely those up to the point of time when initial outlay is recovered. Payback method disregards those costs and benefits beyond the time-horizon of cost-recovery.

Using the above figures, suppose that Project I had no payback after year 10 but legal damages in year 13 for infringement of rights and that Project II has a guaranteed income of £500 per year up to year 20. Even at zero rate of interest, the position is now—

Project I		Project II	
	£		£
Cost at outset	6,000	Cost at outset	6,000
10 years income × £600	6,000	20 years income × £500	10,000
	Nil		
Legal damages, say	3,000	Net advantage	£4,000
Net disadvantage	−£3,000		

Unless the interest factor is very high Project II is now preferable, but payback method takes no account of interest factors and time preference. Imagine that two other projects A and B have identical costs of £11,100. Both have a payback period of three years but the patterns of distribution of cash flows are—

Project A		Project B	
Year	£	*Year*	£
1	10,000	1	100
2	1,000	2	1,000
3	100	3	10,000
	£11,100		£11,100

The payback criterion cannot distinguish between A and B since both cost £11,100 and have a three-year payback period. But surely even if only 2 per cent interest could be earned per annum upon the £10,000 cash flow from Project A in years 2 and 3 it would be worth at least £400 more than Project B. So payback method is defective because it disregards interest and time-preference factors and they are an essential of capital investment rationale.

A third argument against payback method is the impossibility of comparing different-sized investment patterns. If we compare the following projects the problem can be grasped.

Project I			Project II		
Year	*Costs*	*Benefits*	*Year*	*Costs*	*Benefits*
	£	£		£	£
0	800	—	0	1,000	—
1	200	400	1	—	100
2	—	400	2	—	400
3	—	100	3	—	500
4	—	100	4	—	—
	£1,000	£1,000		£1,000	£1,000

Projects I and II have payback periods of four and three years respectively so that by the payback criterion Project II is better, but Project I's initial cost of £800 can be recovered in two years so if it were divisible Project I could be more desirable.

A final argument against payback is the strategic one of planning. Large projects require extended initial investment and will not yield immediate benefits. Consider the two following projects—

Project X			Project Y		
Year	*Costs*	*Benefits*	*Year*	*Costs*	*Benefits*
	£	£		£	£
0	1,000	—	0	10,000	—
1	—	2,000	1	10,000	—
2–10	—	1,000	2–10	90,000	—
11–100	—	—	11–100	—	1,800,000
	£1,000	£3,000		£110,000	£1,800,000

Project X has a payback period of less than a year and yields 300 per cent on cost some time within the ten years. Project Y is a complete loser for the first ten years but when returns come they average £20,000 per annum for the ensuing ninety years. On a payback analysis Project Y would not even be considered, but ignoring interest considerations, the long-term benefit seems very much greater.

It seems a simple method to apply and provides a "rule-of-thumb" guide for excluding many projects and so saves assessment time. Other methods of assessment ignore the time-value of money, for example, taking the cost, apportioning it over the years of useful life and deducting such apportionment from the annual return on a project. But all methods which ignore the time-value of money are doomed to failure as inaccurate criteria of real worth.

Internal rate of return and net present value

Internal rate of return must be distinguished from net present value: it measures an investment's profitability as a rate per cent. It is the rate per cent at which the sum of discounted future benefits equals the sum of discounted future costs, and involves calculating r (the rate per cent) where—

$$\sum_{j=0}^{\infty}\frac{V_j}{(1+r)^j}=\sum_{j=0}^{\infty}\frac{C_j}{(1+r)^j}$$

In this equation V_j and C_j are the benefits and costs respectively for each year j from 0, the present to infinity. The symbol $\sum$ means the sum of the series (of years in this case).

In contrast, net present value is the difference between discounted future benefits and discounted present and future costs, where the rate of discount is the cost of capital or, in some cases, the opportunity cost. It involves computing—

$$\sum_{j=0}^{\infty} \frac{V_j}{(1+c)^j} - \sum_{j=0}^{\infty} \frac{C_j}{(1+c)^j}$$

where c is the cost of capital, the rate at which funds can be borrowed. Thus $r - c$ is the rate of "pure profit" on the project, and a project is only profitable if $r \geqslant c$. It is rejected if $c \geqslant r$. The internal rate of return method of project assessment chooses that which maximizes r, or, in some cases, which maximizes $r - c$, whereas the net present value method chooses that which maximizes net present value, the value computed by applying the above formula.

The internal rate of return method of assessment is popular but presents problems. Manual solutions of r in the first formula above involve "hit-and-miss" methods of calculation sometimes, and some distribution patterns of returns over time have impossible or multiple solutions. An example of the impossible solution is the Porterfield paradox. An investor invests £1 in year 0, receives £2 from the investment in year 1 but has to pay the £2 back in year 2. The internal rate of return in this case is r where—

$$2 + (1 + r)^2 = 2(1 + r)$$

In this case $2 + 2r + 1 + r^2 = 2 + 2r$

$$r^2 = -1$$

$$r = \sqrt{-1}$$

Mathematically this is an impossible solution. Now consider an investment pattern where a company invests £1 in year 0, receives £5 from the investment in year 1 but has to pay back the £5 in year 2. The internal rate of return is r where—

$$5 + (1 + r)^2 = 5(1 + r)$$

In this case $5 + 1 + 2r + r^2 = 5 + 5r$

Deducting $5 + 2r$ and transposing this becomes—

$$r^2 = 3r - 1$$

This equation has two possible solutions 2·6 and 0·38 (260 per cent and 38 per cent). Squaring r approximately for simplicity, at 2·6, the solution is—

$$6{\cdot}8 = 7{\cdot}8 - 1$$

It would be unprofitable for the company to borrow money at higher than 260 per cent because net present value would then be negative.

At 0·38, again squaring r approximately for simplicity—

$$0{\cdot}14 = 1{\cdot}14 - 1$$

The problem is the 38 per cent cut-off point. If cost of capital is 38 per cent for the above project $r = c$, so that net present value is zero. Funds borrowed at more than 260 per cent obviously give the project a negative net present value and funds borrowed between 38 per cent and 260 per cent would give the project a positive net present value, as the curve produced by this project pattern (Figure 6.1) illustrates. But what

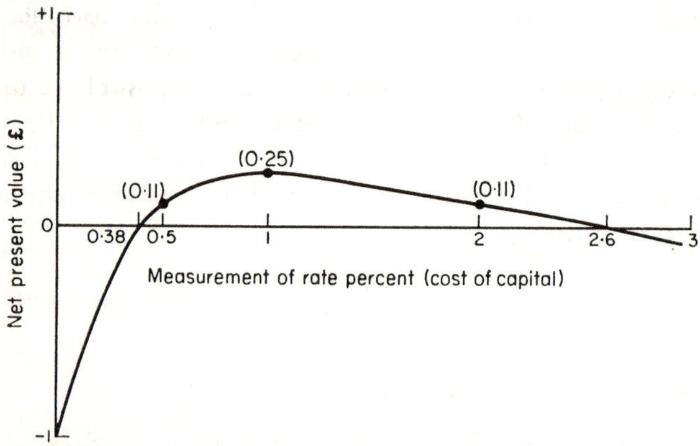

Fig 6.1 The internal rate of return produced by (—1, +5, —5)
Note. This kind of pattern produces the peculiar anomaly that if funds are borrowed freely the project has a net present value of —£1, but if borrowed at 100 per cent it has a net present value of +0·25p.

happens if the cost of capital (c) is less than the lower value of r, if it is less than 38 per cent? Figure 6.1 demonstrates that in this case the project again assumes a net present value which is negative. This is a strange paradox. It means that, if a bank loaned you money interest-free for this unlikely project, you would lose £1, for the project involves paying £1 at year 0, receiving £5 at year 1 and having to pay the £5 back at year 2. But if your bank charged 38 per cent on this project, you would break even, provided that you could also reinvest funds at 38 per cent—and indeed, if your bank charged you 100 per cent interest and you could also reinvest the £5 at 100 per cent interest, you would actually make a profit for net present value would be—

$$£\frac{5}{(1+1)} - 1 - \frac{5}{(1+1)^2}$$

This is simplified to 0·25, so that if 100 per cent is the relevant rate of interest, the project has a positive net present value of 25p.

Obviously, the internal rates of return of 38 per cent and 260 per cent tell us nothing about the real profitability of such a project. We can only predict the worth-whileness of such a project if the cost of capital is known.

Internal rate of return criteria also assume that a project's profitability does not vary with time. Net present value calculations may involve discounting at various rates for different periods if it is expected that capital cost (c) will fluctuate because of anticipated bank-rate or boom conditions, but there is no way of introducing this fluctuation of c into internal rate of return calculations and the rate of return (r) is assessed as a uniform rate which does not vary from period to period. If a project has as many rates of return as years of life, the peculiar project we have examined would have the pattern—

$$(1 + r_1)(1 + r_2) + 5 = 5\,(1 + r_1)$$

where r_1 and r_2 are estimates of the real return in years 1 and 2 respectively. Such an equation would certainly have multiple solutions because r_1 and r_2 are both unknowns.

There is the problem of reinvestment opportunities. If £3,170 is borrowed at 10 per cent to pay for a project which will yield £1,000 per year for four years, it would break even, for $r = c$, since £3,170 is the present value of a four-year annuity of £1,000 at 10 per cent. On the other hand, if the internal rate of return (r) was less than 10 per cent it would be unacceptable and if $r \geqslant (c = 10$ per cent) it would certainly be acceptable. But people do not always borrow money to repay it whenever they like. Redeemable preference shares, debentures and bank overdrafts are negotiated for a fixed term, and in the above example it is likely that £3,170 would remain borrowed for four years and the total repaid at the end of the period. The acceptance criterion would now not merely be whether r $\geqslant$ ($c = 10$ per cent) but depend on the reinvestment opportunities for the net cash flows of £683, since £317 of each year's £1,000 cash flow would be needed to pay 10 per cent interest on the whole loan of £3,170. If these net cash flows of £683 per annum can be reinvested at more than 10 per cent the project is worth while, but if money became cheaper during the life of the project and the investor had contracted to pay 10 per cent upon £3,170, he would be unable to earn sufficient to repay this and the project would not be worth while. Future capital costs and reinvestment rates will probably differ from each other and will not be constant over time. What if the internal rate of return on a project is higher than both borrowing and reinvestment rates in years 1 and 4, lower than both rates in year 2 and came somewhere between borrowing and reinvestment rates in year 3? It would be difficult to rank such a project to compare it with one having a different time-pattern because it involved reinvestment and borrowing rates of later years.

So the internal rate of return criterion presents many problems. These are complexity of calculation, impossible and multiple solutions, the assumption that a project has a uniform rate of return which is constant over time despite boom and recession conditions, and the assumption that borrowing and reinvestment rates are not only always equal, but that they are also constant over the life of the project, whereas this is invariably not the case. But despite these difficulties it can provide a good index of a project's profitability. If the project's internal rate of return (r) is always greater than cost of capital (c) it would seem to be always acceptable.

Let us see how this works out in a capital-rationing situation. In the simple capital-rationing situation there is a ceiling above which one cannot borrow. If this is £10,000, which could be borrowed at $c = 10$ per cent and a given project has an internal rate of $r = 20$ per cent the project is acceptable if it costs less than £10,000. There is a more complex capital-rationing situation, however, where there is no fixed "ceiling" but the cost of capital increases for each additional sum borrowed. The first £3,000 may be borrowed from a bank at 10 per cent, the next £10,000 by issuing shares, which investors expect to yield 15 per cent, the next £15,000 at 20 per cent and so on. So capital is "price-rationed" in steps, and profitability (r) could also be in "steps" because of "plant-capacity", a concept examined later in the book. Let us assume the following steps in project-profitability—

Increments of outlay		*Internal rate of return* (r)
	£	%
	5,000	25
the next	10,000	22
each additional	10,000	... in each case 2 less

The problem is not one of deciding whether to accept or reject such an investment but deciding the level of the investment, given the "step"

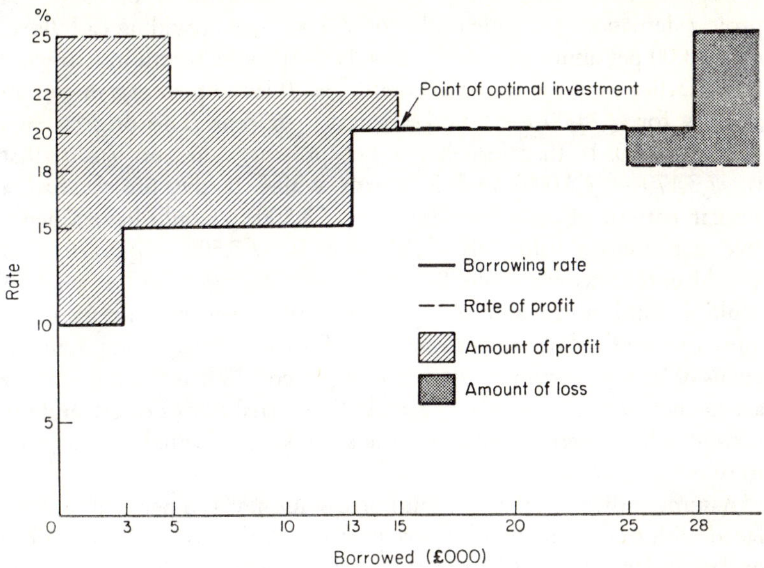

Fig 6.2 Progressive investment with varying rates

case of capital rationing outlined earlier. The solution in such a case is to invest at the lowest point where marginal (incremental) cost of capital equals marginal (incremental) rate of return upon the project.

Figure 6.2 illustrates these step patterns. The optimum return on the project is where borrowing and investing rates start to converge at £15,000. Both "incremental" (marginal) rates converge at 20 per cent. The first £3,000 profits 15 per cent, for $r - c = 25\% - 10\%$. The next £2,000 profits 10 per cent (25% − 15%), the following £8,000 profits only 7 per cent (22% − 15%) and the following £2,000 makes a "profit" of 2 per cent (22% − 20%). Thus the total "profit" on £15,000 is £1,250; an average rate of "profit" (p) of 8·33 per cent, represented by the weighted average internal rate ($r = 23\%$) less the weighted average cost of capital ($c = 14{\cdot}67\%$).

So, despite its difficulties, internal rate of return can be a useful criterion for measuring profitability, especially in a step capital-rationing situation. The net present value method, which we shall now consider in more detail, has not this advantage, but eliminates some of the problems we have discussed.

Suppose that funds cost $c = 10$ per cent and can be invested in a project demanding a single outlay of £3,000 and providing cash flows of £1,000 per annum for four years. Is the project worth investment? In an earlier example we noted that £3,170 is the present value of an annuity for £1,000 for four years at 10 per cent. This project costs only £3,000. It therefore has a net present value of £170 (that is, £3,170 − £3,000) and is worth while. If the project had a similar pattern of cash flows but cost £3,500 it would have a negative net present value of £330 (that is, £3,500 − £3,170) and would not be worth while. Simplicity of calculation and absence of multiple and non-real rate difficulties make net present value an attractive method of project assessment for each project is expressed in terms of its net worth to an investor at present. When it is a matter of acceptance or rejection of a project, both internal rate of return and net present value criteria should give the same kind of signal, to accept or to reject.

Assume, however, that we can borrow money at 8 per cent and are faced with two mutually exclusive projects. Project A requires £3,170 outlay and yields £1,000 per annum for four years. This is like the previous case, but note that now $c = 8$ per cent. Its internal rate of return (r) is, of course, 10 per cent. Project B, however, requires £6,478 outlay and provides £2,000 per annum for four years. £6,478 is the present value of an annuity of £2,000 per year for four years at 9 per cent. So, in this case $c = 8$ per cent, but $r = 9$ per cent. On the internal rate of return criterion project A is better for it has an internal rate of

10 per cent. But net present value seems to prefer B. This is the position—

	Project A	Project B
	£	£
£1,000 for 4 years discounted at 8%	3,312	
£2,000 for 4 years discounted at 8%		6,624
Cost of project	3,170	6,478
Net present value	£142	£146

Project B now appears slightly more attractive because, although it has an internal rate of return of 9 per cent against Project A's 10 per cent, its net present value is £4 more than that of Project A. If the projects are mutually exclusive the solution to this dilemma depends on the capital-rationing situation. If only £3,170 could be borrowed B could not be undertaken anyway, but if £6,478 could be borrowed, the solution depends on what could be done with the excess £3,308 (that is, £6,478 − £3,170) if we chose Project A. If this surplus could be reinvested at 8 per cent, then B would be £4 more acceptable, but if it could be invested at sufficiently more than 8 per cent to compensate for the £4 difference, then A would be the better project. Of course, non-financial considerations such as flexibility or even risk may move the investor to favour Project A anyway.

Intermediate borrowing and lending rates are important. Although it may be convenient to discount all expected receipts and payments on a project at present capital cost (c), unless the rate is contractual this may be wrong. If $c_1, c_2, c_3 \ldots$ are the effective capital costs for years 1, 2, 3 . . ., although normal procedure takes the present cost of capital and discounts the net cash receipts of year 3 by dividing by $(1 + c_1)^3$, year 3's expected cash receipts should be discounted by $(1 + c_1) \times (1 + c_2) \times (1 + c_3)$ and so on. So discounting becomes more difficult but more realistic.

Other methods

Unlike net present value, net terminal value is a method of compounding rather than discounting. Using the symbols employed in the previous exposition it is—

$$\sum_{j=0}^{\infty} V_j (1 + c)^j - \sum_{j=0}^{\infty} C_j (1 + c)^j$$

It ideally compounds cash flows at reinvestment rates. Let us examine Project A again with its outlay of £3,170 and capital cost of 8 per cent with expected flows of £1,000 per year for four years. Net terminal value is the difference between the sinking fund formed by investing £1,000 per year at 8 per cent for four years (£4,506) and the compounded value of £3,170 at 8 per cent after four years (£4,313). It is therefore £193, which is, as expected, simply the net present value compounded for four years, for—

$$£142 \times (1{\cdot}08)^4 = £193$$

Thus both methods produce similar results, but net terminal value as a criterion probably assists us to appreciate that all relevant rates for a period should be considered, not merely present cost of capital. However, it has two distinct disadvantages. It depicts a project's value in the distant future whereas it is more realistic to think of a project's value at the present moment, and when a project with three years' life is compared with one of twenty years' life, it is necessary to calculate net terminal value at year 20, involving unnecessary calculation. Net present value simply discounts both projects to the present time.

The more acceptable methods, therefore, seem to be internal rate of return and net present value, but the former has difficulties of complex calculation, unreal and multiple rates, and the academic unsoundness of constant profitability over time, while the latter may give wrong answers if unequal projects are compared unless the profitability of surplus funds and reinvestment rates are known.

One compromise is value/cost ratio, the ratio of compounded or discounted benefits to compounded or discounted costs. It is—using the previous symbols—

$$\sum_{j=0}^{\infty} V_j (1 + c)^j \Big/ \sum_{j=0}^{\infty} C_j (1 + c)^j$$

The costs C_j for each year and the benefits V_j may be discounted or compounded in exactly the same way as to calculate net present value or net terminal value, as long as one is consistent, but the relationship is expressed as a ratio instead of a subtraction.

This method will not lead to multiple or unreal rates nor involve complex calculations, nor will a small project be rejected simply because it has a low net present or terminal value. If we discount Projects A and B to calculate value/cost ratio we have the following result—

Project A	Project B
$\frac{3{,}312}{3{,}170} = 1{\cdot}04$	$\frac{6{,}624}{6{,}478} = 1{\cdot}022$

Project A is now the more profitable. This method combines the advantages of both major methods and has no distinct disadvantage, but much depends on the objectives of the firm. To those who want immediate returns, net present value is a better criterion, but to those who think of profit as a rate of yield, value/cost ratio is better. No method, however, entirely solves the problem of changing reinvestment costs and rates.

So far we have thought of borrowing and lending rates as equal for a given period and defined capital cost (c) as the cost of funds for a period, whether lent or borrowed. If a project yields $r = 20$ per cent and money is available at $c = 10$ per cent the project is obviously profitable. But if the lending rate is 25 per cent the project is not optimal because there is a better alternative. So, although capital has an explicit cost at which it can be borrowed, it has an implicit opportunity cost, which is more relevant in decision-making. This is the cost of the next best alternative and if there is a better alternative the project is not worth while financially. If Project A is the next best alternative to Project B it is sometimes even legitimate to use the internal rate of return (r) from Project A as the "implicit cost of capital" (c) for discounting Project B and calculate the implicit net present value or value/cost ratio of Project B. The question whether to use borrowing, lending or opportunity costs of capital for calculating net present value is not always clear, but an advanced study of the subject by Hirshleifer in "On the Theory of Optimal Investment Decisions" (see Bibliography) appraises the merits of lending and borrowing rates in two-period and multi-period analyses and some multiple-rate solutions are studied.

Finally, linear programming may be used for project selection in a capital rationing situation and for discovering effective interest rates. If the net present values of four projects are calculated using a given cost of capital and projects 1 and 3 are mutually exclusive, and if funds are restricted to £30,000 in year 1 and £20,000 in year 2 it is possible to programme an optimal use of resources in the following situation—

Project	1	2	3	4
Net present value (in £000's)	20	40	14	45
1st year outlay	7	12	5	15
2nd year outlay	4	16	5	6

This is similar to the linear-programming situation of Chapter 5. The problem can be formulated in the following way, given that capital is rationed and that net present value must be maximized.

$$\begin{array}{llr} \text{Maximize} & 20x_1 + 40x_2 + 14x_3 + 45x_4 & \\ \text{subject to} & 7x_1 + 12x_2 + 5x_3 + 15x_4 & \leqslant 30 \\ & 4x_1 + 16x_2 + 5x_3 + 6x_4 & \leqslant 20 \\ & x_1 \quad + \quad x_3 & \leqslant 1 \\ & x_1, \quad x_2, \quad x_3, \quad x_4, & \geqslant 0 \\ \text{all} & x_1\text{'s integer} & \end{array}$$

Note that a project can usually only be accepted or rejected as a whole and so x_i's must be integer. As there can be no negative solutions all solutions must be values of x_i greater than or equal to zero, so should be 1 or 0 unless a particular project can be doubled. As x_1 and x_3 are mutually exclusive and only one can be accepted they cannot together exceed 1. So if x_1 is 1, x_3 must be 0.

The dual equivalent provides the shadow costs or opportunity costs of the resources, which are the rationed funds in years 1 and 2 respectively so that the solutions to the dual in this case will be the implicit interest rates or maximum opportunity costs of money in years 1 and 2 to make the projects worth while. For simplicity assume that projects x_1 and x_3 are no longer mutually exclusive. The dual version of the above programme would now look like this—

$$\begin{array}{llr} \text{Minimize} & 30y_1 + 20y_2 & \\ \text{subject to} & 7y_1 + 4y_2 & \geqslant 20 \\ & 12y_1 + 16y_2 & \geqslant 40 \\ & 5y_1 + 5y_2 & \geqslant 14 \\ & 15y_1 + 6y_2 & \geqslant 45 \\ & y_1, \quad y_2 & \geqslant 0 \end{array}$$

The solutions y_1 and y_2 will provide the effective "prices" of money in years 1 and 2 respectively, expressed in terms of year 0.

Summary

Methods of project assessment were examined. Payback fails to account for the time-value of money, ignores returns which occur after the time of recovering initial outlay and has no effective means of judging between the intermediate flows of large and small projects. Internal rate of return presents peculiar difficulties: complex calculations and impossible and multiple rates of return. It assumes a constant "rate" of profitability which does not vary over time for any given project, but profitability is never a constant; it is a complex of "annual rates" of profit on a given project. Once it is realized that these are not identical, solution becomes impossible. It also assumes that borrowing and lending rates are similar and constant for every year of a project's life.

Net present value also presents this difficulty but is easier to calculate and does not produce multiple solutions, although it fails as an index of profitability for different-sized projects. Net terminal value is an alternative which presents similar difficulties to net present value.

Value/cost ratio was discussed. This involves discounting or compounding the benefits and costs of a project and expressing the ratio between them instead of their mathematical difference. It succeeds where other methods are weak.

Two kinds of capital rationing were discussed, after a short explanation of explicit and implicit capital costs: the step pattern of progressive investment where the optimal level of investment is that level at which marginal cost of capital is equal to marginal rate of return, and the ceiling pattern of capital rationing which is best solved by an integer linear-programming model. The solution to the programme indicates the best projects to employ and the dual solutions are the effective rates of capital cost for every year of capital rationing.

Questions

1. What are the main disadvantages of payback method? Give illustrative examples.
2. Compare "internal rate of return" with "net present value" as means of project assessment.

3. State two paradoxes associated with "internal rate of return".
4. What are the advantages of value/cost ratio?
5. In what two ways may capital be rationed?
6. Distinguish between explicit and implicit capital costs.
7. Formulate a programme for optimal selection of projects in a capital-rationing situation.
8. How can the dual of this programme be used?
9. Why is reinvestment important in the study of discounted cash flow?
10. Funds cost 5 per cent p.a. but can earn 10 per cent p.a. They may be used for two projects. Project A requires immediate investment of £5,000 but will produce £1,252 p.a. for each of five years, after which there is no income. Project B requires an investment of £1,000 p.a. for each of the first five years, during which there is no inflow of cash, but from years 6 to 10 inclusive there will be a cash inflow of £1,540 p.a. Examine the two projects from the standpoints of payback, internal rate of return, net present value and value/cost ratio. How would you be motivated by the solutions in each case?
11. How would the above situation be affected if an alternative use of funds yielding 11 per cent is discovered, and (i) both projects could be abandoned, (ii) either Project A or Project B had to be chosen for other reasons?
12. How would the above facts be altered if capital cost (c) remained at 5 per cent for the first three years, but rose to 7 per cent in year 4 and remained at 7 per cent until year 7, after which it was expected to rise to 10 per cent until year 10?

Bibliography

W. J. Baumol, *Economic Theory and Operations Analysis* (Prentice-Hall, 1965) (particularly Chapters 18, 19 and 24)

H. Bierman & S. Smidt, *The Capital Budgeting Decision* (Collier-Macmillan paperback, 1968)

B. V. Carsberg, *An Introduction to Mathematical Programming for Accountants* (Allen & Unwin, 1969)

D. Garbutt, *A Simple Introduction to Capital Expenditure Decisions* (Pitman, 1967)

J. Hirshleifer, "On the Theory of Optimal Investment Decision", *Journal of Political Economy*, August 1958

J. T. S. Porterfield, *Investment Decisions and Capital Costs* (Prentice-Hall, 1965)
C. D. Querin, *The Capital Expenditure Decision* (Irwin)
E. Solomon, *The Theory of Financial Management* (Columbia U. P., 1963)
H. M. Weingartner, *Mathematical Programming and the Analysis of Capital Budgeting Problems* (Prentice-Hall, 1963)

7 Annual Accounts and Income Measurement

The previous chapter assumed that it was possible to estimate the income or benefit from a project or from an investment over a number of years. If we could do this with some degree of accuracy, initial decision-making would often be an easy matter, but in fact it is not possible to predict a company's income or the income from a project for more than a few years into the future with any degree of certainty. It is necessary to rely on approximations, based on previous and current incomes, or on the experience of similar investments or projects, or on general trends. It is therefore essential that we should be able to measure current income for two reasons—

(*a*) to be able to estimate future income, although current income figures will have to be adjusted because of general business experience, company trends and other changes; and

(*b*) as a yardstick to compare with previous estimates to discover how accurate were previous estimates when these were made, and to report any differences.

Because of the basic fact of time preference illustrated in previous chapters, and because the prospect of £100 this year has more current value to most people than the prospect of £100 in, say, ten years' time it is convenient to divide time into periods, for example, annual periods for reporting the income of a company, monthly periods for reporting sales and production and weekly periods for reporting cash receipts and payments. In long-term planning annual reports are probably the most important, for the indeterminate future is thus divided into a series of self-made equal annual steps, and management is somewhat like a tight-rope walker, having to adjust its balance at each step and ensuring that it is walking accurately in its predetermined course.

Balance Sheets

A balance sheet is a statement of the financial position of a company or other organization at a given point of time. If all the resources of the organization had a financial value, and if all its liabilities could be quantified, and if it was possible to obtain the total value of a company or organization simply by adding together the values of all its assets and deducting all its liabilities, such as the debts which it owes to others, it would be true to say that the balance sheet gave the total value of a company.

Further, if there were no withdrawals or investments of funds in the company for a whole year, it would be possible to calculate the income of the company for the year very easily. One would simply take the two balance sheets of the company as drawn up at the beginning and end of the year in question, and ascertain the difference between the totals expressed in each. A simple example should make this clear.

EXAMPLE

BALANCE SHEETS OF PAINT AND DYE LTD

	1 January 1972		*31 December 1972*	
	£		£	
Fixed assets				
Freehold premises (factory & offices)	20,000		20,000	
Machinery	18,000		16,000	
Motor vehicles	15,000		10,000	
Furniture & fixtures	9,000		8,000	
		62,000		54,000
Investments in other companies at cost		10,000		18,000
Current assets less current liabilities				
Stock-in-trade: Raw materials	5,000		7,000	
Work in progress	2,000		1,000	
Finished goods	3,000		7,000	
Trade debtors (that is, debts due from the company's customers)	4,000		6,000	
Bank balances	1,000		1,500	
	15,000		22,500	
Less: Trade creditors (that is, debts due to the company's suppliers)	5,000		6,000	
		10,000		16,500
Net worth		£82,000		£88,500

Notes.

(1) Net worth is the stated financial value of the company at the point of time in question. In published accounts it is usually represented by *shares* (that is, amounts invested originally in the company) and *reserves* (that is, amounts accumulated from previously undistributed profits).

(2) I have omitted taxation from this simple treatment of the subject because I wish to distinguish clearly between liabilities and equity (or ownership). Taxation is not an expense (i.e. something deducted in arriving at profit) but an appropriation (or slice) of profit, *after* it has been calculated. Think of it as the State's share of the profits of the business.

Balance sheets of companies usually contain (*a*) a provision for future taxation out of current profits and (*b*) current taxation. The future taxation provision is an estimate of next year's tax based upon this year's profits, while on the other hand amounts due in respect of current taxation appear in the balance sheet as current liabilities. This is sufficient about taxation for the moment. In Chapter 14 I shall deal with the subject specifically from the viewpoint of planning and decision-making.

At a glance it is possible to see that the financial value of the company has increased by £6,500 from £82,000 to £88,500 during the year in question, but this has involved making a number of assumptions about balance sheets which should be challenged.

These are—

(i) unambiguous values of items;
(ii) the "addition" fallacy;
(iii) absence of intangible assets.

(i) Unambiguous values of items We have assumed that each of the items in both balance sheets has a particular unchallengeable value at the point of time in question. Yet premises may be worth more than £20,000, because of a rise in property values since the last date on which the premises were valued. All the other assets are probably valued at "cost less depreciation". Depreciation is simply an allowance written off the cost-price of an asset to account for its estimated deterioration over time. For example, machinery may have deteriorated by £2,000 over the year, hence the reduction in stated value from £18,000 to £16,000. But such things are anyone's guess, and it may not be possible to discover the true value of machinery unless one attempted to sell it—at prohibitive dismantling and transport cost.

The values of current assets (that is, those assets which are held to be converted finally into cash) may be a little better defined. Yet finished goods may only be saleable at £7,000 if there is a market for them, and work-in-progress may be valueless if it can be used for no other purpose, and debts may be difficult to collect immediately at the amount of £6,000 stated. So all the figures in such a balance sheet, although arrived at by a kind of logic, must be regarded as not much more than approximations of their true values on 31 December 1972.

(ii) The "addition" fallacy We wrote earlier of *synergy*, the concept that the value of combination of things may often be more (or less) than the independent values of the components. An extreme example is perhaps that of a prize bull which is purchased for £2,000. Does it follow that, if the creature were to be hacked into pieces, the total value of the pieces, when sold, would be £2,000? Obviously not! There is value in the very combination of the elements which make up the whole. One has only to study the optimization model in Chapter 5 from this standpoint. The very need for an optimization model results from the fact that the ratio between the profits obtainable from the products differ from the ratio between the resources needed.

In a two-resource, two-product model it is easy to find a point at which all resources are used up and profit maximized but when one has a large number of different types of resources this is less easy. There are ten different categories of assets in the above balance sheet, and even if we know them to be correctly valued could we be sure that they were in the correct proportion to each other? Is there too much machinery, or too much of the wrong kind of machinery? Has the company invested too much or too little of its funds in investments in other companies? The question of whether there is a good or bad combination of assets in the balance sheet is an essential factor in deciding the real value of the company as a working unit.

(iii) Absence of intangible assets We have assumed that there is nothing else besides these physical assets, book debts and cash, which can add to the total value of the company at both points of time. Yet the basic lesson of Chapter 3 is that a company has many resources which are unquantifiable. Its management, executive capacities, availability of manpower, geographical position, market accessibility, research and development facilities, among other things, are all valuable. Sometimes an all-embracing item captioned *goodwill* is written into the balance sheet to account for the difference between the total combined and individual values of a company's assets.

Measuring income

Because of these three basic difficulties, balance sheets can normally be regarded as not much more than approximate pictures of the affairs of companies at the times in question. Attempts have been made to standardize the presentation of accounts, and accountants work within the narrow constraints of law and accounting conventions. In many cases investments in companies and withdrawals from them (e.g. payments of dividends) make it difficult to ascertain income simply by examining balance sheets. For this reason sets of accounts are prepared, showing what has happened in the year in question. A larger example will show what these accounts contain.

Zeno Ltd

BALANCE SHEET 1 JANUARY 1971

	£
Capital, authorized, issued and fully paid	
Ordinary shares, 50,000 at £1 each	50,000
Reserves	130,000
	£180,000

Representing the following assets and liabilities

Fixed assets and goodwill	Cost	Depreciation	Net
	£	£	£
Goodwill	25,000	—	25,000
Freehold land	10,000	—	10,000
Freehold buildings	40,000	10,000	30,000
Plant and machinery	80,000	50,000	30,000
	155,000	60,000	95,000
Add: **Current assets less current liabilities**			
Stocks in hand: Raw materials and work in progress		80,000	
Finished goods		70,000	
		150,000	
Liquid assets: Debtors		5,000	
Cash		25,000	
		180,000	
Less **Current liabilities:**			
Trade creditors		95,000	
			85,000
			£180,000

Notes

(1) Balance sheets are usually made up on the last date of a period. The purpose of using 1 January 1971 is to illustrate that the following income accounts are for the whole of 1971.

(2) Note that the accountant has included goodwill. This is his estimate of the difference between the financial value of the company as a whole, and the sum of the financial values of its tangible assets.

(3) Modern balance sheets are usually presented in two parts, one of which shows how the capital of the company is made up, that is, how its ownership is analysed into various classes of shares and reserves, and the other part analyses the items owned into *fixed assets*, those which are acquired for relatively long periods and *current assets*, those which are acquired simply to be converted into cash for the purpose of making profit.

(4) In practice the balance sheet of Zeno Ltd would also include—
    (*a*) current tax liability, listed under "current liabilities", and
    (*b*) provision for future taxation, which would be treated as a deferred (or "long term") liability.

The December 1971 balance sheet of Zeno Ltd (p. 75) includes a dividend paid and proposed. Under the earlier system of Schedule F tax (a form of income tax collected upon dividends distributed) it was necessary to describe dividends as either "gross" or "net" of tax. The system of imputation and tax credits which will be described in Chapter 14 has removed this problem.

ACCOUNTS FOR THE YEAR ENDED 31 DECEMBER 1971

MANUFACTURING ACCOUNT

	£	£
Raw materials and work in progress		
Opening stock on 1 January 1971	80,000	
Add: Purchases during the year	110,000	
	190,000	
Less: Closing stock on 31 December 1971	60,000	
Cost of materials used during the year		130,000
Add: **Direct labour**		60,000
Prime cost		190,000
Add: **Production overhead**		
Indirect costs of manufacturing	34,000	
Depreciation of plant and machinery	16,000	
		50,000
Cost of finished goods transferred to warehouse		£240,000

TRADING ACCOUNT

Sales revenue		375,000
Less: **Cost of sales** computed as follows:		
Stock of finished goods on 1 January 1971	70,000	
Add: Factory production transferred (as above)	240,000	
	310,000	
Less: Finished goods in warehouse		
Stock on 31 December 1971	60,000	
		250,000
Gross profit from trading		£125,000

PROFIT AND LOSS ACCOUNT

Gross profit from trading		125,000
Less: **Other expenditure**		
Administration expenses	41,000	
Selling expenses	65,000	
Depreciation on freehold property	800	
		106,800
Net profit during year		£18,200

Zeno Ltd

BALANCE SHEET 31 DECEMBER 1971

Capital: authorized, issued and fully paid		£
Ordinary shares 50,000 at £1 each		50,000
Reserves		130,000
Profit and loss account: Net profit 1971	18,200	
Less: Dividend paid and proposed (10%)	5,000	13,200
		£193,200

Representing the following assets and liabilities

Fixed assets and goodwill	Cost	Depreciation	Net
	£	£	£
Goodwill	25,000	—	25,000
Freehold land	10,000	—	10,000
Freehold buildings	40,000	10,800	29,200
Plant and machinery	90,000	66,000	24,000
	165,000	76,800	88,200

Add: **Current assets less current liabilities**		
Stocks in hand: Work in progress and raw materials	60,000	
Finished goods	60,000	
	120,000	
Debtors	50,000	
Cash in hand and at bank	20,000	
	190,000	
Less: Current liabilities: Trade creditors	85,000	
		105,000
		£193,200

Explanation The three intervening accounts are a means of exhibiting the way in which the company's increase of £13,200 took place. Note that income was even greater than £13,200 for the company made a profit of £18,200 and distributed £5,000 to its shareholders. There are three stages in arriving at the profit of £18,200—

(*a*) the Manufacturing Account;
(*b*) the Trading Account;
(*c*) the Profit and Loss Account.

A manufacturing company would normally produce all three accounts, but not all the information in them has to be published. Usually an abbreviated form of Profit and Loss Account is published.

The *Manufacturing Account* is a list of the costs of producing goods actually supplied to the warehouse during the year, that is, direct materials, direct labour and manufacturing overhead. "Direct" in this context simply means "directly related to the volume of production". If a large amount is produced the costs of labour and materials will be high, and if smaller amounts of goods are produced they will be lower. As we shall see later, no cost is fully "direct". In the case of materials and labour, however, there is some relationship between cost and production. Indirect costs of manufacturing are factory rates, heating, lighting, factory supervision and similar expenditure. If these are added the total cost of producing goods during the period can be calculated.

The *Trading Account* serves two purposes. Not all goods produced in the period are sold during the period. It is necessary to discover the cost of goods sold, simply by adding to total production cost the cost of finished goods in stock at the beginning of the period, and by deducting the cost of finished goods in stock at the end of the period. The resulting figure called *cost of sales* is then deducted from sales revenue to discover the *gross profit* for the period. In Zeno Ltd's accounts the gross profit is 50 per cent of cost of sales or 33⅓ per cent of sales revenue. This may reflect the company policy to sell goods at cost plus 50 per cent or that profit should be 33⅓ per cent of selling price.

The *Profit and Loss Account* classifies and analyses the remaining costs which have to be written against trading income before net profit can be discovered. These usually fall into four categories—

(*a*) administrative expenses, such as managers' salaries;
(*b*) selling expenses, such as commissions and advertising;
(*c*) distribution expenses, the costs of getting goods to customers;
(*d*) financial expenses, such as bank charges and interest payable.

In the next chapter I propose to examine the accounts of Zeno Ltd to see how they can be inaccurate and misleading, especially in view of the three problems mentioned earlier. In both the manufacturing and trading accounts we have assumed that the opening and closing stocks had uniform value and that there was only one way of computing stock value at a given point of time. As we shall see, there are many. In both the manufacturing and profit and loss accounts there are depreciation charges which appear to indicate the cost of "wear and tear" in the respective fixed assets, machinery and buildings during the period involved, during 1971, but again it is anybody's guess as to how much that wear and tear really was, so that depreciation can be not much more than an approximation. Some accountants argue that it is never really intended to represent the reduction of value of the asset during the period, but is simply a method of apportioning the cost of the asset equitably over the time which it is likely to last.

The other reasons why the accounts could be misleading are that (*a*) the value of the whole is not necessarily the sum of the values of the parts and that (*b*) many intangible assets are not included in the balance sheet. These difficulties were explained earlier, and it was stated that accountants often included a global yet nebulous item in the balance sheet, called *goodwill*, to adjust any discrepancy that may have resulted from either of these two causes. An examination of Zeno Ltd's balance sheet is sufficient to illustrate what usually happens, for goodwill is exactly the same at the end of the year as it was at the beginning, yet this is, of all things, most unlikely for the value of the company as a unit, *vis-à-vis* the environment in which it is operating, is changing from moment to moment.

A final reason why accounts are sometimes inaccurate and misleading is that the very scale of measurement, the unit of currency, is not constant in value. Problems of income measurement can therefore be said to spring from four principal sources—

(*a*) variation of values of stocks-in-trade;
(*b*) methods of calculating depreciation;
(*c*) the treatment of goodwill and other intangibles;
(*d*) the problem of inflation.

Before we can examine them we need to discuss some unwritten rules which accountants often apply when dealing with each of these four problems. They may be discussed under the general topic of conventions and concepts.

Conventions and concepts The usual conventions of accounting are—

(*a*) conservatism
(*b*) consistency
(*c*) materiality
(*d*) objectivity

Conservatism means understating rather than overstating value and profit, but sometimes an accountant finds that it is impossible to understate value without overstating profit. *Consistency* means using the same methods wherever possible. It is a principle which an accountant often pleads as his support when calculating stock prices or the rate of depreciation upon fixed assets, for it is argued that if there is consistency over time any differences due to anomalies in the methods used will counterbalance each other and the effect will be near-accuracy. *Materiality* means not bothering unduly about insignificant items such as small cash balances. Some large companies prepare their published accounts to the nearest units of a thousand pounds. It is probably the greatest concession which has been made to the idea that a balance sheet is only an approximation anyway. Finally, *objectivity* means that the accountant is interested in facts rather than in opinions.

There are four major accounting concepts. They are—

(*a*) the money-measurement concept;
(*b*) the business-entity concept;
(*c*) the going-concern concept; and
(*d*) the cost concept.

The *money-measurement* concept assumes that everything can be valued in terms of a stable unit of currency. The *business-entity* concept distinguishes the business from its owner for all transaction purposes. The *going-concern* concept assumes that the business is likely to last indefinitely. Balance sheet values are therefore not those which may be the result of hasty realization. The *cost concept* values balance sheet items, as we have seen, on a cost basis, and assumes that the total value of a company is the aggregate of the written down costs of all its assets.

The above eight principles are very much like proverbs, like very wise pronouncements, good in themselves but capable of disastrous application. The purpose of the balance sheet should surely be to show not merely the minimum worth of a company at a point of time, but as far as possible the actual worth of the company on that date, for income is really the increase in the value of the company between two points of time, in the absence of investments and withdrawals, and a diminished estimate of the company could be as misleading in this context as an exaggerated one. Consistent application of a depreciation rule or of a stock-valuation principle may adjust matters in the long run, but one economist aptly stated that in the long run we shall all be dead. Great financial disasters usually happen over a short period. Materiality is at least an admission that there is no penny-precision about accounts but it has often been used as an excuse for ignoring inflation and therefore presenting distorted accounts. Objectivity has similarly been used as an excuse for making cost the basis of value, whereas the value of most things is more related to the potential benefit that we are likely to receive from them than to the more objective amounts of "cost" which we paid for them.

This logic highlights the defects of both the money-measurement concept and the cost concept as they are often applied. The business-entity and going-concern concepts impel us to ask "What is the real value of a company as a whole?" It is, if anything, the discounted present value of all the future benefits which will be received from it, that is, the discounted value of its future income.

We have thus reached a rather circular paradox. We cannot know the income of a company unless we know with certainty its respective values, its net worth, at the beginning and end of the period in question, and yet it is impossible to decide its value at both these points of time unless one can estimate the company's future income. There is one way out of the dilemma. We cannot estimate in advance external gains resulting from increases in goodwill, in the values of fixed assets, in stock or in the purchasing power of money, but we can isolate these factors and discover the pure trading income of the company, hoping that the trend of trading income over a number of years will signpost its prospective future income. This, in fact, is what the accountant tries to do. Chapter 8 will discuss how, by isolating external factors, we may do this more accurately.

Summary

The previous chapter's discussion of discounted cash flow assumed that it was easy to estimate future income from a project or company or investment. But we have not such foresight. If there were no further capital raised by a company in a period and no dividends paid by it, income would appear to be the difference (i.e. the increase) in its value between two points of time. The balance sheet of a company is intended to be a statement of its worth, analysed into assets and liabilities, at a given point of time. It raises three basic problems, (*a*) that each item can be accurately valued at that point of time, (*b*) that the value of a company is necessarily the total of the values of its constituent parts, and (*c*) that there are no intangible assets. Income statements are normally divided into three parts which deal respectively with manufacturing, trading and "profit and loss" operations, but these may similarly be affected by the arbitrary nature of valuation, particularly of stock-in-trade and of the depreciation charges against fixed assets for the period in question.

Problems (*b*) and (*c*) lend themselves to a rather global treatment, the insertion of a package item called "goodwill" in the balance sheet, but this is rarely adjusted to show its real worth on the balance sheet. It is normally written down according to accounting conventions. These originated in the prudent-stewardship function of the accountant, but can often produce results which are misleading. Income can be better determined, not from knowing the minimum value of a company at two points of time as conservatism would indicate, but if possible by discovering its real values on those dates. Consistency can often involve the consistent carrying out of rule-of-thumb methods of valuing assets. Materiality and objectivity can be similarly misapplied.

Obviously what matters is the value of the company as a unit, but this is the discounted value of future income, and since we cannot assess the income of a company between two points of time unless we know its value at those two positions the problem is a circular one. The accountant attempts to answer the problem by projecting a trend of future income from current trading income. In the next chapter we shall ask how the unstable external valuation factors which affect profit may be eliminated and a more accurate picture of the company's trading income obtained.

Questions

1. What are the major problems in estimating the future income of a company over a period of years?

2. Why is time divided into annual periods for accounting purposes? What advantages are there in the production of annual accounts?
3. What is a balance sheet? What does it purport to show?
4. Would it be possible to calculate the annual income of a company simply by comparing its balance sheets at the beginning and end of a given year?
5. It is often said that the net worth of a company, as depicted in its balance sheet, is equivalent to its value. What are the three basic reasons why this may not be the case?
6. What are the problems in valuing fixed assets?
7. What is depreciation?
8. Can depreciation be anything more than an estimate of the decline in an asset's value?
9. What is the difference between fixed assets and current assets? Give examples of (*a*) fixed assets, and (*b*) current assets?
10. Discuss the basic problem attached to valuation of stock in trade.
11. How does the accountant attempt to rectify any discrepancy in the balance sheet resulting from the presence of intangible assets or the "addition fallacy"?
12. Why does the accountant prefer to write off goodwill as soon as practicable?
13. What are the main accounting concepts and conventions?
14. Discuss some of the ways in which the application of conventions can lead to distorted and misleading accounts.
15. Upon what does the value of a company at a given point of time really depend?
16. A company used £15m worth of material during a year and spent £20m upon factory wages. Its factory overheads were £4m. Estimated depreciation of machinery was £6m. What was its cost of production for the year?
17. If the above company had stocks of finished goods of £8m and £13m at the beginning and end of the year respectively, what would be its "cost of sales" for the year?
18. In the above case, if sales revenue from the goods produced were £60m what would be the amount of gross profit? What would it be, expressed as (*a*) a percentage of cost; (*b*) a percentage of sales revenue?
19. If the company's administrative and other expenses were £15m for the year what would be the net trading profit?
20. What are the main causes of inaccuracy in the calculation of trading profit in this way?
21. What other gains and losses accrue to a company during a period, besides trading profit?
22. How may inflation result in the distortion of accounts?

23. Prepare a balance sheet from the following figures in respect of April Ltd on 31 March 1972—

	£
Freehold land and buildings	60,000
Machinery and equipment	40,000
Bank overdraft	6,000
Trade debtors	9,000
Stock-in-trade	15,000
Trade creditors	3,000
Motor vehicles	10,000
Office equipment	2,000

The company's capital is divided into 100,000 £1 shares which were issued on 1 April 1971, fully paid. How would you deal with any difference between this amount and the net worth of the company?

24. Would it be true to regard the above difference between issued capital and present net worth as trading profit for the year if it partly resulted from a revaluation of land and buildings, and if they had been acquired on 1 April 1971 at only £45,000?

Bibliography

H. Bierman, *Financial and Managerial Accounting* (Collier-Macmillan, 1963)

H. Bierman, *Financial Accounting Theory* (Collier-Macmillan, 1965)

H. Bierman & A. R. Drebin, *Managerial Accounting: An Introduction* (Collier-Macmillan, 1968)

R. J. Bull, *Accounting in Business* (Butterworths, 1969)

S. Davidson (ed.), *An Income Approach to Accounting Theory* (Prentice-Hall, 1964)

H. C. Edey, *Introduction to Accounting* (Hutchinson, 1963)

E. O. Edwards & P. W. Bell, *The Theory and Measurement of Business Income* (California U. P., Cambridge U. P., 1961)

A. J. Grant, *Accounting Made Simple* (W. H. Allen, 1970)

E. S. Hendriksen, *Accounting Theory* (Irwin, 1965)

F. P. Langley, *Introduction to Accounting for Business Studies* (Butterworths, 1970)

H. Ross, *Financial Statements: A Crusade for Current Values* (Pitman, 1969)

8 Some Problems of Income Determination

In Chapter 7 we stated that, if there were no capital investments in a company during a period and there were no withdrawals from it, that is, no dividends paid by it, the "income" of the company from an economic standpoint would simply be the difference between its values at the beginning and end of the period in question. If its value on 1 January 1972 were £J and its value on 31 December were £D, income (£I) would be simply £D–£J. The dilemma was that real value itself is dependent upon future income, that, to use the previous discount formulae—

$$£J = \sum_{0}^{\infty} \frac{I_j}{(1+r)^j} \text{ and } £D = \sum_{1}^{\infty} \frac{I_j}{(1+r)^j}$$

Hence, the very determination of £I is, in itself, dependent upon values which are dependent upon income themselves, that is, if we try to apply the economists' concept of income, for example, that of Hicks who defined income as "the maximum value which one can consume during a week and still expect to be as well off at the end of the week as one was at the beginning". To try to predict income, understood in this sense, for future periods, would involve trying to predict fluctuations in the values of fixed assets and stock-in-trade, in the purchasing power of money and in "goodwill" resulting from fluctuations in the total value of the company, as well as in operating income. Accountants assume that the operating income of a company will at least present us with a picture of its probable future operating income. With this in view it is necessary to isolate the effect of fluctuations caused by changes in the purchasing power of money, in fixed assets, in stocks and in "goodwill".

Adjustment for inflation

Look at Zeno Ltd's balance sheets and accounts in the previous chapter and assume that Land and Buildings were purchased when prices stood at 100, machinery was purchased in 1967 when prices were 150 except for £10,000 purchased at the end of 1971. January 1971 prices were 200, the 1971 average was 250 and December 1971 prices were 300. How should Zeno Ltd's accounts be redrafted to account for the falling value of the pound?

Zeno Ltd

BALANCE SHEET AT 1 JANUARY 1971 ADJUSTED FOR INFLATION

Fixed assets	Factor	Cost	Deprecia-tion	1. 1. 71 prices	31. 12. 71 prices
		£	£	£	£
Freehold land	200/100	20,000	—	20,000	(30,000)
Freehold buildings	200/100	80,000	20,000	60,000	(90,000)
Plant & machinery	200/150	106,667	66,667	40,000	(60,000)
		£206,667	£86,667	£120,000	(180,000)

Add: **Current assets less current liabilities**

Stock	150,000		
Debtors	5,000		
Cash	25,000		
	180,000		
Less: Creditors	95,000		
		85,000	(127,500)
		£205,000	(£307,500)
Representing equity (in capital and reserves)		£205,000	(£307,500)

Note: At this stage goodwill is ignored

The Balance Sheet at 31 December 1971 may also be converted to take general inflation into account and would look something like this—

Zeno Ltd

BALANCE SHEET AT 31 DECEMBER 1971 ADJUSTED FOR INFLATION

Fixed assets and goodwill	Factor	Cost	Deprecia-tion	31. 12. 71 prices
		£	£	£
Freehold land	300/100	30,000	—	30,000
Freehold buildings	300/100	120,000	32,400	87,600
Plant & machinery	300/150 (*see* p. 88)	170,000	132,000	38,000
		£320,000	£164,400	155,600

Add: **Current assets less current liabilities**

Stock	120,000	
Debtors	50,000	
Cash	20,000	
	190,000	
Less: Creditors	85,000	
		105,000
		£260,600
Equity represented by capital, reserves and year's profit		£260,600

I should explain that price-level indices are economists' devices to measure the rise in prices (or cost of living) or, conversely, the declining value of the pound. There are various types of indices computed according to differing formulae, and they are not the concern of this book. It should be emphasized, however, that a price-level index is only a general indication of a rise in prices. When wage negotiations are carried out because of rises in the cost of living, employers and employees tend to use whichever indices are most favourable to their respective points of view. Such an index is usually computed on the basis of average amounts spent by consumers on various classes of commonly purchased goods. The indices we have used are, of course, exaggerated.

The accounts exhibits show that two processes are involved—

(*a*) partial adjustment of asset values to show income in terms of the ever-changing pound; and

(*b*) full adjustment to measure income for the year in terms of end-of-year prices.

(*a*) If profit is measured in terms of the ever-changing pound after adjusting generally for inflation, and stock is valued at current prices, the profit after adding back interim dividend paid is £55,600; that is, the difference between the January and December values of the company in changing pounds.

Using the balance sheets of Zeno Ltd partially adjusted this is simply—

	£
End-of-year value of Zeno Ltd at end-of-year prices	260,600
Less: January value of Zeno Ltd at January prices	205,000
Income for 1971 in terms of the changing pound	£ 55,600

(*b*) But this is, of course, unsatisfactory. If, however, January 1971 prices are re-interpreted in terms of December 1971 prices, the firm is seen to have made a loss, after adding back the interim dividend paid, for now the end-1971 value of £260,600 has to be compared with the January value of the company in December pounds, i.e. £307,500. Its value has therefore fallen by £46,900. This real loss can be checked by calculating the adjusted trading surplus and then taking into account monetary gains and losses.

1. Calculation of adjusted trading surplus for 1971

		Book value £	Factor	31. 12. 71 prices £
Operating profit for 1971 per accounts		18,200		
Add back: Depreciation		16,800		
Profit before depreciation		35,000	300/250	42,000
Less: Adjusted depreciation:				
Buildings	800		300/100	—(2,400)
Plant	16,000		300/150	—(32,000)
		16,800		
				7,600
		18,200		
Less: Dividend paid		5,000	300/250	6,000
Adjusted trading surplus after dividend payment		£13,200		£1,600

Adequate provision for depreciation on real values now almost eliminates profits after dividend. This is bad enough, but worse is to come. It is obvious that cash depreciates if prices rise. Cash will therefore have fallen in real value during 1971, and so will debts which are contracted in terms of cash. Stock values would normally appreciate in terms of money during rising prices, but we are at present assuming that stock is realistically priced in both January and December balance sheets, and that stock turnover is very rapid. Thus calculation of monetary loss on current assets and monetary gains on current liabilities is an easy matter.

I hasten to add that, although we are treating stock-in-trade as a "monetary asset" for the purpose of simplification at this stage, it is not this kind of easy matter in practice. The prices of stocks-in-trade could only be equated with their monetary equivalents if a company turned over its stocks at a highly rapid rate, if it bought new stocks each day and disposed of them the following day, so that their balance sheet values were always accurate in terms of money. The valuation of stock-in-trade constitutes in itself a problem of great dimensions, but as we shall be dealing with this later in the chapter I ignore it at present for the purpose of illustration. To illustrate how the surplus of £1,600 (which is still a positive surplus although much less than the original £13,200 net of dividend) can be reconciled with the newly calculated loss of £46,900, we have to explain a difference of £48,500—a monetary loss due to price-level changes. This is shown on the following page.

2. Calculation of monetary loss in 1971 due to price level changes

	Stock	Debtors	Cash	Creditors	Net working capital
	£	£	£	£	£
December balances	120,000	50,000	20,000	85,000	105,000
Less:					
January balances	150,000	5,000	25,000	95,000	85,000
Change in book value	−30,000	45,000	−5,000	−10,000	20,000
Changes above adjusted to December prices (× 300/250)	−36,000	54,000	−6,000	−12,000	24,000
January balances at December prices (× 300/200)	225,000	7,500	37,500	142,500	127,500
Projected December balances in December pounds	189,000	61,500	31,500	130,500	151,500
Closing December book values in December prices	120,000	50,000	20,000	85,000	105,000
Monetary loss on working capital	£69,000	£11,500	£11,500	£45,500	£46,500

Add: Cash worth £10,000 in average terms for 1971 held until December and used to purchase plant and machinery, for £10,000. Real December prices were 300/250 average so there was a real loss of £2,000 (i.e. £12,000 − £10,000) in holding cash (*see* p. 85)	2,000
Total Monetary Loss for 1971	£48,500

The real loss of £46,900 resulting from the fall in value of the company in real terms from £307,500 (January value in December pounds) to £260,600 (December value in December pounds) can now be reconciled.

3. Calculation of real loss in value of Zeno Ltd during 1971

	£
Monetary loss and hidden loss in stock values (as above) (2)	48,500
Deduct operating surplus (after paying dividend) (as above 1)	1,600
Real loss in value of Zeno Ltd during 1971	£46,900

The problem of stock-in-trade

In dealing with the general problem of inflation I assumed, purely for the sake of convenience, that stock could be regarded in much the same way as a monetary asset, an asset which could always be converted into cash on the balance sheet date at exactly the price stated in the balance sheet. It was pointed out that this would only be so if stock was being turned over rapidly, that is, if it were being purchased and sold very quickly. In general this does not happen, and the valuation of stock-in-trade presents a problem to the accountant, because the average warehouse contains both old and new stock, some of which has been acquired long ago at old prices, and some of which has only just been acquired.

Accountants at one time had a heuristic (rule-of-thumb) ruling based on the conservative convention that stock should be priced at "cost or market price whichever is lower", and the rule is still observed wherever possible. But which costs are to be used, for the costs of identical units of stock change over time? Shall we use their more up-to-date prices or the prices at which they were acquired, or shall we just take an average, and if so, what sort of average? Should it be "weighted"? The problem is similar to that of calculating those price-indices we mentioned earlier. Two methods which illustrate extremes in dealing with the problem rather than all the possible methods used, are—

(*a*) *First in, first out* (FIFO), which charges earliest stock prices to the manufacturing account and keeps latest prices in current stocks when valued for balance sheet purposes, and

(*b*) *Last in, first out* (LIFO), which charges latest stock prices to the manufacturing account and keeps earliest prices in current stocks when valued for balance sheet purposes.

For the purpose of illustration I assume that the accountant of Zeno Ltd has been using the FIFO method of stock pricing and illustrate the likely way in which he calculated his stock prices. Then we shall see what would happen if instead of using FIFO he decided to use the LIFO method. We shall question both these alternatives and ask whether or not there could be a better solution. For simplicity we shall work from the original Zeno Ltd balance sheets of the previous chapter, ignoring the inflation-adjusted balance sheets until we make a final assessment of the whole problem.

The unamended version of the Zeno Ltd accounts is assumed to be governed by first-in, first-out (FIFO) method. Let us illustrate this—

FIFO method

		£
Opening stock in January 1971, 40,000 units at £2 each		80,000
Add: Purchases in May 1971, 22,000 units at £5 each		110,000
		190,000
Stock charged to manufacturing account	£	
First 40,000 units at £2 each	80,000	
Next 10,000 units at £5 each	50,000	
		130,000
Closing stock in December 1971, 12,000 units at £5 each		£60,000

This agrees with the manufacturing account as shown in the previous chapter. If the accountant wished to use last-in, first-out (LIFO) exactly the same units would be charged from the warehouse to production, but they would be priced differently.

LIFO method

		£
Opening stock in January 1971, 40,000 units at £2 each		80,000
Add: Purchases in May 1971, 22,000 units at £5 each		110,000
		190,000
Stock charged to manufacturing account	£	
First 22,000 units at £5 each	110,000	
Next 28,000 units at £2 each	56,000	
		166,000
Closing stock in December 1971, 12,000 units at £2 each		£24,000

This example is necessarily an over-simplified one. It assumes that there was no manufacture between January and May 1971, for if there had been then stocks would have been priced to production during that period at £2 (the latest price) under the LIFO method.

However, note that production appears to cost £36,000 more under the LIFO method than it does under the FIFO method. This could have two effects. If (to use our illustration in the previous chapter upon which present figures are based) sales revenue is £375,000 and this sales revenue is entirely the result of a sales price dictated by the market, then LIFO accounts will appear to show £36,000 less profit. Obviously materials will appear to cost £36,000 more so profit will appear to be £36,000 less. But the company may be monopolistic and able to dictate its own prices for its products, and the accountant may be using a cost-plus method of deciding selling prices, that is, he may take all costs involved in the production of the product, and add an allocation of overheads or indirect costs and a percentage in respect of allowable profit. Obviously if prices can be decided by the producer in this way the effect of the £36,000 extra apparent cost for materials is quite different for selling prices will be higher, not merely by £36,000 but by £36,000 plus a percentage for overheads and profit, and the accounts will show more not less profit. For our future examples we shall assume that the company is in a market-dictated situation and that it appears to earn £36,000 less under LIFO than under FIFO because costs appear to be £36,000 extra.

A defect in the conservatism of both methods is that neither FIFO nor LIFO shows accurately the current value of stocks on the balance sheet date if prices are continually rising. Even LIFO only shows stocks at the price at the latest purchase as a charge against production, but remaining stocks are valued at outdated prices. Neither method accounts for unrealized holding gains between the date of latest purchase and the balance sheet.

For example, let us assume that the average trade price per unit during 1971 was £8. By this I mean not the weighted average of units in stock, but the average prevailing market cost per unit. Suppose also that the general trade price of such units on 31 December 1971 was £10, and that Zeno Ltd charges its units to production at the annual average trade price of £8 per unit and prices the remainder in its final balance sheet at £10 per unit, taking credit for any gains, though unrealized, in holding such stocks during times of rising prices. To use the exact average of £8 at the beginning of the year requires a great deal of foresight as to what the trade average price will turn out to be, but let us assume this for the purpose of illustration.

Holdings gains can now be calculated and isolated from the company's operating (or trading) profit. The relevance of this calculation will be considered in the complete illustration later in this chapter.

Statement of holding gains upon unrealized stock

	£
Holding gain on first 40,000 units assumed purchased at £2 per unit = 40,000 × (£8 − £2)	240,000
Holding gain on remaining 10,000 units purchased later in the year at £5 per unit = 10,000 × (£8 − £5)	30,000
Total holding gain on stock charged to production	270,000
Holding gain upon units remaining in stock on 31 December 1971 using trade price for year end = 12,000 × (£10 − £5)	60,000
Total gain due to appreciation of stock prices during year	£330,000

The problem of fixed assets and depreciation

At the beginning of this chapter we tried to adjust distortions in accounts arising from the fact of inflation, as a result of the rise in prices or the fall in the value of the pound. We had to assume that prices moved uniformly, that fixed assets, stocks-in-trade and all other assets could be revalued simply by using a percentage index adjustment. The second section of the chapter showed that this would not necessarily give us correct values of stock-in-trade, and in this section the logic of the previous section is applied to fixed assets. The problem of valuing fixed assets has two aspects. In the first place, as with stock-in-trade, prices do not move uniformly; for example, factory prices may rise faster during a property boom than the prices of machinery or motor vehicles. Secondly, there is the problem of estimating depreciation, the financial estimate of the decline in value of a fixed asset during the period. Individual fluctuations of values of fixed assets need not disturb the manufacturing and trading accounts, for they can be treated as holding gains, but income statements ought to be charged with the cost of using the equipment and other assets in question, for the company could not operate without its factory, its machinery, its office premises, its cars and other equipment. It would initially seem logical that the depreciation or "wear and tear" of the assets should be written off during the operating period. In practice there are various methods of doing this, of which the most popular are—

(*a*) the fixed-instalment method;
(*b*) the reducing-balance method;
(*c*) the sum-of-digits method;

(*d*) the annuity method;
(*e*) use-adjusted methods; and
(*f*) revaluation.

There are other methods of providing for the cost of replacement by investment in equities, securities or an insurance policy, but as these do more than write down the cost of the asset in question I do not propose to deal with them specifically.

(*a*) *The fixed-instalment method* simply writes off the cost in equal instalments over the estimated life of the asset. If a machine is purchased for £1,100 and has an estimated scrap value of £100 at the end of its life, and if its life is estimated to be ten years, then amounts of £100 per year will be written off against its cost. Each year the manufacturing account will be charged with £100 and each year, if there are no external fluctuations in the market value of the machine, the machine will appear at £100 less than the previous year in the balance sheet. At the end of the tenth year it will be shown at its scrap value of £100.

(*b*) *The reducing-balance method.* Some accountants argue that the first method takes no account of the higher repair costs in the later years of the asset's life and that it is preferable to write off larger amounts in earlier years. One method of achieving this is to write off an equal percentage of the reduced balance every year. Assuming the above facts, if we wished to write down an amount of £1,100 to a scrap value of £100 in ten years it would be necessary to use an annual rate of over 21 per cent. For clarity of illustration, however, I shall use 20 per cent in the example which follows.

ILLUSTRATION

Year	*Value at beginning of year*	*Annual charge*	*Value at end of year*
	£	£	£
1	1,100 (cost)	220	880
2	880	176	704
3	704	141	563
4	563	112	451
5	451	90	361
6	361	72	289
7	289	58	231
8	231	46	185
9	185	37	148
10	148	30	118

In this table the charge is based on the written-down value at the beginning of the year, so that column 2 is invariably 20 per cent of column 1, and the remaining 80 per cent is carried down to the following year in column 3. After ten years the scrap value is $(0{\cdot}8)^{10} \times$ £1,100 = £118. At about 21·3 per cent depreciation charge per year the scrap value would be £100.

(*c*) *The sum-of-digits method.* This is a compromise between the "straight line" of the fixed-instalments method and the very rapidly diminishing curve of the reducing-balance method. Further, there are reasons why it is an ideal method for leasing and hire-purchase companies because of the method of repayment. One simply adds the "arithmetic progression" of years involved, in this case 10, such that $1 + 2 + 3 + 4 \ldots + 9 + 10 = 55$. Now divide cost price less residual value by 55, that is £(1,100 − 100)/55 = £18·18, and write off 10 × £18·18 or £182 in the first year, 9 × £18·18 or £164 in the second year and so on, leaving £100 balance for residual value in the final year.

(*d*) *The annuity method* needs little explanation after the chapter on compound interest values. It is simply a method of adjusting the straight-line or fixed-instalment method of depreciation to take into account "interest" on the reducing balance. It adjusts the asset value to the time value of money.

(*e*) *Use-adjusted methods.* These are methods which take account of the use of an asset for depreciation purposes instead of the lapse of time. One simply takes the cost of an asset and, assuming no residual value, divides it by the number of units which it is likely to process or produce. If there is residual value, the difference between cost and residual value is treated in this way. Alternatively, the amount to be written off may be divided by the number of hours which the machine is likely to operate or, if the asset is a motor vehicle, by the number of miles which it is estimated to run. One thus obtains either a unit charge or an hourly charge or a mileage charge which may vary from one period to another, and it is obvious that more depreciation will be written off if an asset is well used than during a period when it lies idle. There are, of course, strong arguments against the application of this method, especially in cases where a machine is likely to deteriorate much more by lying idle than by being used, and, of course, the method takes no account of the possibility of obsolescence during the time when the asset is idle.

(*f*) *Revaluation.* It would seem that the most realistic thing to do would be to revalue the asset at the end of each year and write off the difference, but the very use of this method leads to the kind of error which we are trying to avoid. If it is desirable to calculate operating profit, then this should be free from fluctuations resulting from sudden changes in the market values of fixed assets. If fixed assets are revalued yearly trading profit will reflect such revaluations.

There is a solution to the problem. It is to revalue every asset yearly and enter as correct a value as possible in the balance sheet for each date, but to charge manufacturing, trading and profit and loss accounts with a kind of rent charge which will represent the real economic rent which the company would have had to pay for the use of the asset concerned if it did not possess it but had to rent it from an external company, e.g. if it paid rent for its factory and hired its machinery from a leasing company. Any differences between written-down value and the revalued figure would be treated as a random fluctuation in the value of the asset and be accounted for outside the operating accounts. It would be as though the company had set up a hiring department, which allocated assets on hire to the operating departments at an economic rental and took credit for any gains or losses which were made in the capital values of the assets themselves.

Thus, if—

A_1 = the cost of the asset or its value at the beginning of the period;
d = the asset's rent-charge per year charged to the operating accounts;
f = the random fluctuation during the period plus wear and tear;
A_2 = the revalued worth of the asset at the end of the period;

then
$$A_1 - d + f = A_2.$$

The operating department would bear the cost of d, but the company as a whole would either bear the additional cost of $d - f$ or take credit for a random upward fluctuation of $f - d$ as the case may be. Sudden obsolescence would be regarded as a drastic case of $d - f$, while, on the other hand, a sudden windfall due to the appreciation in the value of property would be regarded as a drastic case of $f - d$. The illustration on pages 96–102 will show how this principle is applied.

Goodwill

We have given simple illustrations of how to deal with random fluctuations in the value of a company resulting from a change in the value of money (inflation or deflation), and changing values of stock-in-trade. We have also indicated how it is best to deal with changing values of fixed assets as distinct from the problem of "wear and tear" or depreciation which should preferably be charged to operating accounts at the opportunity cost or economic rent of the asset in question for its use. There will still be a difference between the total assets of a company on any date and its real worth on that date, because of intangible assets and because the value of the company as a whole is never necessarily equal to the sum of the values of its parts. However, if total value and individual values are as accurate as they can be, goodwill can be brought into the accounts purely as a balancing figure. The following illustration demonstrates this.

Illustration We are now in a position to bring the four basic lessons of the chapter, treatment of inflation, distortions due to fluctuations in the value of stock-in-trade, fluctuations of fixed assets and goodwill all together in one large example, as shown in the following pages.

Zeno Ltd

ADJUSTED MANUFACTURING ACCOUNT 1971

	Units	FIFO	Adjusted	
		£	£	£
Raw materials and work in progress				
Opening stock	40,000	80,000	80,000	
Add: Purchases	22,000	110,000	110,000	
	62,000	190,000	190,000	190,000
Holding gain on stock (computed below)			330,000	
Less: Closing stock	12,000	60,000	120,000	
				210,000
Cost of material used	50,000	130,000		400,000
Add: **Direct labour**		60,000		60,000
Prime cost		190,000		460,000
	£			
Add: Production expenses	34,000			
Imputed equivalent of renting machinery & plant	16,000			
		50,000		50,000
Cost of goods manufactured in 1971		£240,000		£510,000

Note: Computation of holding gain on stock

		£
Opening stock:	40,000 units at £2 charged out at £8, 40,000 × £6	240,000
Purchases:	10,000 units at £5 charged out at £8, 10,000 × £3	30,000
Closing stock:	12,000 units purchased at £5 now £10, 12,000 × £5	60,000
Total holding gain on stock		£330,000

Adjusted closing stock is 12,000 units at £10, hence the figure of £120,000; and adjusted purchases are 50,000 units at £8, hence the figure of £400,000.

Zeno Ltd

CONVENTIONAL AND ADJUSTED TRADING ACCOUNTS 1971

		Conventional		Adjusted
		£		£
Sales revenue		375,000		375,000
Less: **Cost of sales**—Opening stock of finished goods Jan. 1971	70,000		70,000	
Factory production transferred	240,000		510,000	
	310,000		580,000	
Closing stock revalued in adjusted accounts	60,000		80,000	
		250,000		500,000
Gross profit in conventional accounts		£125,000		
Gross loss in adjusted accounts				−£125,000

Zeno Ltd

CONVENTIONAL AND ADJUSTED PROFIT AND LOSS ACCOUNTS

		Conventional		Adjusted
		£		£
Gross trading profit (Trading Loss)		125,000		(125,000)
Deduct:				
Administration expenses	41,000		41,000	
Selling expenses	65,000		65,000	
Depreciation on buildings	800			
Equivalent of rent on buildings			4,000	
		106,800		110,000
Net operating profit (Operating loss)		£18,200		(£235,000)

RECONCILIATION OF CONVENTIONAL AND ADJUSTED FIGURES OF NET OPERATING PROFIT

Holding gain upon stock during 1971 (see note to manufacturing account)			£ 330,000
Deduct: Net operating loss from adjusted statement		235,000	
Differences in closing stock revalued	200,000		
	120,000		
		80,000	
			315,000
			15,000
Add: Additional imputed rent on buildings £4,000 − £800			3,200
Net profit per conventional accounts			£18,200

Now let us draw up the January and December balance sheets in terms of the value of money at the two respective balance-sheet dates. Closing stocks will of course be revalued at the above figures, and fixed assets valued at their real values in terms of currency at the respective balance-sheet dates. The real value of the company will be computed at both dates in terms of value of the pound at each of those dates, and any difference between the aggregate net assets and the integral value of the company in terms of discounted income will be regarded as goodwill. Assuming the following revaluation figures the balance sheets will look like this—

Zeno Ltd

ADJUSTED BALANCE SHEETS

	1. 1. 71	31. 12. 71	Changes
Fixed assets and goodwill	£	£	£
Goodwill (included as a balancing figure)	11,000	43,000	32,000
Freehold land (revalued at both dates)	30,000	100,000	70,000
Freehold buildings (revalued at both dates)	64,000	92,000	28,000
Plant and machinery (revalued at both dates)	30,000	20,000	−(10,000)
Carried forward	135,000	255,000	120,000

	£	£	£	£
Brought forward		135,000		255,000
Add: **Current assets less current liabilities**				
Stocks in hand:				
Raw materials, etc.	80,000		120,000	
Finished goods	70,000		80,000	
	150,000		200,000	
Debtors	5,000		50,000	
Cash	25,000		20,000	
	180,000		270,000	
Less: Creditors	95,000		85,000	
		85,000		185,000
Revaluations of the company at both dates		£220,000		£440,000
Represented by real value of ordinary shares revalued in terms of money at both dates		£220,000		£440,000

EXPLANATION OF CAPITAL INCREASE OF £220,000 IN TERMS OF CHANGING MONEY VALUES

	£	£
Appreciation of goodwill (as above)	32,000	
Appreciation of freehold land (as above)	70,000	
Appreciation of freehold buildings (as above) £28,000 + rent equivalent £4,000	32,000	
Appreciation of plant (rent equivalent £16,000 *less* depreciation £10,000)	6,000	
		140,000
Gain from holding stocks		330,000
		470,000
Less: Real net operating loss (computed earlier)		235,000
		235,000
Less: Cash used for plant additions		10,000
Aggregate income during the year		225,000
Less: Dividend distributed during 1971		5,000
Monetary and real increase in real value of company		£220,000

The figure £220,000 explains the difference in value of the company at the beginning and end of 1971 in money terms. However, if the January value of the company (£220,000) is translated into December pounds the converted January value will be £330,000, for prices have risen by 50 per cent during the year. The real income during the year will therefore be only £110,000 in December pounds. How can this be explained?

First let us calculate the monetary loss in net current assets due to the change of prices.

A. Calculation of monetary loss on net current assets

	£	Rate
Opening balance: Net current assets £85,000 in December pounds	127,500	$\frac{300}{200}$
Monetary increase in net current assets during the year from £85,000 to £185,000 = £100,000 converted to December pounds	120,000*	$\frac{300}{250}$
Expected closing balance if there had been no monetary loss	247,500	
Real closing balance of net current assets in December pounds	185,000	
Monetary loss on net current assets during the year	£62,500	

B. Adjusted table of real changes in fixed asset values in December pounds

	January values in December pounds	December values in December pounds	Changed value	Rent converted $\frac{300}{250}$	Real change
	£	£	£	£	£
Goodwill	16,500	43,000	26,500	—	26,500
Freehold land	45,000	100,000	55,000	—	55,000
Freehold buildings	96,000	92,000	–(4,000)	4,800*	800
Plant & machinery	45,000	20,000	–(25,000)	19,200*	–(5,800)
	£202,500	£255,000	£52,500	£24,000	£76,500

C. Computation of real increase in equity in December pounds

		£
Real increase in fixed asset values adjusted to December pounds (table B)		76,500
Stock appreciation converted to December pounds:		
£330,000 at average index × 300/250 =	396,000*	
Less: Monetary loss on net current assets (table A)	62,500	
		333,500
		410,000
Less: Net operating loss (computed earlier £235,000 × 300/250		282,000*
		128,000
Less: Cash used for plant additions £10,000 } × 300/250	12,000*	
Cash used for dividend payment £5,000 } × 300/250	6,000*	
		18,000
Real change in the value of company during 1971 in December pounds		£110,000

A taxation problem

It should be apparent at this stage that one of the greatest problems which arise from using adjusted income and from presenting balance sheets in this revised format is that of determining taxable income for, if corporation tax is based upon income, the company may, for example, find itself quite unable to pay tax on "non-cash" profits which result from large unrealized increases in the value of land.

This would be an even worse problem than that which executors of large estates meet in being unable to pay estate duty upon land, for at least in their case the land is usually sold ultimately.

If the accountancy profession decided to adopt an "unrealized" basis of income determination, the problem could be resolved by legislation to exempt appreciating assets of this sort, but the move from an "income-based" to a "value-added based" system of taxation may solve the problem ultimately without unnecessary legislation to redefine "income" for tax purposes as Chapter 14 indicates.

Conclusion

Note that in the tables on pp. 101–2 average index figures for 1971 converted to December 1971 pounds are followed by an asterisk (*). This rigorous example has shown us that conventionally prepared profit and loss accounts and balance sheets do not necessarily give us reliable figures of operating income for a company, and that they must be adjusted to indicate real operating income after isolating holding gains on stock, price-level changes and changes in fixed assets and goodwill. Operating income must be further adjusted before the real net cash income for a given year can be ascertained. All such figures are historical, and will only be true of the future if things continue as they are at present. It is better for a company to discover its optimal income by calculating its optimal level of sales, optimal sales price, and optimal expenditure on materials, labour and overheads. By discounting such a figure the potential value of the company may be discovered. The process of calculating optimal prices and quantities and monitoring operations to discover variances from optima is known as budgetary control and the accompanying accounting system is called standard costing. This field is explored in the next chapter.

Summary

The chapter has been concerned with problems of income measurement. If the value of a company is really the discounted value of its future income, then there should be some way of estimating such future income. The measurement of the historical income of a company over the previous few years could give us some indication of likely future income, but this assumes that past and present operating income have been correctly measured. Balance sheets and income statements can be distorted by (*a*) the instability of the monetary unit, (*b*) fluctuating values of stock-in-trade, (*c*) fluctuations in the values of fixed assets and (*d*) fluctuations in the total value of the company resulting from the fact of intangible assets and the "addition" fallacy.

We discussed methods of dealing with each of these problems, and in particular examined the problem of "wear and tear" or depreciation. Various methods of calculating depreciation were discussed, such as the fixed-instalment, reducing-balance, sum-of-digits, annuity, use-adjusted and revaluation methods. Revaluation would seem the most accurate, but leads to the dilemma of giving the operating income statement the credit for any fluctuations in the values of fixed assets, the very kind of dilemma which we are trying to avoid. From an economist's standpoint it appears preferable to charge the operating income account with the opportunity cost of the service rendered by the fixed assets, for example, the cost of rent for land and buildings if the company did not possess them, or the leasing charges in respect of machinery or vehicles. The assets would still require to be revalued for balance sheet purposes, but any difference between the fluctuation in the asset's value from one balance sheet date to another and the operating rent charge or opportunity cost of the service which the asset provides would be regarded as a random fluctuation and accounted separately. Thus real operating income over a period of past years can be measured with some accuracy and the trend of future income projected, although there could be a problem in adjusting "income" for taxation. This, however, would not necessarily be optimal income, and future chapters will set the task of correcting the standard future income by further examining the variables upon which such income depends. This is a matter for the application of budgetary control and standard costing.

Questions

1. What are the four reasons why balance sheets and income statements may be distorted?
2. How is inflation measured? Is there such a thing as a uniform rise in prices?
3. What are the methods of measuring usage of stock-in-trade in terms of money?
4. Explain the difference between the FIFO and LIFO methods of stock pricing.
5. What is depreciation? How is it calculated? Does it always correctly measure the wear and tear of an asset during a period? If not, say why.
6. Should fluctuations in the values of fixed assets be taken into account in measuring operating income?
7. What sort of charge should be offset against operating income in respect of a service provided by a fixed asset?

8. How may accounts be adjusted to allow for price level changes? Distinguish FIFO from LIFO. Do either of these methods provide us with real values for calculating income for a period?

On 1 January 1971 there were 10,000 units in stock priced at £1. On 2 January 1971, 5,000 units were purchased at £10 each. 8,000 units were charged to manufacturing account during the year. Discuss with calculations the difference in value, the difference in cost and income for 1971 if FIFO and LIFO methods are used for reporting stock balances and charges. Then assume that the average (standard) price for 1971 was £20 per unit and the standard price was £25 on 31 December 1971. What difference does this make to reported costs and profits?

9. The following are the summaries of the final accounts of Soaring Ltd for 1970 and 1971—

BALANCE SHEETS

	31. 12. 70	31. 12. 71
	£	£
Fixed assets (net)	10,000	9,000
Stocks	2,000	4,000
Debtors	2,500	1,000
Cash	4,500	2,000
	£19,000	£16,000
10,000 ordinary shares issued 1. 1. 70	10,000	10,000
Current liabilities	9,000	6,000
	£19,000	£16,000

PROFIT AND LOSS ACCOUNTS

	1970	1971
	£	£
Sales	24,000	30,000
Cost of sales	16,800	23,400
Gross profit	7,200	6,600
Other expenses	6,000	4,800
Net profit	£1,200	£1,800

The company carries no profit and loss account balances or reserves and all profits after tax are distributed as dividends during the period. January 1970 prices were 100 and June 1970 prices (which can be taken as a good 1970 average) were 125. In December 1970 they rose to 250, the average for 1971 was 375 and the December 1971 index stood at 500. Fixed assets were purchased when the company was incorporated in January 1970 and £1,000 depreciation is allowed upon £11,000 cost per annum. Assume that all other things are equal and adjust the above accounts for inflation.

Bibliography

All the titles listed in Chapter 7 are applicable and relevant, and in addition—

H. R. Anton & P. A. Firmin, *Contemporary Issues in Cost Accountancy* (Houghton, 1966)

W. T. Baxter, *Depreciation* (Sweet & Maxwell, 1971)

W. T. Baxter & S. Davidson (eds.), *Studies in Accounting Theory* (Sweet & Maxwell, 1962) (in particular, the reading by Professor Edey on "Goodwill")

R. S. Gynther, *Accounting for Price Level Changes—Theory and Procedures* (Pergamon, 1966)

J. R. Hicks, *Value and Capital* (Clarendon Press, 1962)

Y. Ijiri, *The Foundations of Accounting Measurement* (Prentice-Hall, 1967)

D. D. Ray, *Accounting and Business Fluctuations* (University of Florida Press, 1960)

R. Sidebotham, *Introduction to the Theory and Context of Accounting* (Pergamon, 1966)

9 Monitoring Devices I: Budgets and Variances

In the two previous chapters we have been concerned with the question of expected income. We have stated that it may be possible to predict the trend of future income if present and past income can be measured with some degree of accuracy. We suggested isolating the effects of inflation and of random fluctuations of assets and goodwill and of confining ourselves to the measurement of "operating income", and assumed that the study of accurate operating income figures for a number of years will provide us with a moving average and so eliminate the effects of cyclical differences from one year to another, and that the trend of the moving average will provide us with figures of "expected income" for a number of future years.

Purists would argue one stage further. They would say that the present value of a company is not the discounted value of its expected future income but of its net future cash inflow, and that the isolation of fluctuations and the calculation of expected future operating income does not provide us with the figure of expected net future cash inflow for a given number of years. What would be the benefit in earning "income" if it were not available in cash but tied up in excess stock-in-trade and debts which were difficult to realize? However, this kind of argument creates needless problems. No sensible management will allow unsold stocks and materials to accumulate nor allow debtors to remain with increasing balances for long periods. Although there is a certain randomness in debtors, creditors and stock balances from one year to another, they should bear some relationship to each other, to operating profit and to the size of the company. A company's cash flow will, of course, be affected by capital receipts from the issue of new shares or loans and by capital payments upon acquiring new fixed assets, but if these can be isolated, and if stocks, debtors and creditors remain reasonably constant from one year to another, expected operating income will be a realistic estimate of the expected net cash flow into the company.

It would seem essential that there should be monitoring devices for controlling the extent to which a company allows itself to be financed by its creditors and the extent to which it ties its income in credit to its customers and in stocks in its warehouses. These devices are a class of accounting ratios which we shall be considering in the next chapter. At the same time we shall be concerned with the problem of explaining a company's cash flow in terms of its "operating profit". At this stage we must reconsider even more rigorously the question of expected operating income. Even if we accept that there is some parity between a company's future operating income and its future cash flow, and that we can predict a company's future earning power from historical operating income figures, we shall have to admit that such estimates are no more than predictions of what will happen if the company carries on operating as it has been doing up to the present. It does not logically follow that the company has been doing its best, and therefore the projected estimates will not be predictions of the company's potential income (or of its optimal income). They will be no more than *normal* expectations. They will not be *ideal* expectations.

The use of standards to predict optimal income

Calculation of optimal income involves the preparation of a budget. Budgets are very much like the income statements or operating accounts of Chapters 7 and 8, with one difference. They are written in advance. The budgeted sales figure is a prediction of the optimum sales figure; the budgeted material cost is a prediction of the optimum material cost, and so on. The prediction of optima therefore involves producing the correct amount (or volume) of specific products and it involves charging the correct prices for them. It involves buying the best quantities at the best prices. If we assume, for simplicity, that stock levels are constant and that there are no credit transactions, an income budget or income forecast could take the form shown on the opposite page.

INCOME FORECAST

	£	£
Optimum sales = optimum price × optimum quantity		XXXXX
Optimum purchases = optimum materials price × optimum quantity	XXXXX	
Optimum labour = optimum wage × optimum hours worked	XXXXX	
Optimum overheads (production and "profit & loss account")	XXXXX	
Deduct: Optimum cost of sales (computed above)		XXXXX
Optimum profit upon quantity sold = Real income from operations		XXXXX

This elementary budget is a very simple form of income statement. Because stocks are assumed to be constant, there is no need to predict a trading account to calculate cost of goods sold, and the inclusion of both production overheads and profit and loss account expenses obviates the need for a "profit and loss account" section. In practice, budgets are much more complicated, for separate budgets are prepared for each department, for each cost centre, for each type of product and for each process. The use of a single statement will help us to understand budgetary control generally.

By such analysis we can see that historical figures do not necessarily provide us with their likely future equivalents; far less can they provide us with optimal future equivalents. Let us isolate and study, for example, the case of material cost.

The 1971 material cost in the previous chapter's illustration could be used as a standard material cost for 1972, but we have already discussed some of the problems of doing so. Consider what would happen, for example, if the unadjusted figure of £130,000 had been used to predict the standard material cost figure for 1972. Even under LIFO the figure was greater and when it was adjusted for real inflation it became a very bad predictor. Historical standards are unrealistic because prices will probably rise again in 1972; because demand for the product may change and a different quantity of components be therefore required or because new technology may increase the company's ability to produce the same product with less or even with different materials.

Ideal standards are often unattainable and the resulting repetition of adverse variances has a discouraging effect upon performance, tending to make budget demands unrealistic. It is clear that the figures used in budget preparation and the standards required to monitor a company's performance must be somewhere between the historical norm and the ideal impracticable standard. It must be a realistic feasible standard as near to the optimum position in the company's feasible area as possible. The purchasing department will be concerned with the minimum price which it should pay for the best quantity and quality of materials of each category required. When actual figures become available they can then be compared with predetermined estimates and a material expenditure variance will be calculated.

Material expenditure variance

In a bicycle production budget for 1971 it is planned to spend £350,000 on tubes at a bulk cost of £1 each but, because of bad handling in manufacturing, 400,000 tubes are required and, because the price rose to £1·25 per unit, actual cost was £500,000. Thus—

	£
Actual cost: 400,000 tubes at £1·25 each	500,000
Planned or budgeted cost: 350,000 tubes at £1·00 each	350,000
Total material expenditure variance	£150,000

It should be noted that the difference (or variance) between the amount which the bicycle manufacturer expected to spend on tubes for the budget period and the actual amount which was spent is the result of two basic causes—

(*a*) an increase in the price per unit (i.e. per tube);
(*b*) an increase in the quantity of tubes used.

A first reaction to learning that there were two basic reasons for the material expenditure variance of £150,000 would be to inquire how much of the variance *in terms of money* resulted from each of these causes. What would have been the variance if there had been no rise of prices, or conversely what would have been the variance if there had been no increase in the quantity used?

Figure 9.1 will illustrate that there exists a problem in this kind of variance analysis, for there will be a common area which results partly from an increase of price and partly from an increase of quantity. Cost accountants have developed a rather arbitrary method of dealing with this common area. They have assumed that standard price should always be used as a means of measuring material usage variance in terms of money, for it is reasoned that the standard price (or budgeted price) is that which should have been paid. The result of this logic is that price variances have to be measured in terms of actual quantity used.

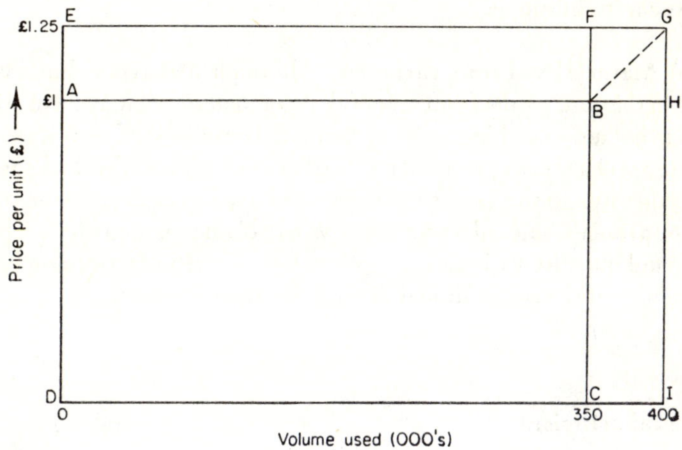

Fig 9.1 The basic pattern of variance analysis

This kind of rule is applied to most of the other expenditure variances such as labour expenditure variance and direct overhead expenditure variances. Thus—

Material price variance = Increase (or decrease) in the price per unit × Actual quantity of units used

Material volume variance = Increase (or decrease) in the quantity used × Standard price per unit

Let us illustrate this with the earlier example:

		£
Material price variance:	£0·25 × 400,000	100,000
Material volume variance:	£1·00 × 50,000	50,000
		£150,000

(a) Material price variance Can this rule-of-thumb division correctly pinpoint responsibility? How did the price variance arise? If it was the result of bad buying, the purchasing department should be blamed for paying 25 per cent too much for the tubes, but it may have been due to unforeseen price changes, in which case planning was at fault, unless it relied upon the purchasing department's forecasts. Perhaps not sufficient advantage was taken of bulk-buying, or perhaps the wrong supplier was selected. In this case, the purchasing department is only at fault if there are no constraints imposed by central management on its choice of supplier.

(b) Material volume variance Although material volume variance in this case results from wasteful use of materials it may have arisen either because machinery is inefficient, because staff are wasteful, because staff are being worked too hard or even because the stocks are of poor quality. So the works manager need not be responsible for overusing materials, and unless we know where blame can be assigned, both price and quantity variances are useless. Let us question more closely the soundness of the conventional division into subvariances.

General criticism

Both the variances in Figure 9.1 are adverse. *ABCD* is the budgeted cost of materials and *AEGI* is the actual cost of materials, so that the total adverse material cost variance is represented by the area *ABCIGE* and convention divides this area into *AEGH* (material price variance)—£100,000—and *BCIH* (material usage variance)—£50,000. These variances are unfavourable but, if *ABCD* had represented the actual material cost and *AEGI* had represented the budgeted material cost, both variances would have been favourable. There is no more a valid reason for including *BFGH* in material price variance than for including it in material usage variance. Some have wanted to divide it diagonally as the dotted line indicates, and to call *ABGE* material price variance and *BCIG* material usage variance. Others have wished to regard the total area *BFGH* for all practical purposes as a separate variance. Obviously it is an area of interdependence. It did not arise from a price-change any more than from materials wastage.

But are not price and quantity interdependent anyway? In a sales situation they usually are, for more can be sold as price becomes lower. Raw materials can be purchased at lower prices per unit as bulk becomes greater, unless the buying optimum is exceeded, after which marginal cost begins to rise. Marginal cost is the incremental cost, that of buying the additional unit. It tends to rise after bulk-buying advantages have been obtained and fixed overheads have been recovered. Further, because it is an elementary economic fact that marginal revenue per unit falls as larger quantities are offered for sale, marginal revenue is represented by the downward-sloping line in Figure 9.2. Economists say that the optimum level of production is where marginal cost equals marginal revenue, a situation similar to that which we encountered in discussing optimal finance with rising capital costs and falling internal rate of return in Chapter 6. The reason for this is clear. Profit is the area between marginal cost and marginal revenue in Figure 9.2. Total profit is the total area between the two curves up to any given level of output. After the intersection, marginal cost is higher than marginal revenue so a marginal loss begins to occur for every additional unit produced and this offsets the profit triangle on the left-hand side of the diagram, *MKZ* in Figure 9.2. As marginal loss is zero at the point of intersection, profit at this level of output is the triangle *MKZ*.

Demski introduces a further argument against the conventional method of material cost variance analysis. In Figure 9.2 a uniform rise in the cost of every material unit used would result in a uniform rise in marginal cost from MC_0 (*KLM*) to MC_1 (*ABC*). Before the price change optimal output level was at X_0 vertically below the point of intersection *M* where the largest profit area *ZMK* was possible. At any output level higher than X_0 losses would be incurred which would have to be deducted from *ZMK* to give the net figure of total profit. A uniform increase in materials cost is represented by the line MC_1. X_0 is now no longer the optimum point of production for at X_0 profit now becomes *ZAB* less *BCM*. If the firm moves to level X_1, however, where the new marginal cost curve MC_1 intersects the marginal revenue curve, it is at least sure of profit *ZAB*. The price change has altered the whole budget situation. Convention would report pure price-quantity variances, either at *AKMC* if output continued at X_0 or at *AKLB* if the company shifted its output level to X_1. Neither of these variances is very useful. If the price change was unforeseeable no one should be blamed. If the planning department changes its output level from X_0 to X_1 as soon as rises are apparent, it should be praised for doing so. So material cost variances should be analysed not on the conventional price/quantity basis, but to indicate whether they are avoidable or unavoidable. Often they result from bad planning and Bromwich argues that it is better to analyse material cost variances into planning and performance variances. By appraising the situation afterwards one can sometimes tell what the

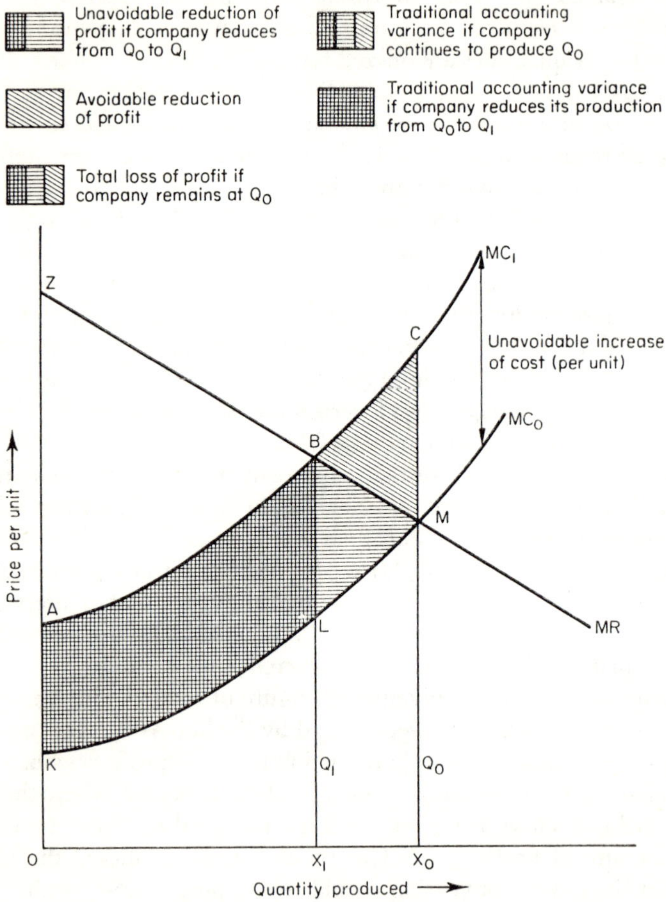

Fig 9.2 The real effect of a uniform rise in material (or other unit) cost

real optimum should have been and divide variances into planning variances (differences between budgeted cost and real optimum) and performance variances (differences between actual cost and real optimum). This method of analysis can also be applied to labour, overheads, expenses and sales.

Accountants defend the conventional analysis, arguing that the amount of time it would take to calculate real variances after considering all economic factors would be astronomical for there is in practice a multitude of components for many products, and mix variances are sometimes also computed to show the difference between the standard mix of raw materials in a product and the actual mix of materials in the finished article. However, computers have made calculation much easier and a more realistic and analytical appraisal of variances should now be possible.

Labour variances

As a product contains so many units of various raw material components, so it may be conveniently described as containing a given number of "standard hours", that is, of expected hours of labour to be spent upon it. The conventional method of analysing labour variances is similar to that employed for material cost variances. Labour cost variance is divided into a labour rate variance indicating the difference between standard and actual hourly rates and a labour efficiency variance showing the difference in the time which it has taken to do a particular job.

ILLUSTRATION

For example, Pronto pays his factory hands £1 per hour to manufacture a budgeted quantity of Spanish guitars. Labour was budgeted at £2,000 for it was estimated that 2,000 standard hours would be taken over the job, and employees were paid previously at £1 per hour for other jobs. However, wages rise to £1·50, but only 1,800 hours are taken over the job.

Thus—

	£
Budgeted cost of labour: 2,000 standard hours at £1	2,000
Actual cost of labour: 1,800 hours at £1·50	2,700
Adverse labour cost variance	−£700

The method of analysis is similar to that employed for material cost variances, thus—

	£
Adverse labour rate variance: 1,800 hours at 50p	−900
Favourable labour efficiency variance: 200 hours at £1	200
Adverse labour cost variance (as above)	−£700

Pronto's 50 per cent rise in hourly rates has been offset to some extent by apparent greater efficiency. But perhaps his workers were more efficient because they were paid more. Convention would blame trade unions for the 50 per cent rise in labour cost and congratulate the workers for a saving of £200, but there is probably interdependence between both, making analysis unnecessary. The behavioural effect of wage increases may be better production initially, but less efficient production as cost of living rises and workers become more militant again. Who knows? Once behavioural interactions are taken into account, possibilities are infinite.

The problem of overhead absorption—direct and indirect cost

Accountants like to know the selling prices at which costs can be recovered and a small profit made, but real selling price often bears little relationship to such cost-plus prices. It is reasonably easy to compute how many standard hours of labour and units of material should go into each unit of a finished article, but it is difficult to absorb overhead costs into computing optimal selling price per unit on traditional lines, for overhead costs are indirect. Indirect labour, materials and expenses may, for example, include bars of soap used by office staff, catering staff wages and computer power, for none of these costs can be directly allocated to each unit which comes off the production line.

Power cost may rank as a direct expense if a meter is installed on each machine to show the exact amount of power expended on a given unit of production, and such direct expenses may be analysed traditionally, and price and quantity variances calculated. Real overhead is indirect, and absorption of indirect costs is a problem to the accountant in cost-plus pricing calculations, for such costs may be fixed or variable. Up to a point, rent is fixed and does not vary with production. £5,000 rent may be paid for a factory regardless of whether 10 or 10,000 units are produced. Some overheads, however, may have a variable element, for example, telephone calls. Many telephone calls are of an administrative nature and would be made anyway, yet there is probably a very strong relationship between the cost of telephone calls and the number of "units" which a company produces and sells. It may be possible to compute a regression relationship between production and telephone cost, i.e. telephone cost = fixed telephone cost + (variable telephone cost × number of units produced).

Isolating variable costs from fixed costs

Many other costs, apart from telephone expenses, fall into the category of being part variable and part fixed, and it is difficult to isolate the fixed element from the variable element. One method of doing so is to plot the costs and volume in respect of each category, telephone, heating and lighting, electricity, etc., and to find the line of best fit. The other method is to use a regression formula upon a number of observations, where x represents output and y represents cost and n is the number of observations. The following example in which there are only three observations and a simple cost/volume relationship will illustrate the method of isolating fixed and variable elements in each category of cost.

Observation	Output (x)	Cost (y)	x^2	y^2	xy
		£		£	£
1	2	11	4	121	22
2	5	20	25	400	100
3	4	17	16	289	68
	$\Sigma x = 11$	$\Sigma y = 48$	$\Sigma x^2 = 45$	$\Sigma y^2 = 810$	$\Sigma xy = 190$

It may be done diagrammatically using the line of best fit (see Figure 9.3), but the formula for this type of problem is that variable cost (v) is—

$$\frac{n\Sigma xy - (\Sigma x\Sigma y)}{n\Sigma x^2 - (\Sigma x)^2}$$

The derivation of this formula may be found in textbooks of statistical theory. Applying it to the problem, variable cost is seen (from the workings columns) to be—

$$\frac{(3 \times 190) - (11 \times 48)}{(3 \times 45) - 11^2}$$

This is—

$$\frac{(570 - 528)}{(135 - 121)} = £3$$

From the variable cost of £3 we can find approximate fixed cost by solving $(\Sigma y - 3\Sigma x)/n$, the 3 in the formula being variable cost. This is

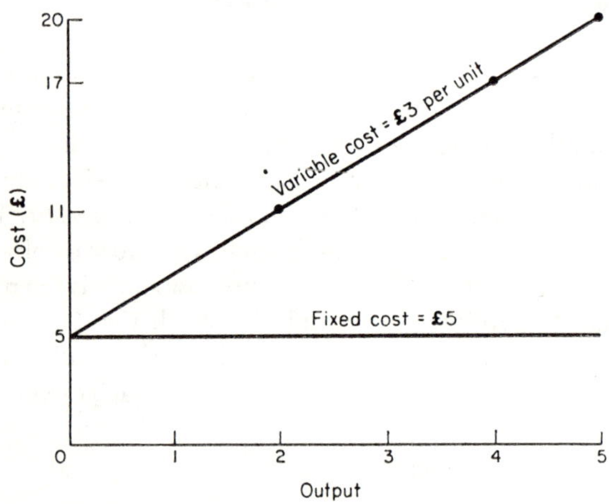

Fig 9.3 Separation of fixed and variable costs by diagram

(48 — 33)/3 = 15/3 = £5. If these values (fixed cost = £5 and variable cost = £3) are substituted in the above observations, total cost works out exactly in each case. The formula is used to estimate fixed and variable elements where there is no exact pattern.

But how can fixed overhead be "absorbed" by production units so that each unit bears its fair share of overhead? The accountant estimates the total number of units to be produced during a period, divides this by the total estimated overhead for the period and simply absorbs such overhead cost by adding it to the cost per unit, either before or after it is taken into stock; that is, either at time of manufacture or when the unit is sold. But, of course, expected production will not be exactly produced, nor will expected overhead cost be exactly incurred. Variance analysis therefore poses interesting problems.

Traditional method of overhead variance analysis

Figure 9.3 illustrates the normal professional treatment of overhead variances. Overhead variance is the difference between actual overhead cost and overhead absorbed by production on the above basis. This is partly due to inefficient working so that standard hours of production

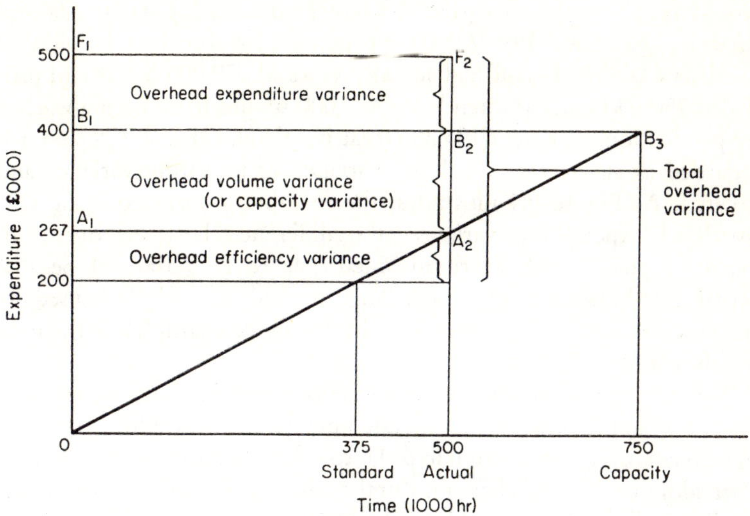

Fig 9.4 Variances resulting from overhead absorption

may be less than actual hours worked. Overhead under-absorbed for this reason is called "overhead efficiency variance". Perhaps employees did not work actual hours anyway because of strikes, machine breakdown or lockouts. Overhead under-absorbed or overhead over-absorbed for this type of cause is called "overhead volume variance" or "idle time variance". If these two absorption variances are detected and isolated, the real overhead expenditure variance remains.

In Figure 9.4 suppose that all variable costs have been isolated, and that fixed overhead is being analysed. It is expected to be £400,000. It is also expected that 750,000 standard hours will be worked during the period, 1 standard hour for 1 unit produced, so that expected production is 750,000 units. By dividing £400,000 by 750,000 an overhead absorption rate of 53p per standard hour (or 53p per unit) is calculated. At the end of the period it is discovered that only 375,000 units have been produced, and that it took the operatives 500,000 hours to do it, so 375,000 standard hours work were produced in 500,000 actual hours. If overhead is absorbed either on a standard hour or on a unit basis, overhead absorbed will have been only £200,000 (that is, 375,000 × 0·53), so that the remaining £200,000 budgeted overhead has not been absorbed into production. If operatives had successfully produced 500,000 units in the 500,000 hours they actually worked £266,667 would have been absorbed (that is, 500,000 units at 0·53) so that £66,667 (that is, £266,667 less £200,000) was under-absorbed because of inefficient labour. If staff had actually worked 750,000 hours and produced 750,000 units as intended £400,000 would have been absorbed by production, so that £133,333 (that is, £400,000 less £266,667) is regarded as an overhead volume variance or idle time variance and isolated. As Figure 9.4 illustrates, the remaining variance is the true overhead expenditure variance, the difference between overheads expected and actual overheads incurred. It is £100,000 because actual overheads are £500,000. This method of analysis is used by accountants for fixed overheads (as in the above example) or for total overheads.

This method of variance analysis accepts absorption costing, a costing system which "slices" overheads and absorbs them by adding them to the direct costs of production in order to calculate the sale price of a unit after adding a "profit" element. But the whole philosophy of absorption costing is difficult to uphold, for prices are often market-determined. Price determination is considered in the next chapter. A more immediate question is, "What use is this method of analysis for monitoring overhead expenditure?" Surely, very little. Persons in control of administrative expenditure, staff salaries, cleaning and rent, cannot be held responsible for factory inefficiencies or for machine breakdown resulting in under-absorption of overhead expenditure. The only relevant variance for monitoring overhead expenditure is overhead expenditure variance, illustrated by the top rectangle in Figure 9.4. This amount, £100,000 in the example, must be further analysed to show whether inefficiencies have resulted from over-using telephone, from rising cleaning, heating and rent costs or from bad planning.

The two absorption variances, idle time and overhead efficiency variances are of no use in monitoring overhead expenditure. They may tell us that 125,000 standard hours were lost because of inefficiency or that 250,000 hours were lost because of failure to work, but such information is of no use in monitoring overhead expenditure. It could be of some use to a works manager.

Sales variances

Traditional accounting divides sales revenue variances using the pattern of Figure 9.1, isolating sales volume variances from sales price variances. In theory a large adverse sales price variance would indicate poor pricing and a large adverse sales volume variance would indicate poor salesmanship. Yet price and quantity are interdependent. Any salesman can sell more simply by lowering the price, and sales managers often understate the quantity they are likely to sell in a budget period so that volume variances always appear favourable. It is difficult to predict selling prices for they are dictated by the market, and although sales prices may not be under-estimated by sales managers because they are frequently cost-determined, yet possibly neither sales price nor sales quantity are realistically budgeted.

The interdependence problem—an illustration

A short example illustrates the effect of interplay between price and volume. Suppose that direct cost (that is, direct materials, direct labour, etc.) of producing transistor radio sets is £5 per unit and that the monthly sales budget is 500 sets at £10 each, a budgeted "contribution" (that is, sales less direct costs) of £5 per unit. Actually, sales are discovered to be 1,000 transistor radios at £6 each, a sales revenue of £6,000.

Convention would analyse this variance of £1,000 (i.e. £6,000 less £5,000) as follows—

	£
Favourable sales volume variance: 500 extra sets sold at £10	5,000
Adverse sales price variance: price reduction £4 on 1,000 sets	4,000
Net favourable sales revenue variance: 1,000 sets sold at £6 less budgeted revenue 500 at £10	£1,000

But has the sales manager really contributed £5,000 to the company by selling 500 extra transistors at £10. No, for he has only sold them at £6 each and they cost £5 each direct cost to manufacture, so that the additional contribution from selling 500 extra sets is £500 at the most. Further, the 500 sets expected to be sold were expected to produce £5,000 revenue and therefore £2,500 (i.e. 500 × £5) contribution. The sales manager has made only £500 (i.e. 500 × £1) upon these, thereby losing £2,000. Hence his action in reducing price by £4 and selling 500 extra units has resulted in an adverse variance of £1,500, that is, £500 from the extra units sold less £2,000 lost on existing units.

This £1,500 can also be calculated in the following way—

	£
Total conventional sales variance (favourable)	1,000
Less direct cost of producing 500 extra units at £5 per unit	2,500
Adverse variance (as above)	−£1,500

But of course the fall of price from £10 to £6 may have nothing to do with the sales manager's selling campaign but be dictated by market conditions. Suppose that competitors produce similar transistor radios for £6 each. In such an event the sales manager can be credited with selling 500 extra units, but only with the additional contribution of £500 (i.e. £1 per unit). Most probably the sales manager could not, even in optimal conditions, have doubled his sales without reducing price. Subsequent appraisal may decide that 1,000 units could have been sold if price had been lowered to £8. The sales manager succeeded in doubling his sales by selling at £6 per unit. The position is therefore—

	£
Economic gain from selling 1,000 units at a realistic contribution of £3 (i.e. £8 less £5) per unit as against 500 units at the budgeted contribution of £5 (i.e. £10 less £5) per unit: £3,000 – £2,500	500
Real adverse variance from selling 1,000 units at an actual contribution of £1 (i.e. £6 – £5) as against realistic contribution of £3 per unit	2,000
Real adverse variance £1,000 (as above) less £5 direct cost upon 500 extra units: £1,000 – £2,500 (as above)	–£1,500

So analysis of sales variances is most difficult. Favourable volume variances are often overstated because salesmen under-estimate likely sales and because sales volume variances often do not take account of direct costs of producing extra quantities sold. At best extra quantities sold merely improve the contribution received by the company. Sales volume and sales price variances are interdependent and the only way to solve the dilemma is by afterwards trying to estimate at what price the quantity actually sold could have ideally been sold.

Summary

A company's real worth is the discounted value of its future earnings, and adjusted historical income statements are useful in predicting what future earnings should be expected. Strictly, future earnings should be expressed in terms of cash flows, but there should be some similarity between profits and net cash inflow when allowance has been made for capital receipts and payments and fluctuations in stocks and credit. Other devices are available for monitoring such fluctuations. Even if such fluctuations did not exist, however, and even if cash income and net operating income were synonymous, historical trading and profit and loss accounts would only provide us with expected future income. They would not provide us with optima for budgetary control and for setting standards. These optima should be arrived at by calculating from optimum prices and quantities the optimum figures of sales revenue, material cost, labour cost and overheads. Such calculations imply that actual prices and quantities may afterwards be obtained and that optimum figures may be compared with actual figures of sales revenue, material cost, labour cost and overheads and the differences (variances) obtained.

It is natural that we should wish to know, in each case, how much of the variances resulted from a change of price and how much can be attributed to a change in quantity used (or sold). The feedback diagram in the early chapters implies that all analysed variances must be useful in initiating action of some kind. Compare this with the thermostat. The traditional method of overcoming the "common area" problem is to use actual quantities for measuring price variances and standard prices for measuring volume variances. Strictly the common area should be halved and attributed equally to price and usage changes. However, the very existence of the common area, although insignificant in most real-life cases, is a precursor of a far greater problem, that there is always an interdependence between price and quantity.

For example a rise of material cost per unit will lead to an increase of marginal cost and therefore to a change in the optimal level (or volume) at which the company should produce. Figure 9.2 illustrates that there is an area of avoidability and one of unavoidability in the traditional accounting variance. Labour variances indicate the same interdependence feature. Increased wages may, for a while, lead to a better standard of work and to a decrease in the actual hours necessary to do a particular job.

Overheads present us with a different kind of problem. They are strictly understood to mean indirect expenses, but some kinds of expenses are composite and contain both direct and indirect elements. The mathematical method of separating direct and indirect elements from each other is to use a linear regression formula or to plot the relevant costs in respect of each volume of output on a graph and to draw the line of best fit.

Indirect expenses are usually "absorbed" by production, that is, the accountant normally calculates the best method of spreading overheads so that each unit produced will bear its fair share of overhead in determining a selling price. At the end of a period there will be some difference between actual overhead spent and the amount of overhead absorbed, that is, added to the cost of production. The difference between absorbed overhead and actual overhead is not useful in monitoring overhead expenditure because some of it is due to idle capacity and some may be due to under-efficiency. By isolating these variances the true overhead expenditure variance may be obtained.

Sales variances are probably the best illustration of the interdependence problem for it is evident that price reduction will lead to an increase of quantity sold. If there is therefore an increase of sales quantity but a reduction of price it would be a little more realistic to calculate the optimum price at which the quantity actually sold could have been sold in the prevailing trade circumstances.

Questions

1. Discuss the relationship between expected future profit and expected cash flow.
2. Illustrate diagrammatically the relationship between price variance and quantity variance in the case of materials, labour and sales. Is there any economic argument against this kind of variance analysis in each of the three cases?
3. Illustrate with a diagram how a rise in marginal cost per unit may lead to a change in the optimal level of production.
4. The following are the budgeted and actual profit statements of Loser Ltd. Calculate variances as far as is possible.

Budget prepared for 1971		*Actual figures available in December* 1971	
	£		£
Sales 4,000 units × £8 each	32,000	Sales 5,000 units × £7 each	35,000
Less: Cost of sales:		*Less*: Cost of sales:	
Materials 2,000 units × £5	10,000	Materials 2,500 units × £6	15,000
Labour 6,000 hours × £1	6,000	Labour 5,000 hours × £2	10,000
Overhead	9,000	Overhead	10,000
Cost of sales	25,000	*Cost of sales*	35,000
Profit	£7,000	*Profit*	NIL

5. From the following observations of experience calculate the fixed costs for the firm and the variable cost per unit which you consider most probable.

Year	*Output*	*Cost (£)*
1968	905	2,108
1969	1,000	2,167
1970	795	2,031

Use the formula provided for this purpose. Slide rules or logarithm tables may be employed.

Bibliography

L. R. Amey, *The Efficiency of Business Enterprises* (Allen & Unwin, 1969)

H. R. Anton & P. A. Firmin, *Contemporary Issues in Cost Accountancy* (Houghton, 1966)

J. Batty (ed.), *Developments in Management Accountancy* (Heinemann/ICMA, 1968)

H. Bierman, *Topics in Cost Accounting and Decisions* (McGraw-Hill, 1963)

M. Bromwich, "Standard Costing for Planning and Control", *Accountant*, April/May 1969

J. S. Demski, "Variance Analysis using a Constrained Linear Model", in Solomons (below)

M. J. Gordon, "The Use of Administered Price Systems", in C. P. Bonini (ed.), *Management Controls—New Directions in Basic Research* (McGraw-Hill, 1964)

C. T. Horngren, *Cost Accounting: A Managerial Emphasis* (Prentice-Hall, 1967)

C. Moore & R. K. Jaedicke, *Managerial Accounting* (S. W. Publishing, 1963; Arnold, 1965)

D. Solomons, *Studies in Cost Analysis* (Sweet & Maxwell, 1968)

10 Monitoring Devices II: Ratios and Funds Statements

The methods of comparison used in Chapter 9 were absolute, that is, they were expressed in terms of differences between a standard and an actual. The standard was to be regarded as the assumed optimum and the difference or variance was intended to pinpoint the difference in absolute terms between the predetermined optimum and the actual result.

The need for ratios

It should be evident that such variances can be subjected to the kind of criticism which was levelled against net present value as an investment planning criterion in Chapter 6. It is that an absolute amount often fails to give the kind of information which a ratio can give. To say that there is a variance of £600 between actual sales and budgeted sales revenue means something quite different if budgeted sales are £1,000,000 and actual sales are £999,400 from what it would mean if budgeted sales were £1,000 and actual sales £400. In the first case the difference is only 0·06 per cent, whereas in the second case the difference is 60 per cent. In the first example the result would be insignificantly different, but in the second example the result could be absolutely disastrous.

In capital investment theory it was shown that net present value and internal rate of return both had their respective uses, and the use of the profitability index was intended to be a compromise between the two methods of appraisal, because net present value does not, of itself, express the amount of gain in terms of the capital invested. We could adopt the same procedure for all variances. We could express them as percentages of the budgeted or predetermined relevant optima. The use of this logic would imply that the above sales revenue variances should be expressed as

0·06 per cent and 60 per cent respectively instead of using the comparatively meaningless £600.

The use of ratios does not end at this point. Indeed, accountants rarely calculate budget variances in terms of percentages unless they wish to know whether a variance is significant enough to be investigated. Instead, ratios are used to measure profitability and liquidity against historical yardsticks and against the experience of comparable companies.

Profitability ratios

The study of profitability ratios stems directly from the consideration of internal rate of return as a criterion for investment appraisal. In short it is desired to know the profitability of the company's capital and, as turnover (or sales revenue) is most often the basis of profit, all the various kinds of expenditure can be expressed as a proportion of sales.

Thus—

$$\frac{\text{Profit}}{\text{Capital}} = \frac{\text{Profit}}{\text{Sales}} \times \frac{\text{Sales}}{\text{Capital}}$$

Illustration Using the unadjusted final accounts of Zeno Ltd in Chapter 7 the ratios would be—

$$\frac{18{,}200}{180{,}000} = \frac{18{,}200}{375{,}000} \times \frac{375{,}000}{180{,}000}$$

This could be expressed in percentages as:

$$10{\cdot}1\% = 4{\cdot}8\% \times 208\%$$

In many cases the use of return on investment ratio will determine the precise meaning of capital for calculation purposes, for the first of the above three ratios could be used to measure—

(i) profitability of equity capital;
(ii) profitability of total long-term commitment; or
(iii) profitability of net assets relevant to trading.

(i) Profitability of equity capital Equity is the ordinary share capital of a company. It need not obtain its capital (in the wider sense) merely by issuing shares. It could arrange to issue debentures (loan certificates) at a fixed rate of interest. In some cases long-term overdrafts from a bank must be regarded as capital. A paper presented by R. E. V. Groves and R. Harrison at the conference of the Association of University Teachers of Accounting in Cardiff in September 1971 argued the case for regarding bank overdrafts as capital items, and some companies include long-term overdrafts as capital in their balance sheets.

In contrast with this more general view of capital, the profit/equity capital ratio simply measures the profitability of equity capital. It is expressed as net profit/equity and measures the profitability of the company simply from the standpoint of the company's members or equity shareholders. As Zeno Ltd in Chapter 7 has no debenture-holders and no other sources of income besides its trading income, the ratio 10·1 per cent in the illustration can be regarded as a profit/equity ratio.

(ii) Profitability of total long-term commitment There is often considerable difference between equity capital (or ownership capital) and capital in the economic sense. If the company has borrowed capital at a fixed rate of interest, either from debenture-holders (that is, non-members, who have invested money in the company at a fixed rate of interest) or from a bank, the total profitability of capital as a long-term commitment may be calculated simply by adding back to net profit any fixed interest payable during the period, and by adding the total amount loaned to the equity share capital, i.e.

$$(1)\ \frac{\text{Net Profit} + \text{Debenture Interest Paid}}{\text{Shares} + \text{Debentures}};\ \text{or}$$

$$(2)\ \frac{\text{Net Profit} + \text{Debenture Interest Paid}}{\text{Total Assets} - \text{Current Liabilities}}$$

If the Zeno Company had decided to borrow £300,000 at 10 per cent interest and had paid 10 per cent (i.e. £30,000) in debenture interest before arriving at its figure of net profit, there would be very little difference between the net profit/equity ratio and the operating profit (shares + debt) ratio, for the borrowing ratio differs very little from the net profit/equity ratio of 10·1 per cent. However, if it had borrowed its

£300,000 at 20 per cent, the profitability of its long-term commitment would have been—

$$\frac{\text{Net Profit} + \text{Debenture Interest}}{\text{Shares} + \text{Debentures}}$$

$$= \frac{18{,}200 + 60{,}000}{180{,}000 + 300{,}000} = \frac{78{,}200}{480{,}000} = 16{\cdot}3\%$$

The difference between the two ratios would now indicate that the company's activities could be much more profitable if it did not have to pay its debenture-holders as much as 20 per cent. This ratio is often a more accurate criterion of the earning power of the company.

(iii) Profitability of net assets relevant to trading By adding back the debenture interest paid in the above example, we were able to arrive at a figure of operating income. This was because it was assumed that the company had no other sources of income. It may, and often does, both borrow from the public and have investments (either shares or debentures in other companies or other sources of income such as Government stock). In such cases the investments should be excluded in calculating the profitability of the company's net trading assets, even though the very ownership of such assets, such investments in other companies, may from the point of view of "synergy" give the company the kind of trading advantage which it would not otherwise have.

There are two ways of expressing this ratio—

$$(1)\ \frac{\text{Net Operating Income}}{\text{Total Assets} - \text{Investments} - \text{Current Liabilities}};\ \text{or}$$

$$(2)\ \frac{\text{Net Profit} + \text{Debenture Interest} - \text{Investment Income}}{\text{Equity} + \text{Debentures} - \text{Investments}}$$

If the income of £78,200 in the previous example had not been entirely operating income, but if £8,200 had been derived from a very highly profitable 41 per cent dividend from a £20,000 investment in the Plato Company Ltd, then both investment and investment income should be excluded in order to calculate true operating income and true operating assets, and the earning power of the trading section of the company would be—

$$\frac{18{,}200 + 60{,}000 - 8{,}200}{180{,}000 + 300{,}000 - 20{,}000} = \frac{70{,}000}{460{,}000} = 15{\cdot}2\%$$

The very high profitability of a very small investment outside the company now makes a difference of over 1 per cent in the true operating worth of the company, for if these investments were excluded the operating worth of the company's net relevant capital would only be 15·2 per cent. It may, of course, be even lower than this, for the acquisition of its shares in Plato Ltd may have given other benefits of a synergist character, selling, production, purchasing or acquisitional benefits which in themselves may even outweigh the difference of 1·1 per cent in the earnings of the company's total fixed capital.

The pyramid of ratios

Let us now simplify the example and exclude any difference which may be due to the company's issuing loan capital or to the company's acquisition of shares in other companies. Let us return to the original balance sheet of Zeno Ltd in Chapter 7. Figure 10.1 illustrates the pyramid of ratios. It continues the process of analysis which we commenced earlier in the chapter. If a trading company cannot sell its products it cannot earn its operating income. The profitability of the company's capital must therefore depend upon its selling power. The other functions of the company may be expressed in terms of sales. The earlier analysis of the company's profitability ratio may now therefore be more accurately expressed as—

$$\frac{\text{Operating Income}}{\text{"Operating" Capital (or net relevant assets)}} = \frac{\text{Operating Income}}{\text{Sales Revenue}} \times \frac{\text{Sales Revenue}}{\text{"Operating" Capital (or net relevant assets)}}$$

The first of these ratios expresses the rate of return which the company earns by trading from those net assets which are relevant to trading, that is from its fixed capital minus any investments in other companies. The second ratio expresses its operating income as a percentage of its sales revenue and is an administration and production criterion. If the production department (in the case of a manufacturing company) or the buying department (in the cases of both manufacturing and trading companies) is able to reduce its expenditure per unit, and if the company's administration is able to reduce its overheads, then operating income will be a higher proportion of sales revenue.

The third of these ratios is a device for monitoring the sales function of the company. The higher the ratio of sales in proportion to capital, the more likely that the company has a healthy sales department. We must not, of course, forget the lessons of the previous chapter. A sales manager can increase the turnover figure, or sales revenue figure, simply by reducing the price per unit. It is essential that none of these ratios be studied in isolation. Both the profit/sales ratio and sales/capital ratio should be analysed further.

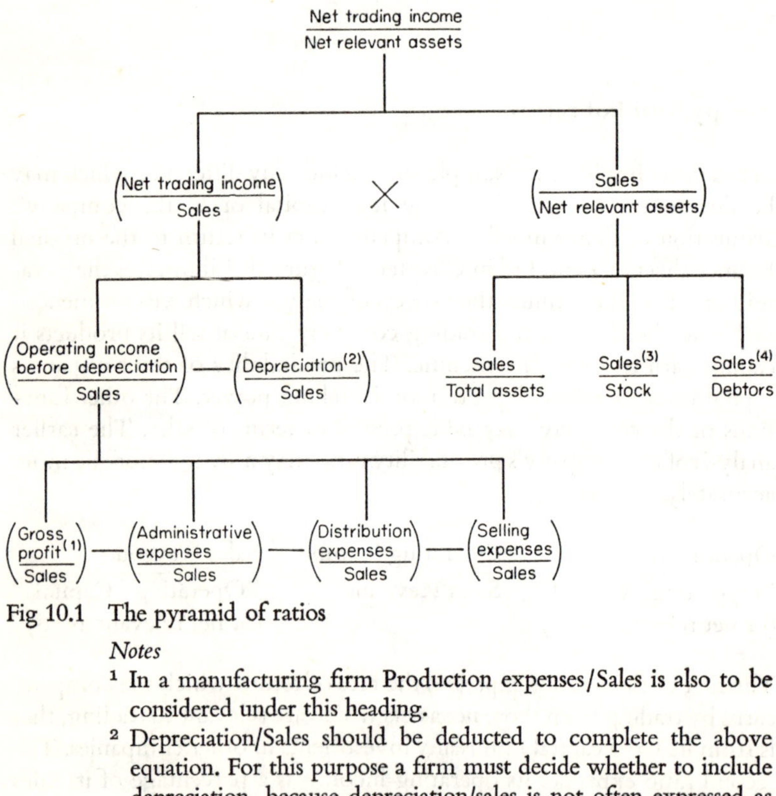

Fig 10.1 The pyramid of ratios

Notes

1 In a manufacturing firm Production expenses/Sales is also to be considered under this heading.

2 Depreciation/Sales should be deducted to complete the above equation. For this purpose a firm must decide whether to include depreciation, because depreciation/sales is not often expressed as a ratio.

3 Sales/Stock indicates stock turnover, but this is more usually expressed as Cost of sales/Average stock or (2 × Cost of sales)/(Opening stock + Closing stock).

4 Sales/Debtors is often inverted to Debtors/Sales × 365 to indicate days sales on books.

A whole family of ratios may be derived from the profit sales ratio. Hence—

$$\frac{\text{Net Profit}}{\text{Sales}} = \frac{\text{Gross Profit}}{\text{Sales}} - \frac{\text{Administration Costs}}{\text{Sales}} - \frac{\text{Selling Costs}}{\text{Sales}} - \frac{\text{Depreciation}}{\text{Sales}}$$

that is—

$$\frac{18{,}200}{375{,}000} = \frac{125{,}000}{375{,}000} - \frac{41{,}000}{375{,}000} - \frac{65{,}000}{375{,}000} - \frac{800}{375{,}000}$$

in the Zeno accounts on page 74. Alternatively in the above case, a percentage set of manufacturing, trading and profit and loss accounts could be constructed showing how much of sales revenue is used up by various direct costs, expenses, depreciation and stock adjustments. If prices were not affected by inflation and if sales quantity were constant it would then be possible to make comparisons with previous percentage accounts for other years, but the procedure is of doubtful value because both prices and sales volume will have changed, and thus the ratio of fixed costs to sales will be different. The use of profit and loss account ratios and the expression of profit and loss account and other income-statement items as percentages of sales has another, and even more fundamental, limitation, for it assumes that comparison with previous years is a useful yardstick. It is only useful if historical standards are not regarded as necessarily optimal, and if all the adjustments of Chapter 8 are carried out.

In constructing the pyramid of ratios in Figure 10.1 I assumed a trading company. I assumed that depreciation/sales is a meaningful variance. It could be meaningful if depreciation represented (as I suggested in Chapter 8) the leasing charge or the opportunity cost of using the assets specified. Often depreciation/sales is not regarded as a meaningful ratio. If I had assumed a manufacturing company it would be possible to calculate production expenditure/sales and this could be regarded as, for example—

$$\frac{\text{Direct Materials}}{\text{Sales}} + \frac{\text{Direct Labour}}{\text{Sales}} + \frac{\text{Production Overhead}}{\text{Sales}} + \frac{\text{Factory Depreciation}}{\text{Sales}}$$

The limitations of all these ratios must be realized, i.e. if they are to be used for historical comparison there are strong arguments against using previous history as a yardstick for measuring present operations. They may, however, serve to show in some cases the general direction in which the company is moving.

Stock control and stock turnover

It has already been noted that cash flow depends not only upon operating income nor even upon total income, but upon those fluctuations of stock and credit which may take place and need to be monitored. Optimum stock levels are difficult to calculate and formulae which assist in stock control are found in some operational research textbooks. A safeguard against stockpiling is to ensure that the ratio closing stock/cost of sales (or, during periods of fluctuating prices, closing stock in units/year's sales in units) is kept constant. Stockpiling is only desirable in an inflationary situation where holding gains on stock outweigh both the cost of holding stock (i.e. additional warehouse rent and interest tied up) and the cost of obsolescence. Obsolescence is a particular danger so stock turnover may be measured by means of a stock turnover ratio expressed either as—

$$\frac{\text{Cost of Sales}}{\text{Average Stock}}$$

or as—

$$\frac{2 \times \text{Cost of Sales}}{\text{Opening Stock} + \text{Closing Stock}}$$

A high rate of stock turnover means that stock is priced realistically, and a low rate of turnover may not only mean that some stocks are priced in the stores at outdated prices but could mean that some stocks are obsolete and should be sold cheaply or dumped.

The above devices are intended to monitor the level of stock-in-trade so that operating income may be realized in cash and not countered or offset by stockpiling. It should, however, be clearly stated that, although trading income is more easily realizable in cash if there is no stockpiling, there are occasions when, as was indicated in Chapter 8, stockpiling is desirable because of the holding gains which can be obtained by buying at an earlier date. If the rise in the average prices of stock concerned exceeds the rent of extra warehouse space to contain the stock and the interest costs of extra capital tied up in the stocks, then it pays to buy stock when it is not needed and to hold it. If this kind of action will result in shortage of cash at a critical period then obviously it ought not to be pursued.

Illustration In the unadjusted balance sheet of Zeno Ltd in Chapter 7 the ratio

$$\frac{\text{Closing Stock}}{\text{Cost of Sales}} = \frac{120{,}000}{250{,}000} = 48\%$$

All this stock is not saleable, for some of it is in the process of production, and the figure of finished goods may be more appropriate in this case—

$$\frac{\text{Closing Stock of Finished Goods}}{\text{Cost of Sales}} = \frac{60{,}000}{250{,}000} = 24\%$$

As we stated, it may be better to express the ratio as—

$$\frac{\text{Average Stock of Finished Goods}}{\text{Cost of Sales}}$$

if there is a pronounced increase in the company's sales during a given year. On the other hand if there have been wild fluctuations in prices either of these ratios could be translated into units.

The stock turnover ratio may also be calculated using the figures from the unamended balance sheet of Zeno Ltd. In this case I shall use only the figures relevant to finished goods—

$$\frac{2 \times \text{Cost of Sales}}{\text{Opening Stock} + \text{Closing Stock}}$$

$$= \frac{2 \times 250{,}000}{70{,}000 + 60{,}000} = \frac{500{,}000}{130{,}000} = 3{\cdot}85$$

There is a limitation on the value of this ratio for it only expresses the rate of turnover of stock as an average. It does not preclude the possibility that the company may have kept some stocks in its warehouse for a number of years. Only by computing the stock turnover ratios for every item of stock will it be possible to discover redundant lines, and even then they should not be discarded for they may have other value to the company quite apart from their use in manufacturing and trading.

Ratios for monitoring credit

Credit fluctuations must also be monitored, for increases of debtors and decreases of creditors will reduce the net cash income for a given period, while increases of creditors and decreases of debtors will increase net cash income. An increase of sales usually involves an increase of debtors and an increase of purchases usually involves an increase of creditors, but if debtors are increasing at a faster rate than sales a collections campaign is needed, and if creditors are increasing at a faster rate than purchases the company may lose the goodwill of suppliers. The ratios for monitoring these relationships are—

$$\frac{\text{Debtors at end of year}}{\text{Sales}} \text{ and } \frac{\text{Creditors at end of year}}{\text{Purchases}}$$

These ratios may both be multiplied by 365 and expressed as "days sales on books" or "days purchases on books" respectively. Using the balance sheet on page 75 the position would be—

$$\text{Days Sales on Books} = 49, \text{ i.e. } \frac{50{,}000}{375{,}000} \times 365 \text{ and}$$

$$\text{Days Purchases on Books} = 282, \text{ i.e. } \frac{85{,}000}{110{,}000} \times 365$$

But like should be compared with like and if the volume of purchases or sales is fluctuating considerably it may be better to use average debtors and average creditors for the year instead of the above end-year figures. The only reason for the conventional ratios above is that they are easy to calculate. From the information which we have in the balance sheets of Zeno Ltd average debtors are only £27,500 and average creditors £90,000. This may mean that many of the sales have taken place in recent months and the debtors' ratio is not as bad as it appears. On the other hand the creditors' ratio is somewhat worse if the average for the year is taken. These ratios are only the genesis of credit control. A company should examine the age of its debts and discover which of its debtors are the most troublesome. Its own creditors must be kept under review and it must discover why these are not being paid promptly if its creditors' ratio is rising. It may be to the advantage of the company to increase its creditors in a time of inflation, but conversely it may result in sudden inability to pay immediate demands and lead to financial difficulties.

Liquidity ratios

We have dealt with methods of measuring the earning power of the company and the sources of such earning power. We have shown that all the company's trading expenditure items can be expressed as a percentage of sales. We then looked at those two factors which may often convert a healthy trading profit into a poor cash inflow or even a net cash outflow; we looked at fluctuations in stock and in credit and at the tools which can be used for controlling stock and credit. The previous paragraph indicates that it is necessary to look at cash itself and its availability. Can the company pay its debts? In particular, can it pay its trade creditors? How does its ability to do so (or otherwise) compare with its liquidity position in a previous year?

There is a need to measure the company's liquidity as a ratio. An easy ratio used for this purpose is current ratio (that is, current assets/current liabilities) indicating the general health of a company's working capital. In the balance sheet on page 75 the ratio is 190,000/85,000, or 2·23, which is quite healthy as it is greater than the ratio of 2:1 acceptable in most businesses. Acid-test ratio or liquidity ratio (current assets less stock/current liabilities) is a more accurate means of assessing a company's creditworthiness. Stock is deducted from the numerator because stock values are uncertain. In our example £120,000 of the £190,000 current assets is stock, but much of it is work-in-progress which could not be sold easily, and the company may have difficulty in selling finished goods in a hurry during liquidation. So the company only has £70,000 in monetary assets with which to pay its creditors (£85,000), and if it realized its debtors (£50,000) and used all its cash (£20,000) it would still have to find £15,000 to complete payment of its debts.

Liquidity ratio should be 1:1 but in this case it is 70,000/85,000 (or 0·83). This means that, although the company's working capital position is sound, it may not be able to produce sufficient monetary assets with which to pay debts in a hurry.

Funds statements

From the use of percentages for the purposes of monitoring we can now return once again to the use of absolute differences in monitoring.

Just as variances are normally expressed in absolutes so the difference between the cash flow of a company and its operating profit can also be described as an absolute, that is, as a difference in terms of money. There will in nearly every case be such differences, for it is obvious that no company will keep its creditors, its debtors and its stock levels absolutely constant from one year to another. As we stated in Chapter 8 it may also raise capital or purchase capital items, such as fixed assets. Such capital receipts and payments will affect the working capital which it has (that is, its current assets less its current liabilities, or its net current assets). Fluctuations of stocks, debtors and creditors will do more than merely affect working capital. They will affect the actual cash balance of the company.

One of the major drawbacks of liquidity ratio and current ratio is that they are purely static. They may, as an historical comparison between the ratios of two periods, indicate that a company's working capital has changed, but they will not tell us how it has changed. A funds flow statement can mean one of two things. It may mean a statement to show on an historical basis where working capital came from and how it has been applied or it may show where cash has come from and how it has been applied.

A "working capital" statement will show those movements during the year which have affected the amount of working capital available. These will be—

Sources of Working Capital	*Uses of Working Capital*
Profits from trading	Losses on trading
Issuing more share capital	Paying dividends
Issuing debentures	Redeeming debentures or preference shares
Sales of fixed assets or long-term investments	Purchase of fixed assets or long-term investments.

The funds position of a company is affected by transactions involving the gaining of revenue or the transfer of capital items into revenue or revenue items into capital. It is not affected by transactions involving current assets and current liabilities only or by transactions involving fixed assets or long-term "capital" items only.

Depreciation needs special attention when measuring the flow of funds and the alteration of the company's working capital position, for although it is a charge against revenue for the calculation of profit it is not an expense in the true sense. The company spent its money on purchasing the fixed asset initially. Any depreciation written off the asset in future years will not involve extra spending. It should therefore be added back to profit for the calculation of working capital changes.

The other type of "funds" statement goes a little further and shows what other items, apart from increases or decreases in working capital, have affected the company's cash position. They are—

Sources of Cash	*Uses of Cash*
Sales of stock-in-trade	Purchases of stock-in-trade
Decreases of debtors	Increases of debtors
Increases of creditors	Decreases of creditors

Illustration Let us look again at the original unamended balance sheet of Zeno Ltd in Chapter 7, this time from the viewpoint of measuring (*a*) changes of working capital and (*b*) changes of cash. The company's working capital (that is, its net current assets) has increased from £85,000 to £105,000 and its cash has decreased from £25,000 to £20,000. Why have these changes taken place?

In some respects this is a simple example for there are purchases but no sales of fixed assets and long-term investments, nor is there issue or redemption of debentures. However, depreciation has been written off and a dividend paid. Let us prepare a two-part statement showing (*a*) change of working capital and (*b*) an explanation of the decrease in the cash balance.

Zeno Ltd
FUNDS FLOW AND CASH DISPOSITION STATEMENT
YEAR ENDED 31 DECEMBER 1971

		£
Net profit for the year		18,200
	£	
Add back: Depreciation (i) Freehold Buildings	800	
(ii) Plant & Machinery	16,000	
		16,800
Inflow of working capital from operating profit		35,000
Dividend paid during the year		5,000
		30,000
Deduct: Purchase of new plant and machinery		10,000
Carried forward		20,000

(I) **Increase of working capital** (£105,000 less £85,000) (brought forward)		20,000
Add: Decrease of stock-in-trade (£120,000 – £150,000)		30,000
		50,000
Deduct: Application of cash:	£	
(*a*) Increase of Debtors (£50,000 – £5,000)	45,000	
(*b*) Decrease of Creditors (£85,000 – £95,000)	10,000	
		55,000
(II) **Resultant Decrease of Cash Balance** (£25,000 – £20,000)		–£5,000

Summary

The chapter deals with two other kinds of monitoring devices, ratios and funds statements. Variances could, of themselves, be completely meaningless unless there is a yardstick against which they are measurable. All the types of variances calculated in Chapter 9 can be expressed in the form of a ratio or percentage of the standard against which they are comparable. The advantage of doing this is that one thinks in terms of significance rather than in terms of absolutes. The difference between expressing a variance as an absolute and expressing it as a ratio is very similar to the difference between net present value and profitability ratio in Chapter 6.

But the use of ratios does not end there. They can be used to measure profitability and fluctuations in stock and credit, and also to test the liquidity of the company. The profitability of capital may be expressed in terms of the return on capital which could be paid to equity shareholders but this is not a criterion of the company's profitability in the economic sense, the real return on the real capital invested. So two adjustments have to be made. Debentures and debenture interest must be added to capital and net profit respectively, and investments in other companies and income from such investments should be deducted. The result is the company's real earning power, net operating income/net relevant assets.

Figure 10.1 shows the pyramid which can be constructed. The

company's selling efficiency can be measured in terms of its ratio of sales to net relevant assets, while cost efficiency can be measured by expressing all items of cost as percentages of sales. Percentage accounts can be prepared so that income statements of various years can be compared with each other. This has its limitations, particularly in the historical nature of the comparison.

Good profitability may be frustrated by stockpiling or by debt accumulation. A company can safeguard against unnecessary stockpiling by keeping its closing stock/cost of sales ratio constant or by means of the stock turnover ratio, cost of sales/average stock. Such a ratio is only a rough guide. It is preferable to calculate such ratios for each line of stock being sold and to express such ratios in units as well as in monetary terms, for this is a safeguard against fluctuating prices.

The ratios of debtors to sales and creditors to purchases are only rough indications of the extent to which a company is burdened by unpaid items. It is normal to use "end of year" debtors and creditors but in seasonal business the use of yearly averages may be preferable. Both these ratios are only rough guides. If the debtors/sales ratio has increased considerably during a year it is necessary to investigate for reasons. This may involve classification of debtors into age categories and estimates of likelihood of payment. The creditors/purchases ratio should not increase unduly. It may be an advantage to accumulate trade creditors balances in times of inflation for not only does the company borrow money without paying interest but it ultimately repays in pounds which have decreased in value. The great disadvantage in the accumulation of accounts payable is that cash may not ultimately be available to pay sudden demands from suppliers, with risk of insolvency.

Liquidity ratios monitor the company's ability to pay short-term debt. Current ratio is easy to calculate, but has the disadvantage of assuming that stock-in-trade (including unsaleable work-in-progress) can be easily realized. The "acid-test" ratio is more realistic.

These ratios indicate that changes in the company's liquidity may have taken place but they do not show how they have occurred. The third kind of monitoring device is the funds statement. This type of statement shows why a yearly profit will not necessarily result in a similar increase of cash. It is best prepared in two parts showing (*a*) how profit has been offset by other items in increasing or decreasing working capital and (*b*) how accumulation and dispositions of stocks and credit items have, together with changes of working capital, produced either an increase or decrease in the cash balance of the company.

Questions

1. Critically assess the liquidity position of Mr Kaye from the following Balance Sheet—

BALANCE SHEET OF N. KAYE AT 31 DECEMBER 1971

Fixed Assets (written down by depreciation during previous years)		£ 3,000
Current assets	£	
Stock	10,000	
Debtors	100	
Cash	900	
	11,000	
Less: Current Liabilities—Creditors	5,500	
		5,500
		£8,500
Represented by Capital and Reserves		£8,500

2. A freelance salesman is able to produce the following figures in respect of his business at the beginning and end of 1971.

	1 Jan	31 Dec
	£	£
Warehouse and fixtures	2,765	2,936
Motor car	880	660
Stock of goods	432	382
Due from debtors	736	867
Due to creditors	95	69
Cash at bank	79	93

During the year his weekly drawings amounted in total to £1,632, but he paid into the business bank account a £25 prize received from his private holding of Premium Bonds.

Prepare opening and closing balance sheets (i.e. at 1 Jan. and 31 Dec.) and compute the profit (or loss) for 1971.

3. Calculate the profitability of the salesman's capital in the above example.
4. How is profit/capital ratio of the salesman affected by the fact that he could have been employed at a salary of £2,000 p.a. if he had not been in business on his own account?
5. How would the profit/capital ratio of the salesman in ques. 2 be affected if he had borrowed £1,000 from a friend at 20 per cent interest?

6. From the figures in ques. 2 prepare a statement showing sources and dispositions of—

    (*a*) working capital;
    (*b*) cash.

7. With the help of ratios assess and interpret the stock, credit and liquidity positions of the freelance salesman.
8. Explain the two ratios used in monitoring credit. What are their limitations?
9. If cost of sales is £3,000 and opening stock is £500 and closing stock £1,000 what is the stock turnover ratio?

Bibliography

Many of the books mentioned earlier are relevant but particularly the following—

H. Bierman, *Financial Accounting Theory* (Collier-Macmillan, 1965)
R. J. Bull, *Accounting in Business* (Butterworths, 1969)
R. K. Jaedicke & R. T. Sprouse, *Accounting Flows: Income, Funds and Cash* (Prentice-Hall, 1965)
S. A. Tucker, *Successful Managerial Control by Ratio-Analysis* (McGraw-Hill, 1961)

11 Pricing and Contribution

Our discussion of variances, ratios and funds statements as monitoring devices has only served to emphasize the importance of setting the correct standards. We saw that one of the weaknesses of using accounting ratios as monitoring devices was that they were often based on historical standards. Real budgetary control involves discovering what is optimal. It involves deciding—

(*a*) what costs shall be paid;
(*b*) what quantities (or volume) shall be produced; and
(*c*) what shall bc the selling price of the product.

All these three decisions are important. Usually a company cannot dictate its costs, and selling prices are generally dictated by the market, by convention or by legislation, so that the major decision left to the company is to determine its optimum output level given a level of fixed costs and a limitation of demand for its product. There is an optimum price at which to sell a product and an optimum quantity to produce, but accountants differ from economists in methods of calculating these optima.

Historical cost Accountants calculate prices by taking direct costs of labour, materials and expenses and absorbing indirect cost. A percentage is added for profit. This is the cost-plus method of pricing discussed in Chapter 9. It is an unsound method for determining real value or real selling price because costs are historical and as they fluctuate they become irrelevant even for present pricing. Direct materials costs fluctuate and even if the annual average trade prices are used as in our adjusted profit and loss account of Chapter 8, they will be irrelevant at some future time when the product is actually sold. Wage rates will have changed. Even if all direct costs are stable, the absorption of a slice of fixed overhead into the cost of each unit produced on the basis of budgeted output or expected labour is unscientific and useless unless both overhead costs and actual output can be predicted. Nor are any direct costs really direct, for identical units do not have exactly the same amount of labour spent upon them nor do they contain exactly the same amount of material. As both materials and labour costs fluctuate even the calculation of direct cost is a matter of convenience, and as historical costs they are irrelevant, inappropriate and distortionate.

Linearity Because of the absorption of overhead in the suggested selling price of the product, cost-plus pricing is sometimes called

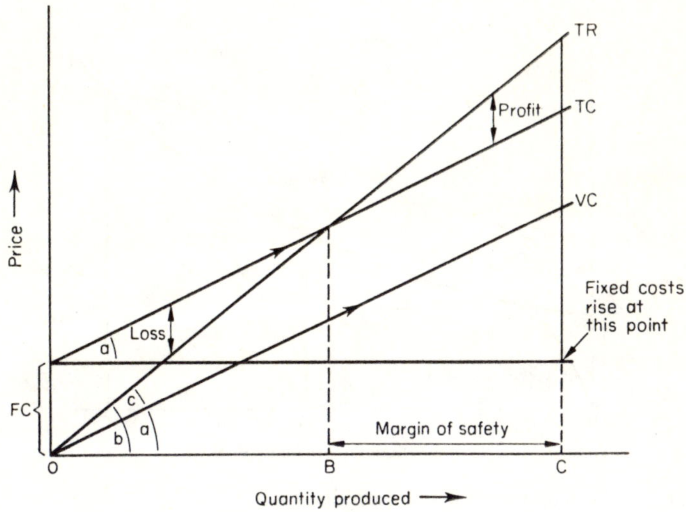

Fig 11.1 The accountant's break-even diagram
Key: *FC*, fixed cost; *VC*, variable cost; *TC*, total cost; *TR*, total revenue; *a*, marginal cost; *b*, marginal revenue; *c*, contribution per unit; *B*, break-even point; *C*, capacity

"absorption pricing". It assumes linearity of costs and ignores the effects of demand, failing to reflect the effects of competition in selling adequately. Figure 11.1 illustrates the type of break-even chart used by an accountant to discover at what volume of production a company will be likely to make the highest profit, given the limits of its plant size and capacity. It is *linear*. The term *linear* means that there is an assumption that all the functions in the model are straight lines. Total revenue is linear in the accountant's model, implying that any amount produced can be sold at constant average price irrespective of output level, and that there is always enough demand to absorb supply of the product regardless of the volume of output. This is economically unacceptable. A company cannot keep increasing output expecting to sell it unless price is lowered. Similarly the linear relationship between total output and cost is unsound because of diminishing returns. For example, a firm may not be operating as efficiently at full capacity as it would at slightly lower than full capacity.

A study of the differences between break-even charts in Figures 11.1 and 11.2 indicates the distinctions between accountants' and economists'

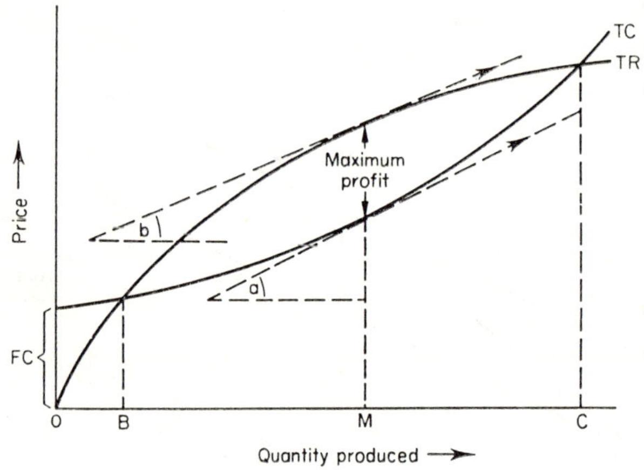

Fig 11.2 The economist's break-even diagram

models. The three principal functions involved are fixed cost, variable cost and sales revenue. The accountant's margin of safety is the horizontal distance between break-even point and capacity, between *B* and *C*. The accountant's linear model indicates that if marginal cost equals marginal revenue, that is if $a = b$, then contribution (c) must be 0 and the company cannot make a profit in such conditions. The economist says the reverse, as Figure 11.2 illustrates. He says that as *TC* (total cost) and *TR* (total revenue) are respectively concave and convex and doubly intersect each other maximum profit will be obtained where the distance of *TR* above *TC* is at its greatest and where their tangents are parallel to each other. Here $a = b$, that is, marginal cost equals marginal revenue, and profit is maximized. The first intersection in the economist's diagram is the equivalent of the accountant's break-even point and the second intersection in the economist's diagram is the equivalent of the accountant's "capacity level" (*C*). The philosophy of each model is different. The economist's curve functions prevent easy determination of fixed and variable costs by linear regression in the manner described in Chapter 9, but if linear regression is sensibly used it can be an efficient method of determining approximate fixed and variable costs, for many companies operate sufficiently near to the economic optimum to be unaffected by the extreme sections of both curves. However, the accountant would recommend producing as near to capacity level as possible while the economist would recommend producing at *M*, where marginal cost equals marginal revenue.

Neither the economist nor the accountant provides break-even models or pricing systems which are completely satisfactory. The economist envisages a market situation, so that the decreasing gradient of the total revenue curve (*TR*) reflects the effect of decreasing demand on total revenue, but rarely is quantity purchased so highly sensitive to price changes. The accountant's price model is easy and efficient and appears to be fair and factual, but would only be suitable where the company could dictate price. The economist's price model would use the best market price in every situation but this would mean having a prophetic sensitivity to future market trends, and changing prices so often that salesmen and customers would be irritated and confused.

Overhead absorption We have dealt with the historical-cost and linearity objections to the accountant's model. A third objection is to the principle of overhead absorption. Even in job costing, where most costs are direct and it would seem difficult to go wrong, treatment of overheads can cause embarrassment. Professor Flower in "The Case of the Profitable Bloodhound"[1] carefully studied Ferranti's treatment of overheads in pricing the Bloodhound missile contract.

In this case, previous experience had shown that Ferranti's overheads had been about 564 per cent of direct labour. So it appeared that the Bloodhound contract could be priced in the normal manner by adding direct material and labour costs, allocating 564 per cent of direct labour in lieu of overheads and adding a percentage to total cost for profit. Because direct labour was estimated at £1·3 million, overheads were estimated at about £7·4 million (i.e. 564 per cent of direct labour), and the project was priced accordingly. By magnificent saving, labour costs

[1] In Carsberg and Edey (eds), *Modern Financial Management.*

were actually reduced to only £573,000 and overheads were only about £3·1 million, so that by saving labour and overheads and yet charging its previously estimated price, Ferranti added nearly £5 million to its profit. The case shows that an overhead rate often magnifies a small difference in the base upon which it is calculated—in labour costs in this case—and that unrealistic prices result from this treatment, despite attempts to be methodical and accurate.

Jointness A fourth argument against cost-plus pricing is the problem of jointness. In job costing a small difference in direct costs can result in a wide difference of price. When large quantities of an identical product are manufactured the problem is aggravated by failure to estimate fixed costs and volume of production. How much more difficult must such estimation be if a whole vector of different resources is being jointly used to produce a vector of dissimilar products, joint-products and bi-products! Consider, for example, the syrup and cough-linctus example of Chapter 2 and ask how overheads can be absorbed even in this two-product, two-resource example. To take another example, is it logical that, say, 10,000 units of product *A* should bear 30 per cent of fixed overhead costs and 7,000 units of product B should bear 70 per cent of fixed overhead, given that the same service is being provided for both products by such overheads?

The "plus" in cost-plus A fifth argument against cost-plus pricing is against the "plus" in cost-plus. A percentage is added for profit because it is assumed that a company will be able to sell the product at total price. The profit-loading percentage is calculated by planning a given internal rate of return on capital invested, and by assuming a relationship between capital employed and total annual cost of production (including overheads). Thus—

$$\begin{array}{c}\text{Percentage of}\\\text{Profit-loading}\end{array} = \frac{\text{Capital employed}}{\text{Total annual cost}} \times \begin{array}{c}\text{Planned internal rate of}\\\text{return on capital employed}\end{array}$$

It can be seen that the very basis of cost-plus method of adding a percentage to "cost" for profit leans very heavily upon a planned and expected return on investment, that is, upon having a constant internal rate of return or rate of profitability upon capital. One of the lessons of Chapter 6 was that internal rate of return is not constant from one period to another and that there are fluctuations in the profitability of capital. If this is appreciated the concept of adding a percentage to cost in order to calculate selling price purely to make a given rate of return upon capital must be regarded as unsound.

Reconciliation between the two concepts

The criticism that prices are cost-determined and that costs are historical is valid, but the relevance of the criticism depends upon the extent of discrepancy between historical and present costs. The methods outlined in Chapter 8 could be reapplied in this context. Work-in-progress could be charged with unit and labour costs as they currently exist at the time of production and any holding gain upon raw materials treated quite separately. If production is a long process and raw material costs have changed during the process there is no reason why prices of partly finished goods should not be updated so that selling price will really reflect current raw material prices and current labour costs. The same treatment could be applied to overheads.

Linearity is an accountant's over-simplification but in practice cost and price functions do not follow the curved pattern of the economist. Break-even charts of real-life situations are somewhere in between these extremes with step-patterns, kinked linear functions and linear functions of different gradients at different levels of production. Figure 11.3 is an example of such a chart.

The accountant's treatment of overhead assumes that it is possible to add an equitable share of indirect expenses to the price of each unit in order to arrive at a fair selling price per unit. If it is really possible to predict the optimum volume of production and calculate the share of overhead to be borne by each unit at such level of production there is no reason why overheads should not be absorbed in the traditional way. But the calculation of a fair price based on such a method is no real predictor of the price which the market will pay. The Ferranti case does not illustrate what normally happens in overhead absorption. It shows us the kind of anomaly which can result from the use of such time-honoured methods.

The accountant's treatment of jointness is not perfect but at the very least the defence can be made that it is the best possible treatment under the circumstances. It would be ideal if management could decide at every moment the company's optimum level of production and if it could calculate by means of linear programming the optimum transfer prices for the jointly used commodities at that level of production. The accountant's methods of dealing with jointness are arbitrary but not completely unreasonable.

Similarly, the arbitrary nature of the percentage used to represent profit in the cost-plus method is not an indication that the use of percentages is unreasonable. If market price can be predicted and the company operates at its optimum level, the percentage added to cost as a profit factor is simply the ratio of profit to cost at the optimum level.

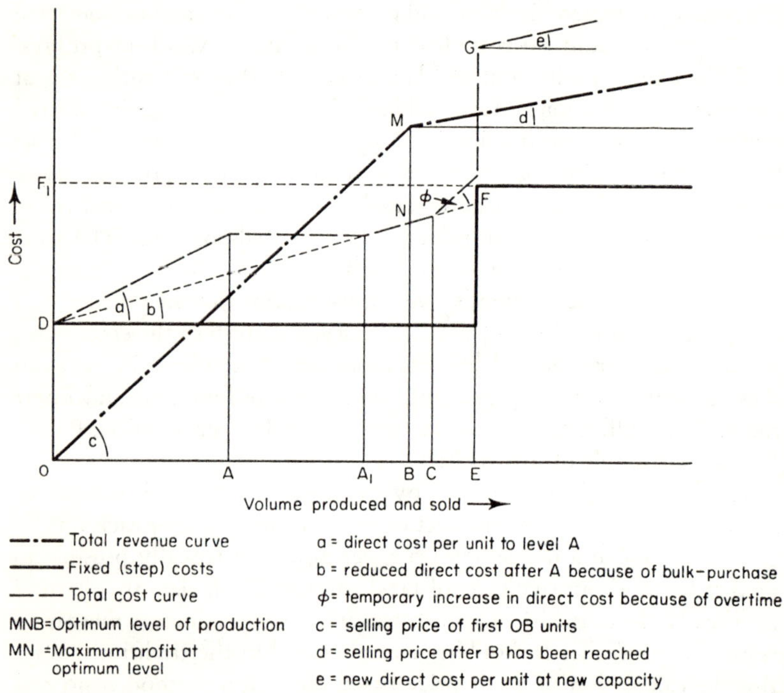

Fig 11.3 A reconciliation of accountants' and economists' break-even charts

In Figure 11.3, for example, it is *MN/NB*. The real criticism of the use of percentages for profit factors in the accountant's cost-plus calculations does not really spring from the validity of the method, but from the way in which the method is employed.

Figure 11.3 is one example of a possible real-life situation, poised midway between the economist's and accountant's models. Total revenue is linear up to M, where the market is satisfied at price c, but the company can sell more than OB units by lowering its price to d, after it has already sold OB at c. Originally direct cost per unit is a (representing, shall we say, material cost of a_1 and labour cost of a_2), but if it purchases OA_1 at a bulk rate it can do so at the same price as it would have paid for OA at the old rate, so that new material cost of b_1 and the existing labour cost of a_2 make up a new direct cost of b per unit. At C there is an increase of ϕ per unit because labour has to work overtime, and when OE is reached there is a vertical rise in fixed cost from OD to OF, because capacity has been reached and it is now necessary, for example, to construct a new factory, and there is a similar rise in the total cost curve which will rise at e after the sharp vertical increase from F to G. The optimum number of units to produce is OB, where the distance between total cost and total revenue curves is at its greatest at MN. It can now be seen that the real decision is not, "At what price shall we sell?", but "At what level of production will contribution (or profit) be maximized?" Figure 11.3 also illustrates an indeterminate break-even point, lying somewhere between A and A_1. Note the two intersections.

Contribution The use of the term "contribution" at this stage of the argument makes definition necessary. Earlier we stated that the accountant defined contribution as the difference between marginal revenue and marginal cost, that is, the "direct profit" per unit. Obviously, contribution is not profit in the fullest sense, because the company will still have to pay its fixed costs out of contribution before it can make a profit. Break-even point in the accountant's model is the point at which contribution is equal to fixed cost. If the company produces a lower number of units it incurs a loss. But in the more sophisticated sense contribution is relevant profit, and much of real decision-making can be carried out simply by listing the relevant costs and benefits of a decision, ignoring all irrelevant costs and benefits and deciding whether the course of action is worth while. The technique is a common-sense one which can be applied to make-or-buy decisions, to rent-or-buy decisions and to decisions whether to close down a branch, a subsidiary or a department. The following example requires a decision as to new means of producing product A. Is the company to take up the new method, or continue producing as previously. There are no rules to learn. All that is required is a common-sense "contribution" approach to all relevant costs.

EXAMPLE

Should a company change its production method, given the following information?

Information regarding Product A	
Estimated future demand	10,000 units
Present selling price	£4 per unit
Material cost	£1 per unit
Selling price (if new process is used)	£5 per unit
Material cost (if new process is used) due to better quality material	£1·25 per unit
Cost of new machinery for new process	£1,000
Scrap value of old machinery	£250
Scrap value of 500 units existing stock of old material	£50
Cost of removing old machinery	£500
Additional labour cost to operate new machinery	£0·50 per unit

Comparison of relevant costs		£
Extra revenue from 10,000 units at (£5 − £4) per unit		10,000
Less: Extra labour costs 10,000 × 50p per unit =	£5,000	
Extra material costs 10,000 × 25p per unit =	£2,500	
		7,500
Net difference in revenue contribution		2,500
	£	
Less: Cost of removing existing machinery	500	
Deduct scrap value of existing machinery	250	
		250
		2,250
Less: Cost of new machinery		1,000
		1,250
Add back: Scrap value of existing materials		50
Net advantage of making the decision		£1,300

The computation appears to show an advantage from transferring to the new means of production, but much depends upon whether the demand for the 10,000 units is immediate or not. If it is spread over, say, five years and the company has a high cost of capital, it may not pay to make the change, for immediate costs may be outweighed by the fact that future benefits have to be discounted.

The argument that only relevant costs should be considered in decision-making has all sorts of implications, but the principle is simple. One considers only the additional benefits of making a decision, deducts additional costs and asks whether the difference (that is, the contribution) is positive or negative. Past costs have to be ignored, as should book values of machinery which will be scrapped if the decision is made. The only relevant features of discontinuing a foregone alternative are the relevant costs and benefits of discontinuing, and of having to dispose of machinery, labour and materials. Applications are endless and there are no complicated rules to learn. One simply computes the relevant differences in cost and revenue between taking and not taking the particular decision. The method can be applied to decisions whether to make or buy a product, whether to rent or buy a piece of machinery, whether to lease or buy equipment, whether to rent or buy land, or whether to close or maintain a division. The problem of divisional control and departmental interdependence are both complex matters, however, and we shall deal with them in more detail in the next chapter.

Summary

The accountant's cost-plus pricing method takes the costs incurred to produce a unit and adds a percentage for profit. However, costs are not uniform, and they are historical and irrelevant. If overhead is absorbed in some arbitrary way, calculation becomes unrealistic. Costs and demand are not linear; that is, total revenue and total cost curves are not straight lines. Accountants' and economists' break-even charts illustrate different methods of approach. The accountant's absorption costing tends to distort small differences in the basis of absorption as in direct labour in the Ferranti case. The very rationale of absorbing joint overheads is unscientific. Further there is no rational basis for the profit-loading which is added to allocated cost as a fair estimate of profit. Yet this method of pricing gives a speedy and apparently fair method of determining price in some situations.

In the accountant's defence it is argued that, although cost and revenue functions are not entirely linear, they are not entirely non-linear. Historical costs are not always completely irrelevant for much depends upon whether inventory prices have been kept up to date. The validity of the jointness, absorption and cost-plus arguments depends upon the way in which the methods are applied. If the optimum level of production can be calculated, linear-programming methods can be employed to deal with overheads and jointness.

The company cannot decide its selling price if the relevant price is market-determined, so it should decide instead at what output-level maximum contribution is earned. Relevant cost is a simple yardstick for all such decision-making, not only for decisions whether to expand or contract production but whether to discontinue a division, whether to buy new machinery or premises, whether to rent or buy equipment or whether to make or buy components for a product.

Questions

1. Criticize the accountant's method of price determination.
2. Are historical costs relevant for pricing direct labour and direct materials?
3. Revenue is £5 per unit. Direct cost is £2 per unit. Fixed costs are £9,000. Draw a break-even chart and calculate (*a*) break-even point; (*b*) margin of safety if capacity is 6,000 units; (*c*) profit from producing and selling 5,000 units; (*d*) the level of production at which £1,000 profit is made; (*e*) the level of production at which the company will incur a loss of £2,000 if it sells all its units.
4. What is the disadvantage of using direct labour as a basis of charging overhead in contract pricing?
5. Why are the economist's total cost and total revenue curves respectively concave and convex?
6. Outline the argument against adding a percentage to cost in lieu of profit.
7. Decisive Ltd has a division A which produces component X. 10,000 such components will be required per year for the next five years. Raw materials cost £1 per unit and labour costs £20,000 per annum, including the salary (£1,500 p.a.) of a supervisor who would continue in employment even if the division were closed. Division A's overheads are £10,000 per annum, including £2,000 per annum apportioned central overheads. The division's labour charges could be reduced by £10,000 per annum if a new machine is purchased for £37,000. It will last five years and have no scrap value afterwards, but if it is installed existing machinery will have to be scrapped for £1,000. The new machinery would require material

costing £1·50 per unit, but it is doubtful whether the finished product will be more valuable.

Existing raw materials stocks were purchased for £2,000 but can be sold for only £800, and there is a stock of 3,000 ready-made components. A company in the locality manufactures identical components and the supplier is prepared to sell them to Decisive Ltd for £4 per unit.

The company can borrow money at 10 per cent per annum. Prepare comparative computations and advise management whether to continue running division A as previously, run the division with improved machinery or close the division completely.

Bibliography

H. Bierman, *Topics in Cost Accounting and Decisions* (McGraw-Hill, 1963)

H. Bierman & A. R. Drebin, *Managerial Accounting: an Introduction* (Collier-Macmillan, 1968).

B. V. Carsberg & H. C. Edey (eds), *Modern Financial Management* (Penguin, 1969). (In this work the readings by Baxter and Flower are particularly relevant.)

E. Jones, *Finance for the Non-financial Manager* (Pitman, 1972)

A. R. Oxenfeldt, *Industrial Pricing and Market Practices* (Prentice-Hall, 1951).

J. Sizer, *An Insight into Management Accounting* (Penguin, 1970).

G. J. Stigler, *The Theory of Price* (Macmillan, 1952).

12 The Problem of Transfer-pricing

We ended the previous chapter by describing the contribution approach to relevant costing. We stated that the common-sense criterion of relevance could be used by the management of a company in deciding whether to close down a division. One of the problems of divisional assessment, particularly if a product is processed by one division after another, is that of deciding the price at which a partly finished product (later called the "intermediate product") can be sold internally from one division to another. Obviously the amount of profit which a division is allowed to make must itself be a criterion in assessing its performance, and the uncritical use of "cost-plus" methods to arrive at transfer prices can distort an assessment of divisional performance.

If there is a market for the intermediate product then by the simple criterion of relevant costs it is logical that the transfer price of the partly finished product should be fixed at current market price.

For example, in a bicycle company, divisions A to G make components: A makes frames; B makes wheels; C makes tyres. Each division supplies the assembling division H, and H supplies completed bicycles to the selling division I. If there is an outside market for frames, wheels, tyres, etc., then each component division can be regarded and treated as a separate firm. Division A will sell frames and division B wheels to division H at their current wholesale market prices, for this is the relevant opportunity cost of the transfer. If division B did not exist, division H would have to buy wheels from an outside supplier at market price and if the firm had no assembling centre, division B would sell wheels to an outside assembling company at current market prices. In practice there may be some difficulty because there could be several prices for a given component, and because of the difference between buying and selling prices, in view of the selling costs which B would have had to incur and the purchasing costs (even if only the time and worry of its purchasing officer), which H would have to spend. So transfer price would be located somewhere between the relevant net selling benefit to B and the relevant net opportunity cost to H. In this case each division could be treated as a separate company and an unprofitable division could, in theory, be discontinued.

The real transfer-pricing problem arises when divisions are integrated, i.e. fully interdependent, and when it is not possible to sell the partly finished product.

But problems can arise before we get to this stage. Suppose that if company has four divisions. Division 1 passes partly finished goods to division 2, division 2 to division 3 and division 3 to division 4. Even a there is a market price for the partly finished unit at each stage, company policy, strategic advantage and jointly shared overheads may all dictate that divisions 2 and 3 must be continued, regardless of their contribution. Yet for control purposes each division should be informed of the level of production, transfer price and the level of profit which it should make in order to maximize the total profit of the firm.

To do this divisional managers should prepare schedules of their respective divisional costs of processing all quantities of units up to a stated maximum so that the divisional marginal cost (that is, the divisional cost of producing each extra unit) can be calculated.

In Figure 12.1(i) the unshaded areas under curves MC_1, MC_2, MC_3 and MC_4 graphically represent the marginal costs of each processing division and *a*, *b*, *c* and *d* are the fixed costs of each division. The firm's total profit will be maximized where total marginal cost equals total marginal revenue. By adding the divisional marginal costs ($MC_1 + MC_2 + MC_3 + MC_4$) total marginal costs are calculated and the total marginal cost curve (*TMC*) of Figure 12.1(ii) can be drawn. Total marginal cost equals total marginal revenue at *P* where *TMC* intersects *MR* and the optimum quantity Q_1 is produced, and the total area under *TMC* is the total cost of producing this optimum quantity. By consulting divisional schedules again, the central management can now calculate the marginal cost for each division to produce the Q_1th unit, *OA* for division 1, *AB* for division 2, *BC* for division 3, etc., and to determine transfer prices *OA* for division 1, *OB* for division 2, *OC* for division 3, etc., so that division 1 will spend the "area" under MC_1 for Q_1 units, selling them for OAT_1Q_1 and making a profit represented by the lowest shaded area. Division 2 will spend the total area under MC_2 by purchasing Q_1 units from division 1 at OAT_1Q_1 and by spending additionally the unshaded area in its own rectangle upon its own processing costs. It will sell its partially completed units to division 3 at OBT_2Q_1 making its own profit represented by the second-lowest shaded area in Figure 12.1(i) and so on. As the total shaded area in Figure 12.1(ii) equals the sum of the shaded areas in Figure 12.1(i), profit is being maximized, yet if the shaded areas of Figure 12.1(i) are compared with each other there is no

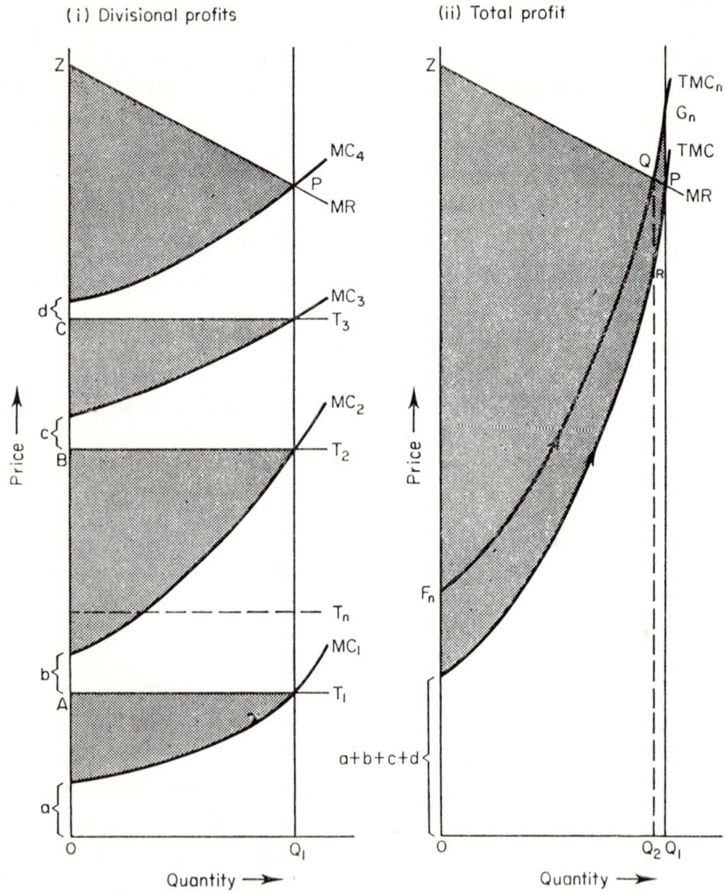

Fig 12.1 Determination of transfer prices

parity between the divisions. To maximize the total profit of the company divisions should not necessarily earn equal profit, nor should they earn profit at a given rate of return on capital invested in them. If they attempted to do so, to suboptimize, the profit of the company as a whole would fall. Suppose, for example, that division 1 decided to provide central management with a false schedule of costs such that it could charge an extra $T_n - T_1$ per unit to division 2 by making its transfer price T_n instead of T_1. The effect would be to add an extra rectangle $T_n - T_1$ high to all the costs of Figure 12.1(i) and to shift all assumed costs up by that amount so making everything above T_n in Figure 12.1(i) $T_n - T_1$ higher.

Central management would now draw a new but false cost curve TMC_n in Figure 12.1(ii) and the new curve F_nQG_n would be assumed to be the marginal cost curve of the company, so producing a false optimum at Q_2 and division 1 would make super-profit $(T_n - T_1) \times Q_2$. In Figure 12.1(ii) this is the area between *TMC* and TMC_n to the left of the vertical line *QR*. By moving from its true optimum at Q_1 to the false optimum at Q_2 the company as a whole would have lost the triangle *PQR*, that is, the whole area between the two *TMC* curves (true and false) immediately below *MR*. Obviously central management must provide a firm check on divisional cost schedules to ensure that there is no suboptimization.

This model operates when there is need to control divisions but when one cannot dispense with a division because of interdependence. Between the two extreme situations, independence and interdependence, there is a range of possibilities. If market price should be used when divisions are mutually independent and marginal cost at optimal output used when divisions are interdependent it follows that in intermediate cases transfer price must come somewhere between the two extremes. Now consider how difficult it is to apply the cost-plus method of pricing to transfer-pricing unless a company can calculate correctly its average costs for each division at optimum output and correctly allocate profit so as to determine exactly what percentage profit upon cost each division should earn.

It is not impossible that it should be able to do so. Let us look at Figure 12.1 again and ignore the false curve which was drawn to represent fictitious costs incurred by division 1. In (ii) the shaded area represents profit and the unshaded area below it represents cost. Obviously if OQ_1 was known to be a consistently optimal level of production, the company as a whole could budget to produce at volume OQ_1 and it could calculate the proportion between unshaded and shaded areas and add it to each unit produced to obtain the selling price per unit. In (ii) the sloping marginal revenue curve complicates matters, but if we apply the same logic to diagram 12.1(i) and again assume a static position the white area in rectangle OAT_1Q_1 is the total divisional cost and the shaded remainder of the rectangle is the total divisional profit. If this was static for any length of time it would be possible to calculate the transfer price at point 1 simply by adding to the cost of each unit a percentage which represented the ratio between the shaded and non-shaded parts of the rectangle. The same methods could be used for divisions 2, 3 and 4, but note that the percentage has to be different in each case. In the diagram the percentage to be added in respect of profit at T_2 seems to be larger than that at T_1. It is not simply a matter of adding a fixed percentage in respect of divisional profit at the end of each process, but one of calculating the optimum percentage to add at each point.

The message of the chapter is clear. In process costing involving a number of divisions it is incorrect to fix a transfer price for the product simply by adding a percentage to cost, for if each of the company's activities are necessary and the divisions are mutually indispensable they will not make the same level of contribution to the company at a volume of production which optimizes the position of the company as a whole.

If there is a market price, the intermediate product must be priced from one division to the next at market price, for if this were not done, the supplying division could suboptimize if the price were lower than market price simply by selling its products to the outside market and the buying division would not be able to purchase them except at market price from an outside source. Alternatively if transfer price were higher than market price the buying division could suboptimize at the expense of its supplier simply by buying from outside.

If there is no market price and the company as a whole produces at a point where marginal cost equals marginal revenue, transfer price must be the aggregate of marginal costs at the company's optimum level. Care must be taken to see that each division does not include fictitious costs for these will tend to distort the production plan of the whole company and alter the point of apparent economic optimum. It will not simply be a matter of the erratic division obtaining benefits at the expense of the company as a whole, but the very profit of the whole company will be less if suboptimization is carried out.

Summary

The contribution approach to relevant costing highlighted the possibility of using relevant costing for finding out the advantages of retaining or closing a division. If the activities of the division are entirely separate from those of other divisions this should present no problem but in some cases there is interdependence and one obvious example of such interdependence is the use of a transfer price in process costing, that is, a price at which an early division in the process sells its output to another division for further processing.

Relevant costing in the previous chapter used opportunity cost, that is the cost of the next best alternative. If the supplying division is unable to sell its output to the buying division it may decide to sell it to the outside market, if there is a market for the intermediate product. Similarly if the buying division (using the term "buying" to mean buying internally) is unable to purchase the intermediate product from the supplying division, it will obviously try to buy it externally from the outside market. It follows that, where there is a market price for the intermediate product, transfer price should be market price, for in either case the divisions concerned could suboptimize at the expense of the company as a whole by selling their output or buying their partly made components in the external market.

Where there is no market price for the intermediate product transfer price must be fixed at the point of optimal production by consecutively adding the marginal costs of all previous processes. Division 1 would therefore price its product at mc_1, that is, equal to its total marginal cost at the volume of optimum output, but division 2 would fix its transfer price at $mc_1 + mc_2$, that is, at the aggregate marginal cost of the whole process up to the point of transfer, and this process of adding marginal costs of each division would continue in subsequent processes.

There could still be suboptimization—that is, the case of one division bettering itself at the expense of the company as a whole—simply by the division charging subsequent processes with false costs. Real cost control is necessary if the system of using marginal cost for transfer-pricing is not to be abused.

Questions

1. What is the fallacy of using return on investment as a criterion to assess the profitability of a division which processes a product and is indispensable to the company as a whole?

2. Is cost-plus (using the same percentage "profit" for each division) a sound method of arriving at a transfer price in this context?
3. What are the two ways in which a division may suboptimize (*a*) if there is a market for the intermediate product and (*b*) if there is no market for the intermediate product?
4. Marginal costs of division A are £8 per unit at the optimum level of production. The unit is then transferred to division B which incurs a marginal cost of £10 per unit, and afterwards to division C which incurs a marginal cost of £7 per unit. If there is no market price for the unit what are the respective transfer prices at which the product should be transferred—

   (*a*) from division A to division B?
   (*b*) from division B to division C?
   (*c*) from division C to division D?

5. How would the above position alter—
   (*a*) if there was a market price of £10 for the product of division A?
   (*b*) if there was a market price of £26 for the product of division C?
6. Discuss the case of suboptimization by a division's adding fictitious costs to its cost schedule? What methods could be used to counteract this fault?

Bibliography

K. J. Arrow, "Optimization, Decentralization and Internal Pricing in Business Firms", *Contributions to Scientific Management*, Stanford, 1955

P. W. Cook, "Decentralization and the Transfer Price Problem", *Journal of Business*, 1955

J. R. Gould, "Internal Pricing in Firms When There Are Costs of Using an Outside Market", *Journal of Business*, 1964

J. Hirshleifer, "On the Economics of Transfer Pricing", *Journal of Business*, 1956

G. J. Stigler, *The Theory of Price* (Macmillan, 1952).

13 Return on Investment and Divisional Control

At the end of Chapter 11 we hinted that relevant costing (that is the use of the "contribution" or opportunity-cost approach in decision-making) is a useful tool for discovering whether or not to close down a division of a company. Chapter 12 indicated that there were problems in divisional control, particularly in pricing partly finished units which are purchased and sold internally by one division from and to another. Study of the subject indicated that in some companies there is interdependence, that is, it is impossible to close down a division if it does not appear to be profitable in any case because it performs a function which cannot be performed outside the company. The company may be technologically dependent upon the division, or it may not be able to buy its partly finished goods elsewhere.

If we isolate such cases and return to the "internal rate of return" criterion of profitability of Chapter 6, we may now ask whether we can use some similar criterion to assess the efficiency of a dispensable division, that is, to discover whether it would be better to keep or to close down a division which could be discontinued without injury to the company as a whole. May we not also discover if such a criterion can be used to assess the efficiency of any division even if it cannot be closed down?

Return on investment

Traditional accountants use "return on investment" as a rough yardstick for this purpose, that is—

$$\frac{\text{Income from the division}}{\text{Average capital invested in the division}}$$

But the matter is not as easy as it seems, for in the case of each division we have to decide what is capital for the purposes of the analysis and what is income for such purposes. We also have to decide what capital can be attributed to the division and what income ought to be attributed to it. It is the consideration of all four of these problems which makes return on investment a difficult criterion to apply in practice. Let us ask a few questions about each of these to illustrate the difficulty of the situation.

(i) Distinguishing income from capital It is easy to say that the denominator of the fraction should be "capital" and the numerator should be "income". But how can certain costs be treated? How should holding gains on stock be treated? Should the division be given credit for holding them and should they be added to the income of the division for the purpose of calculating return on investment? Conversely they could as easily be regarded as an appreciation of capital. Similarly the division's income could be distorted by inflation. Is this to be regarded as an appreciation of income, when it is, in fact, completely outside the control of the division, or should capital be adjusted to take account of inflation? In the above case much will depend upon whether the financial policies and stock policies are centrally or divisionally controlled. If they are centrally controlled then obviously the division should not be credited with holding gains resulting from keeping goods in stock, and if the financial policy of the company is centrally controlled the division should not receive benefits of holding out on creditors in times of inflation.

(ii) Collection of debts The above paragraph has only described one problem of defining the borderline between capital and income. Holding gains and inflation effects could be treated as accretions of capital or as divisional income, or conversely they could be left out of the divisional assessment altogether. The same applies in reverse. In times of inflation, although two divisions may have the same operating income one may gain in contrast to the other, simply because it has a better debt-collecting policy. If divisions are autonomous in their debt-collecting roles, then cash-flow and income could almost be regarded as synonymous. If the debt-collecting is outside divisional control and is carried out by a central debt-collecting department, then divisions should be assessed on their respective accounting incomes, and no regard should be had to the amount of cash income which a division has received for a particular year. Otherwise a division with high income in uncollectable debts would seem to be a better division than one with less income and no debts at all.

(iii) Research and development—capital or revenue? There is the added question of defining where a division's expenditure on research and development should appear in the fraction. Should divisional research and development, training costs and advertising appear

Add large expenditure expected to benefit a specific division over a long period to capital — when calculating the division's rate of return on investment	Deduct small expenditure expected to benefit a specific division in a short period from income — when calculating the division's rate of return on investment
Add large expenditure expected to benefit the firm as a whole over a long period to capital — when calculating the company's rate of return on investment. Do not apportion this expenditure to divisions	Deduct small expenditure not expected to benefit any specific division, but necessary for normal operations from income — when calculating the company's rate of return on investment. Do not apportion this expenditure to divisions

Fig 13.1 General pattern of treatment of research and development, training, educational and advertising costs

as costs and be deducted from income, so reducing the numerator of the above ratio, or should they appear on the balance sheet as assets and so be added to the denominator (capital invested) in the above ratio? There may be no tangible benefit from such expenditure for some years and the Rolls-Royce and Vehicle & General experiences are reminders that such expenditure should not be capitalized (that is, added to capital, and made to appear as an asset) unless some tangible return is reasonably certain. For divisional purposes expenditure should not be included in any case unless it is applicable to the division and it should not be capitalized unless there is reasonable certainty of ultimate benefit. Figure 13.1 illustrates the position.

(iv) (a) Problems of jointness: cash balances Return on investment has other problems. How should centrally held cash balances be treated for purposes of defining capital of a particular division? What must be done with joint fixed overheads, where several divisions may benefit?

(iv) (b) Problems of jointness: treatment of depreciation and fixed assets Besides problems of definition there are added problems of control of capital. A divisional manager who has no say in the amount of capital invested in his division cannot be held fully responsible if the division is not functioning at optimal level. Even if he has such a say, assets may not be valued correctly because the company's depreciation policy may be unrealistic. If depreciation on assets is unrealistically computed a divisional manager may either scrap assets and buy new ones too frequently or, alternatively, continue to use them when they are obsolete and unserviceable.

Return on investment or net residual income?

Figure 13.2 illustrates a further problem. Suppose that a company borrows money at a rate (cost of capital) represented by angle *a*. It is able to allocate fixed costs to divisions and in this case the division's costs are *OZ*. For every pound of capital invested in the division it will expect a return sufficient to pay its *a* per cent, cost of capital, *BX* for *OX*, *FY* for *OY*, *MN* for *ON*, *HC* for *OC* and so on. This is a more complex kind of break-even chart than Figure 11.2 because it deals with net income, whereas normal break-even charts deal with gross income. The division will not break even unless it invests OQ and receives *PQ* income. Its margin of safety is anywhere between Q and C, and at C capacity is reached, and there will be no extra income for the division unless the company invests a further *CJ* in the division, so the curve *ZPADKGI* is parallel with the horizontal axis between G and *I*. After *I* more capital has been invested, possibly in new factory premises, so the performance curve rises sharply.

Now suppose the divisional manager is told to maximize his marginal return on investment, but is able to decide how much capital is invested in his division. He will invest at point *ABX* where marginal return on

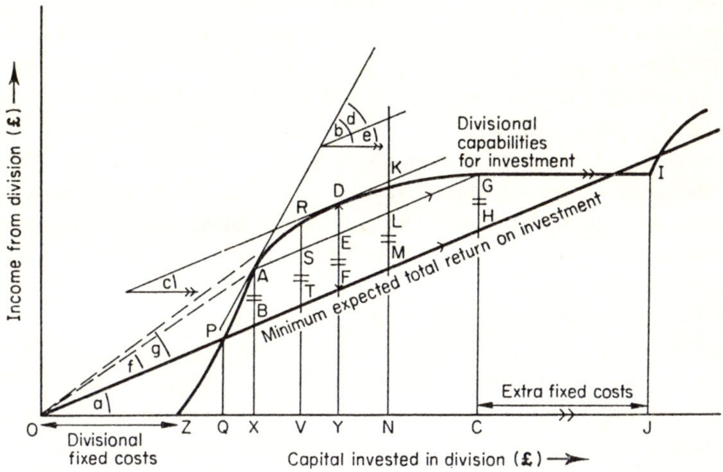

Fig 13.2 Return on investment and net residual income

investment is the tangent to the curve at *A*, or the gradient or angle *b* in the inset. At this point, as $a = e$, marginal return *b* will be much greater than the company's cost of capital ($a = e$), but the actual average contribution is only the angle *f*, the difference between internal rate of return and cost of capital at point *A* (that is, the angle *AOB*). If the divisional manager is instructed to maximize his average return on investment, he will do so at *RSTV*, where $\widehat{ROV}$ is the rate of return and $\widehat{TOV}$ is the cost of capital so that average contribution rate is the difference $\widehat{ROT}$, or *g*, which is greater than *f*. For illustration purposes, suppose cost of capital ($a = c = e$) is 12 per cent and rate of return at this point ($\widehat{ROV}$) is 22 per cent, there would be a net average contribution rate of 10 per cent. The distance in vertical terms between the capability curve and the minimum income curve (or cost of capital) represents the divisional contribution at each level of activity, sometimes called the "net residual income". As *RST* is larger than *AB*, net residual income is greater at this point, but if the division had operated at *ABX* its net residual income *AB* would be no greater than if it had operated at full capacity, for *AB* = *GH*.

At *RST* the position is better than at *AB* but maximum net residual income is at neither of these positions. It is at *DEFY* where the division's income is *DY* and after paying *FY* interest the company is left with *DEF* net residual income. As *DEF* is *DE* greater than *AB* and *GH*, net residual income is *DE* more at this point than if the company had operated the division either at full capacity or where marginal return on investment seemed greatest, and as *DEF* is greater than *RST* contribution is higher at this level of output than it would have been if the company had simply decided that the division should maximize average return on investment.

The case against net residual income

However one weakness of the net residual income argument is that it suffers, in much the same way as the net present value concept, from being an absolute rather than a relative concept. Surely if maximization of profit of each division will result in maximization of the profit of the whole company it is essential that the profitability of each division, i.e. the ratio between contribution and outlay in the division, should be maximized. An even more fundamental weakness of net residual income as a criterion for divisional control is that it assumes that the company should run each division at a level of investment and output where the division's contribution to the company is at its highest. This is unsound. The company should run each division at a level of investment and output where it will maximize the contribution of the company as a whole, otherwise problems of suboptimization, already discussed with reference to processing, will again appear. The criterion for divisional control is therefore not "Is the division maximizing its return on investment? nor is it "Is the division maximizing its net residual income?"

but it is "Is the division being successfully run at a level of output where it successfully maximizes the profit of the company as a whole?".

Linear programming for divisional control

We have already applied this yardstick in the processing situation of Figure 12.1 where the divisions were vertically combined and where one division supplied its output to the next at a transfer price for processing further. If divisions are horizontally associated and use joint resources the problem of running each division at a level of output where it successfully maximizes total profit is a matter of mathematical programming. In Chapter 5 a two-product, two-constraint linear problem was discussed and it was illustrated in Figure 5.1 and solved graphically and by the simplex method. Now instead of thinking in terms of products we must think of the divisions which produce them, and our rationed constraints are not simply labour and materials as in the simple syrup–linctus problem but will include all relevant resources which must be rationed to the divisions. Fixed costs can be ignored but the rationable services which they provide must be brought into the mathematical programme. Rent, for example, buys floor-space which must be rationed between divisions because each division needs a given quantity of floor-space to produce a given quantity of its specific product. The mathematical programme will be simply an advanced version of the two-product linear programme, but the term "linear" has been avoided, because we abandoned the assumption that everything was linear earlier in this chapter. Try to imagine what Figure 5.1 would be if all its straight-line functions were curves. Now try to picture such a diagram drawn in a number of dimensions.

Such a programme could provide the optimum level at which each division should be run to maximize total company profit, and the dual solution of the programme will provide the shadow prices or opportunity costs for each of the constraints or rationed resources.

Divisional optimum not always best for the company

So, in all kinds of divisional control, where there is strategic indispensability the real criterion is not one of return on investment or net residual income but, "Is each division maximizing the total company profit?" Marginal cost provides the solution in a processing situation and mathematical programming can provide the solution in a multi-product situation, and in both cases the real optimum could be anywhere in Figure 13.2. It could, for example, be at *KLMN* as conceivably as anywhere else. Problems will still arise for management if, say, division A over-uses floor space and division B under-uses it, because one division may be suboptimizing and the other may be inefficient. Variances will still be reported, some having easy explanations and some posing problems for the behavioural scientist.

Summary

Relevant costing is a means of deciding whether or not to continue or close down divisions, but the question of divisional performance assessment is complicated by problems of transfer-pricing. Even if methods of calculating transfer prices are agreed, there are still problems of technological, demand and strategic interdependence. Any method of divisional performance assessment must take these factors into account.

The traditional method of divisional performance assessment is "return on investment", that is, to take the income from the division for a given period and calculate the rate of return on capital invested in the division. But this immediately raises the earlier problems of income measurement. How should divisional gains from holding stocks or from inflation be treated? Should the division collect its own debts? If it does not collect debts it should obviously be assessed on the basis of accounting income, that is, income before payment of debts, not on its actual cash income. The problem of treating research and development is a company problem as much as a divisional one, but if they are treated as capital, should the "capital" be allocated to divisions and if they are charged against income, how should this be treated in divisional income?

There are other specific problems of jointness, particularly the treatment of joint cash balances and depreciation of divisional fixed assets.

Even if there are no problems of jointness or of definition, return on investment has its limitations as Figure 13.2 illustrates. Much depends upon what is required from the divisional manager, but circumstances could occur where a division is run at very low levels of output merely to maximize return on investment. Net residual income is an alternative method of assessment. This involves charging the division with the cost of capital and discovering at what level of output it will make the highest net contribution (in absolute terms) to the company. This method bears much the same relationship to return on investment as net present value bears to internal rate of return in capital budgeting. It is limited by the same criterion, that it is an index of profit, not of profitability; that it measures profit in absolute amounts, not in terms of outlay.

An even greater limitation in the value of both methods is that they cannot adequately deal with cases where there is technological, demand or strategic interdependence between divisions. Here, what is optimal for the division may not necessarily be optimal for the company as a whole. In the vertical or process case which was discussed in Chapter 12, the real procedure is to fix an optimum for the whole company, taking, for example, the $MC = MR$ criterion, and fix standards accordingly, rewarding or penalizing divisions in respect of their adherence to such standards.

In what may be termed a "horizontal" case, where divisions make and sell entirely different products but use the same resources, the real solution may be found by mathematical programming. In this case the products are the divisional products, but the resources are the joint resources which they have to use. Such methods provide criteria for dealing with fixed costs. While linear programming is used for the purpose of illustration in Chapter 5, it should be emphasized that the real picture may be as far removed from the conventional linear programme as the real-life situation is removed from the traditional simple break-even chart.

Questions

1. Show by means of diagrams why a processing company's transfer prices should be based upon marginal cost, and discuss the effect of suboptimization.
2. What criteria help to determine how research, development, training and advertising costs should be treated in calculating divisional return on investment?

3. Discuss the merits and demerits of return on investment and net residual income as devices for divisional control, illustrating your answer graphically.
4. Divisions A, B and C produce different units of production. Formulate a model to help management determine the level of output for each division, given the following information per unit—

	Division A	*Division B*	*Division C*	*Total available*
Contribution	£2	£6	£5	
Materials (units)	4	3	1	18,000
Labour (hours)	1	2	3	40,000
Floor-space (square feet)	100	150	400	4,000
Salesmen's time (per 1,000 units)	3 hrs	6 hrs	4 hrs	2,500 hrs

5. How can linear-programming be employed to deal with the problem of joint costs in divisional control?
6. Illustrate how divisional managers can often manipulate depreciation figures to give misleading return on investment results.

Bibliography

The references to books on corporate strategy are relevant.

L. R. Amey, *The Efficiency of Business Enterprises* (Allen & Unwin, 1969)

W. J. Bruns & D. T. DeCoster, *Accounting and its Behavioural Implications* (McGraw-Hill, 1969)

B. V. Carsberg, *An Introduction to Mathematical Programming for Accountants* (Allen & Unwin, 1969)

J. Dearden, "New System for Divisional Control", *Harvard Business Review*, 1966

C. T. Horngren, *Cost Accounting: A Managerial Emphasis* (Prentice-Hall, 1967)

D. Solomons (ed.), *Studies in Cost Analysis* (Sweet & Maxwell, 1968) (particularly for the penultimate article by J. M. Samuels and reply by Bernhardt)

D. Solomons, *Divisional Performance Measurement and Control* (Irwin, 1965)

A further empirical study of return on investment was produced by R. C. Morris of the University of Bristol, "The Book-Yield as a Performance Evaluator". This paper was given at the Southern Area AUTA Conference in Cardiff on 25 September 1971.

14 Taxation and Investment Decisions

In the middle chapters of this book we moved from the long term to the short term, from capital budgets to income budgets. Having looked at the problems of the short cycle, of income budgets and income measurement, we can now return to long-term budgets and to some of the factors which affect capital decisions. We shall look at gearing and dividend policy later and in both these cases the system of taxation will be an important factor in deciding whether a company can lower its cost of capital either by its leverage policy, that is by the proportion of "loan capital" which it issues, or by varying its dividend policy, that is by increasing or decreasing the amount of profits which it distributes to its shareholders. We shall also be looking at another kind of capital decision in this chapter. We shall look at the decision to invest in plant and machinery or in some other kind of project and see how the benefit of such a decision can be affected by the system of taxation, particularly by the rate of tax, by the timing of tax collection and by the kind of allowances given by the Revenue authorities. Much of this will be of an academic nature, for this book is being written at a time when 100 per cent depreciation allowances are being given by the Inland Revenue in respect of purchases of machinery and when a system of imputation is being introduced so that companies who distribute their profits are not unfairly taxed compared with those who do not. The illustrations are important, however, for planners and managers both have to decide how to optimize the use of resources in a changing environment. The taxation "environment" is continually changing; it is being altered by yearly budgets and frequently by mini-budgets, and this chapter will help to isolate some of the signals in the changing tax environment which can act as red or green lights (as the case may be) in helping to decide whether to go ahead with a particular project.

It is clear therefore that this chapter will not be a descriptive résumé of taxation allowances, such as those for blind persons, children, daughter's services, dependent relatives, earned income, housekeepers, life assurance, old age, small income or wife's earned income. Neither will it be a "book-keeping" treatment of taxation, one which will state the various entries that appear in the taxation account when dividends are paid. The first of these methods of dealing with the subject would be adopted by an exponent of taxation, and this book would need to be revised every year, or even more frequently, in order to keep it up to date. The second approach would be adopted in an accounting textbook designed to meet the more technical demands of the subject. It would not tell us how a company's situation could be optimized given certain tax constraints, and how to decide strategies for doing so. In examining some of the strategies it will, of course, be necessary to state what some of the constraints are at the time of writing, but an exhaustive description of the constraints is not intended. I shall deal first with two small examples from personal taxation which will require very little explanation of the present system, but illustrate simply the effect of circumstances on investment decisions of persons. Then I shall give a short history of company taxation to illustrate how tax circumstances can affect company decisions. This will be followed by an "investment appraisal" example, and the chapter will end with the impact of value added tax upon such decisions.

1. Personal decisions

For the purpose of the two small examples which follow I shall assume the basic rate of personal taxation is the "standard rate" of 38·75 per cent in force at the time of writing, although it is highly probable that under the new graduated system to replace income tax and surtax the basic rate will be 30 per cent. I shall ignore the graduation and make 38·75 per cent the "marginal" or "maximum" rate for illustration, while the average rate for each person could be as low as 25 per cent or even 20 per cent depending upon the reliefs and allowances which can be claimed. The examples are (*a*) Building society interest and (*b*) Life assurance relief.

(a) Building society interest Suppose that B pays at basic rate, while E is an exempt person, a pensioner, and both have £100 to invest. Debenture interest is 8 per cent and building society interest is 6·125 per cent. If B invested in debentures his interest of £8 would be taxed and he would receive £4·90 (£5·60 after the new basic rate of 30 per cent). It would pay to invest in a building society. E, however, is exempt. He can cheerfully receive his dividend and submit a repayment claim to make his total receipts £8, i.e. £1·87 more than £6·13 he would have received from a Building Society. B, on the other hand receives the equivalent of gross dividend from the Building Society of £10 (assuming 38·75 per cent basic rate) or rather less, £8·75, if the new suggested basic rate of 30 per cent personal tax is adopted.

(b) Life assurance relief Many investments have built-in life assurance. Not only are the assurance bonuses (the equivalents of profit) free of ordinary income tax, but there is also a normal tax-relief on two-fifths of premiums paid, subject to restrictions on income and sum assured; so that the investor saves 15½ per cent (that is, two-fifths of 38·75 per cent) on premiums paid. For example, it costs only £8·45 per month to save £10 per month. Unit trusts, such as Barclays' Unicorn, building society investments, such as Legal and General's "Money-builder" and property bonds, such as Abbey Life investments, have life assurance advantages and the ideal investor can reap large benefits. But few investors are ideal, and life assurance cover reduces with age and ill health, so that the investor's circumstances and marginal tax rate are both relevant for investment decisions.

These are two small illustrations of the way in which tax circumstances can affect the value of an investment decision. It is advantageous for the person who pays tax at "standard rate" to invest in a building society, as against one who does not. It is advantageous for a healthy person to hold or take out a maximum amount of life assurance combined with investment as against one who could be classed as a "bad insurance risk". Now let us apply the same reasoning to company taxation, and see how a company can optimize in the face of tax rules, but before doing so it will be of some benefit to outline the history of corporate taxes in the United Kingdom.

2. Company taxation

Until 1965 company profits suffered "income tax" in much the same way as the earnings of individuals or the profits of traders and partnerships. Tax was paid by the company and dividends paid to shareholders net of tax. Unlike building society interest which has been considered earlier, however, these payments could be the basis of a claim for repayment of tax. A normally taxable person would not be able to make such a claim, but a pensioner or some other person who would not normally be subject to taxation would be able to recover the tax already deducted at source from the Inland Revenue. Companies also paid another form of tax known as "profits tax" which had been introduced during the Second World War as "excess profits tax". The subject of this tax was the company rather than the individual. In other words, the "untaxable" shareholder could not file a claim with the Inland Revenue for repayment of profits tax, because this, unlike income tax, was levied on the company.

The Finance Act 1965 separated corporate taxation from individual taxation but did so in such a way that a company stood at a tax disadvantage if it distributed its profits. Corporation tax was to be levied upon the profits of the company and income tax deducted at source on dividends which were distributed. Individuals could file repayment claims for the repayment of income tax deducted at source if they were not liable to taxation, but not for repayment of corporation tax. Rates of tax were such that a company would now be at a disadvantage if it distributed more than 40 per cent of its profits but at an advantage if it retained more than 60 per cent of its profits. The following example will clarify the position. Let us assume £140,000 profit.

Pre-1965 position

	£	£	*Percentage of profit*	
Profits		140,000		(100)
Income tax on profits (41·25%)	57,750		(41·25)	
Profits tax at 15%	21,000		(15·00)	
		78,750		(56·25)
		61,250		(43·75)
Less: Dividend (39·39%) net of tax at 41·25% on dividend		32,402		(23·14)
Retained profits		£28,848		(20·61)

Post-1965 position

	£	£	*Percentage of profit*	
Profit		140,000		(100)
Less: Corporation tax at 40%		56,000		(40)
		84,000		(60)
Less: Dividend of approx 39·39% net of tax at 41·25%	32,402		(23·14)	
Income tax on dividend	22,750		(16·25)	
		55,152		(39·39)
Retained profits		£28,848		(20·61)

As can be seen, after the revision of the tax system a company which did not distribute any of its profits would only have needed to pay 40 per cent of its profits in tax, compared with 56·25 per cent under the old system. On the other hand, companies which distributed all of their profits, or the greater part of their profits, were at considerable disadvantage under the new system compared with the old. Corporation tax, under the 1965 legislation, was obviously a good thing for encouraging companies to retain their profits for investment purposes but could be regarded as unfair by those companies who in normal circumstances, or at least in circumstances prior to the 1965 Act, would have considered distribution to have been the wisest policy.

Obviously the system is a good one at a time when it is considered socially undesirable for a company to distribute its profits, but not so good at times when companies are expected to distribute as much as possible, for example, to increase general spending power. The disadvantage of the 1965 system is that unless special provisions are made to reduce personal tax on dividends it is inflexible. It is biased against companies which distribute their profits. Various suggestions have been put forward for having a single company tax in which there is no discrimination against the distribution of profits. In the United States one attempt to alleviate the "double taxation" effect was to give the individual taxpayer credit of 4 per cent of the dividends received plus a complete exclusion of some dividends from total income. This system was then changed by withdrawing the 4 per cent credit and raising the excluded dividends to 100 dollars, provided that they were received from "domestic taxable corporations". For people receiving less than £50 per year income from companies this kind of action had some meaning, but could hardly be considered a serious attempt to deal with the double taxation situation where hundreds of pounds are involved.

Various systems of remedying the situation have been suggested, among which were (*a*) a two-rate system, involving a special rate for dividends and (*b*) the system of "imputation" which was proposed in the budget of 1972, to take place with effect from 1 April 1973. It is probable that this system will be adopted shortly after this book is published. Income tax will not be deducted under Schedule F from distributions after 5 April 1973. Instead, when the company makes distributions of profits and pays dividends, it will be liable to pay an advance sum equivalent to three-sevenths of the distribution in lieu of corporation tax. The effect is very much that of a unified system of taxation without the disadvantage of "double taxation" on distributed profits, for the company's deductions of corporation tax can be offset against its final tax liability for the year's profits and individual members can offset tax deducted at source against their final liability to tax, or even reclaim tax if they are "untaxable" persons. As the rate of credit is only three-sevenths but the rate of corporation tax is expected to be 50 per cent (possibly 40 per cent for companies whose annual profits do not exceed £15,000), it is evident that not all tax payable can ever be claimed against personal allowances or repaid to "untaxable" persons. There will be an element of pure company tax in the structure, just like "profits tax" in the old pre-1965 two-tier system.

EXAMPLE

A company makes profits of £12,000 so that it pays corporation tax of 50 per cent (i.e. £6,000) leaving a balance of £6,000 to distribute. If it decides to distribute £3,500 of this balance the effect would be to provide an advance corporation tax credit of three-sevenths of this net sum (i.e. £1,500) against the £6,000 corporation tax. The sum of £1,500 would be deducted and paid to the Inland Revenue as soon as the £3,500 in dividends was distributed, leaving £4,500 to be paid when corporation tax on the current year's profits becomes due in about twelve months' time. The shareholder who receives, say, £35, would have a £15 credit to be offset against his personal tax liability on the dividend "grossed up" to £50. The proposed basic rate of taxation, if the suggested changes are implemented, will be 30 per cent, not 38·75 per cent, so that if the taxpayer pays tax at basic rate (30 per cent) no claim for repayment nor additional payment will be necessary. If he is "exempt" or "untaxable" he will be able to claim the additional £15 from the Inland Revenue, but if he pays the higher rates of graduated personal tax (the equivalent of the present surtax) he will be required to pay additional tax at the higher rates on the "gross" dividend received. A company could not possibly convert all its burden of corporate taxation into credits, because, even if it distributed the whole £6,000 "taxed" net profits of the year, the credit available to shareholders would only be three-sevenths of £6,000 or £2,571 in practice (it would not be 30 per cent of £12,000 = £3,600). Both these amounts are smaller than the £6,000 corporate taxation which it would be liable to pay.

I have mentioned and outlined both these systems of company taxation, pre-1973 and suggested post-1973, because they illustrate how the tax "environment" can be a determining factor in strategic company decisions whether to distribute or not distribute. In the pre-1973 "environment" the company's shareholders benefit by not distributing, whereas in the post-1973 situation one can conceive at least the theoretical possibility of a company being owned by a large number of "exempt" persons. Although the imputation system tries to maintain balance between distributing and non-distributing companies, in the hypothetical case of a company owned by a large number of "exempt persons" it would be in the interests of shareholders to distribute as much as possible.

This taxation problem, although it is relevant, is not the only factor to be considered by a company in making the dividend decision. Other factors will be considered in Chapter 15.

3. Investment appraisal

The following example will illustrate how capital decisions are affected by tax legislation. For this purpose operating income and net cash flow are assumed to be identical.

Mechanics Ltd has a relevant capital cost of 10 per cent, and the directors can increase the company's income if they purchase equipment costing £20,000. The figures of extra income per annum resulting from the purchase are those in the second column below. The low figure of £4,500 in year 1 is because of anticipated teething troubles. Is the project worth while?

Year	*Increased income due to purchase of machinery*	*Present value factor 10%*	*Increased income in present value terms*
	£		£
1	4,500	0·909	4,091
2	6,000	0·826	4,956
3	6,000	0·751	4,506
4	5,000	0·683	3,415
5	4,000	0·621	2,484
6	3,000 (with scrap)	0·565	1,695
	Gross present value		21,147
	Less initial investment in year 0		20,000
Net present value (equivalent of 5·5% value/cost ratio net)			£1,147

The initial impression is that the investment is worth while. Now, for absolute simplicity, let us suppose that corporation tax is immediately payable on all cash flows as they are earned and can be immediately recovered on all cash spent. The net effect of this simple treatment of taxation would be to reduce each of the above figures by the amount of the tax. The investment would still be worth while but the net present value would be the net equivalent of £1,147 after tax had been deducted. Whether we take the traditional rate of about 40 per cent corporation tax or the possible new unified rate of 50 per cent company tax the positions would be similar as the following illustration proves.

		40% Corporation tax		*Suggested 50% tax*	
	Gross	Tax	Net of tax	Tax	Net of tax
	£	£	£	£	£
Gross present value	21,147	8,459	12,688	10,573	10,574
Initial outlay	20,000	8,000	12,000	10,000	10,000
Net present value	£1,147	£459	£688	£573	£574

The real-life situation is not so simple, however, for tax legislation can alter the worth-whileness of an investment in two ways—

(*a*) not all capital expenditure is immediately allowed for tax purposes;
(*b*) tax is normally assessed on the profits of the previous year so that there is an interval between the receipt of income and the payment of tax based on it.

(*a*) In the circumstances of writing this book, the first of these problems has been at least temporarily removed, for the Chancellor in his last budget announced that companies would be allowed to write off 100 per cent of expenditure on machinery in the year in which the outlay was incurred, except in the case of motor vehicles. Up until this year most large machinery investments, however, were subject to "capital allowances" or depreciation allowances. Just as the businessman or company does not bring all capital expenditure into account in the period in which it is incurred, but spreads it over a period as the examples in Chapter 8 indicate, so the Inland Revenue used to allow businesses to write off only a certain proportion of their capital expenditure each year. This procedure is still adopted in the case of motor vehicles. Machinery, on the other hand, was subjected to a kind of depreciation allowance system for tax purposes in which a large slice of the expenditure was written off during the first year and the balance in progressively smaller instalments over successive years. Before July 1971 the first year's allowance stood at 60 per cent and the balance of capital expenditure was allowed on a "reducing balance" depreciation scheme of 25 per cent per year, whilst between July 1971 and April 1972 the initial "chunk" of expenditure was raised from 60 to 80 per cent. The effect of a 60 per cent tax allowance will be examined more closely later in order to show how the very good, encouraging picture presented by the above figures can be thrown into reverse simply by introducing this complication.

These examples will seem, perhaps, now to be of purely academic interest to illustrate this point, but it must be remembered that there could, in theory, be a reintroduction of periodic writing down of machinery for tax purposes, and that motor vehicles purchased cannot even now be brought into account for tax purposes entirely in the year in which they are purchased.

(*b*) The timing of tax payments is still important even in a situation in which there are 100 per cent depreciation allowances for it does not necessarily follow that the situation depicted earlier will be an accurate one. The benefit to the company will not be £574 net of 50 per cent corporation tax. There is a lag of about twelve months between receipt of income and payment of tax, or between expenditure and the tax claim for repayment. It is true that the effect of this is minimized by the imputation system by which a company will make an advance payment of some of its corporation tax as soon as it pays a dividend to its shareholders so that high profits will be reflected by high dividends and vice versa, but for the sake of illustration I shall ignore the effect of imputation tax, and assume that the company retains all its profits, so that the effect of a twelve-month "delay" in the payment of tax can be clearly seen. There will, in most cases, be a lapse of more than twelve months, for companies do not receive cash flows at the end of each year, but evenly or otherwise throughout each year, and we shall assume in these examples that the investment, although undertaken in year 0, was offset against the profits of year 1 and therefore the credit not claimed until year 2. The credit would probably not have been a repayment, but purely a reduction in the company's general liability. We must assume that the company has a large number of other investments, and that this is one among many. We therefore consider, not total profit, but additional (or incremental) profit and additional (or incremental) expenditure throughout these examples. The final cash flow of £3,000 actually included £1,000 for the realization of scrap.

In year 1 the whole of £20,000 could be offset against the extra income of £4,500 giving a credit of £15,500. Let us take the lower (40 per cent) corporation tax figure for the sake of comparison. The corporation tax credit at this hypothetical rate of 40 per cent would be £6,200 and this would be offset against the 2nd year's profits if the 100 per cent allowance had not been claimed in year 0.

Project evaluation with 100% allowance

Year	*Gross income*	*Corporation tax*	*Net income*	*Present value factor (10%)*	*Present value*
	£	£	£		£
1	4,500	—	4,500	0·909	4,091
2	6,000	6,200 Cr.	12,200	0·826	10,077
3	6,000	2,400	3,600	0·751	2,704
4	5,000	2,400	2,600	0·683	1,776
5	4,000	2,000	2,000	0·621	1,242
6	3,000	1,600	1,400	0·565	791
			26,300		20,681
7	—	1,200	1,200	0·513	615
	£28,500	£3,400	25,100		20,066
Less: Initial cost of investment in year 0					20,000
Positive net present value (less than 1% value/cost)					£66

Note that in theory the benefit of the 100 per cent writing down allowance seems already to have vanished. In fact the position is not as bad because cash flows are received throughout each year and not at the end of each year. Further, it is unlikely that the period for recovery of tax on the investment would necessarily be as much as two years. However, corporation tax figures, as can be seen, are based on the figures of gross income of the previous year in each of the above cases.

Investment grants could be more beneficial if they are immediately recoverable. If, however, there is a lag between payment and recovery this should be taken into the discounting calculation.

Investment allowances differ from investment grants. Allowances are based on the recognition (in most cases) of periodic decline or deterioration in value, by offsetting a large initial "slice" of expenditure in the year of purchasing equipment and periodic instalments of the balance of expenditure in subsequent years. Although 100 per cent first-year allowances are obtainable at the time of writing they are the exception. In all other events some expenditure, however small, remains to be written off against profits for tax purposes in subsequent years. Development grants, on the other hand, are actual payments of money in lieu of expenditure to encourage investment in equipment and machinery and buildings. At present both investment allowances and development grants can be obtained. The current budget proposals deal with purchases on or after 22 March 1972 and allow 20 per cent of investment expenditure to be reclaimed in development areas and 22 per cent in special development areas, subject to conditions of safeguarding existing employment and straightforward modernization. Capital allowances will be given on the full cost of the new equipment, ignoring the fact that part of the cost (20 or 22 per cent as the case may be) is met out of grants.

It will be seen that if grants are paid immediately the effect will be to reduce initial cost figures by 20 or 22 per cent. The initial cost of £20,000 in year 0 would now be reduced by £4,000 or £4,400 as the case may be, leaving a net present value of either £4,066 or £4,466, depending on whether or not the investment is in a special development area. These are only examples, and the position may change at any time, but they do serve to illustrate that an investment grant payable immediately could be better than an apparently substantial investment allowance to be claimed against tax payable in more than a year's time.

Smaller first-year allowances As we stated earlier, 100 per cent first-year allowances are historically exceptional, although they can be claimed at the time of writing this chapter. In previous years, first-year allowances on machinery were rarely more than 40 per cent. Before the mini-budget of July 1971 it was possible to claim a first-year allowance of 60 per cent of the cost of equipment. This was increased in July 1971 to 80 per cent and in March 1972 to 100 per cent. We do not have to look at first-year allowances lower than 60 per cent in order to illustrate the disincentive of having to spread capital expenditure claims over a number of years for tax purposes. Let us calculate the net present value of Mechanics Ltd's project assuming that only 60 per cent of expenditure can be claimed as a first-year allowance against profits for tax purposes and that remaining expenditure has to be written off on the reducing balance method at 25 per cent. This would have been the position if, say, Mechanics Ltd had acquired (or desired to acquire) its equipment in April, May or June 1971 and if the depreciation allowances had not been subsequently altered.

Revised computation assuming that allowance had only been 60% We shall calculate first the capital allowances and then the tax payable assuming a rate of 40 per cent corporation tax.

(i) CAPITAL ALLOWANCES

	£
Initial investment in year 0	20,000
Investment allowance in year 1 (60%)	12,000
	8,000
Writing-down allowance in year 2 (25%)	2,000
	6,000
Writing-down allowance in year 3 (25%)	1,500
	4,500
Writing-down allowance in year 4 (25%)	1,125
	3,375
Writing-down allowance in year 5 (25%)	844
	2,531
Writing-down allowance in year 6 (25%)	633
	1,898
Residual value on sale (included in £3,000)	1,000
Balancing allowance	£898

(ii) CALCULATION OF TAX PAYABLE ASSUMING A 40% RATE OF TAX

Year	*Extra income*	*Capital allowance*	*Net extra income*	*Corporation tax (40%)*
	£	£	£	£
1	4,500	12,000	7,500 Cr.	3,000 Cr. (*a*)
2	6,000	2,000	4,000	1,600
3	6,000	1,500	4,500	1,800
4	5,000	1,125	3,875	1,550
5	4,000	844	3,156	1,262
6	2,000 (net)	1,531	469	188
(*b*)	£27,500	£19,000	£8,500	£3,400

(*a*) The £3,000 credit figure is not necessarily a tax repayment because the company will probably have other income in year 1.

(*b*) The totals are merely for checking purposes.

The project can now be evaluated. Note that tax is payable the year after income accrues.

(iii) PROJECT EVALUATION

Year	*Gross income*	*Corporation tax*	*Net income*	*Present value factor (10%)*	*Present value*
	£	£	£		£
1	4,500	—	4,500	0·909	4,091
2	6,000	3,000 Cr.	9,000	0·826	7,434
3	6,000	1,600	4,400	0·751	3,304
4	5,000	1,800	3,200	0·683	2,186
5	4,000	1,550	2,450	0·621	1,522
6	3,000	1,262	1,738	0·565	982
			25,288		19,519
7	—	188	−188	0·513	−96
	£28,500	£3,400	£25,100		19,423
Deduct initial cost of investment in year 0					20,000
Negative net present value of project					−£577

Notice the difference now! What previously appeared to be a positive net present value of £1,147 (value/cost ratio of 5·5 per cent) has now been converted into a negative net present value of £577 (or a negative value/cost ratio of nearly 3 per cent). Obviously the timing of depreciation allowances for tax purposes matters very much from the standpoint of investment appraisal.

4. Value added tax

The illustration which we have just given involving a 60 per cent first-year allowance is dated. The previous illustration involving a 100 per cent depreciation allowance and investment grants depicts more accurately the situation at the time of writing. It can be seen that the impact of 100 per cent capital allowances and 20 or 22 per cent investment grants has been to remove an unfair imbalance in taxation particularly in the case of a firm's wishing to undertake large-scale expenditure to enhance the profitability of a business from which returns on investment are not expected for a considerable time. Just as proposed tax reforms in this case relieve hardship of a company incurring considerable capital expenditure, so proposed corporation tax reforms, as was seen earlier, relieve hardship of companies wishing to make large dividend distributions.

Value added tax is another proposed tax reform, intended to prevent an unfair tax burden resulting from making one financial decision as against another. It may ultimately replace other taxes for this reason.

At the time of writing, a draft explanation of value added tax has been set out in the recent Finance Bill and a White Paper on the subject, *Value Added Tax* (HMSO, 37p), has been issued. The draft clauses are impregnated with such phrases as "the Treasury may by order make provisions . . ." indicating that there is some flexibility and indeed vagueness in the legislation at present. The principle of value added tax, however, is by no means vague and we shall consider how the tax may affect investment and financial decisions.

The tax is to be payable by a registered person or business supplying goods or services. Payment will be made to Customs and Excise and businesses are generally liable to registration if the annual turnover is more than £5,000. "Goods or services" is a general description. Certain goods in the essential categories of food, books, fuel, construction and medicine are zero-rated for the purpose of the tax and property, insurance, postal, finance, education and health services will also be exempt. Gifts of goods will not be exempt from the tax but gifts of services may be exempted.

The principle of collection is quite simple. The proposed rate is 10 per cent. If a manufacturer purchases inputs he will pay tax in the invoiced price indicated by the invoice, and when he sells his manufactured product he will collect tax from customers by inclusion of value added tax in the invoice sent to customers. The balance of tax will be paid to the Customs and Excise.

EXAMPLE

Suppose that X Ltd purchases components A and B for manufacturing a product C which it sells to customer Y. If the manufacturers of A and B have fixed net retail values of £10 and £20 respectively upon A and B, they will be required to collect value added tax on their sale and thus to charge X Ltd gross amounts of £11 and £22 respectively, in both cases adding 10 per cent to the cost of the good. X Ltd will thus have already paid £3 value added tax upon its product, C. If C has a net retail value of £50, X Ltd will add 10 per cent of £50 (i.e. £5) to the cost of product C and invoice it to Y at £55. Although it collects £5 from C, it will be entitled to deduct the £3 which it has already paid to the manufacturers of components A and B and to pay the net value added tax of £2 (i.e. £5 − £3) to the authorities.

It would appear that, as it seeks to spread the incidence of tax evenly over all stages of production, value added tax is one step further in the direction of an entirely "fair" tax system. Another significant feature of the tax is its collection period. In most cases it will not be more than three months between the date of invoicing and the date of payment to the authorities, and thus if the tax will finally take the place of corporation tax, the lag of over twelve months from expenditure to repayment claim will disappear, and there will be no significant time-interval for discounting purposes. There is no distinction between capital and revenue expenditure, so that companies which undertake large capital purchases will gain from the standpoint of value added tax, and if value added tax replaces company taxation the two complicating factors mentioned earlier, (*a*) non-availability of immediate tax relief and (*b*) time-lag in payment of taxation, will have both been successfully buried.

Summary

The message of this chapter is a uniform one. By means of two illustrations from personal taxation we showed that personal tax circumstances mattered in determining whether or not a decision would be profitable. Building Society investment is better for a taxable person than for an exempt person. Insurable persons can improve the value of investment by combining it with life assurance.

In theory the same is true of company investment. However, a short study of the history of company taxation in recent years indicated that the present tendency is to remove circumstantial imbalance. For example, whereas a company had, from 1965, to pay a higher proportion of its profits in tax if it paid large dividends this is no longer true, and whereas a company may have been required to tie up a large capital outlay for a number of years before being able to claim tax-relief the position has now been rectified by a system of 100 per cent capital allowances and investment grants. The chapter concluded by illustrating that value added tax may be another step towards a "fair" system of taxation by reducing the time-lag before payment (or repayment) of tax and by spreading tax at a uniform rate fairly over stages of production.

Questions

1. An executive taxpayer is taxed at an average of 50 per cent of his personal income although his basic rate is only 30 per cent. He pays 75 per cent on the top £1,000 of his income. What is his relevant rate for deciding whether he should invest in shares to receive an extra £500 income?
2. A pensioner asks whether he should cash his 8 per cent local authority loan and invest in the Happywide Building Society which advertises "a gross yield of 9½ per cent to taxpayers at basic rate". How would you advise him?
3. Illustrate the effect of the imputation system on the distribution policy of a company.
4. Show how the investment policy of a company is affected by the introduction of 100 per cent first-year allowances and the reintroduction of investment grants.
5. How is value added tax collected? Show how its introduction has helped to spread the impact of tax over the stages of production.

Bibliography

J. Sizer, *An Insight into Management Accounting* (Penguin, 1970) (for a large worked example of the effects of tax in capital budgeting prior to the introduction of 100 per cent capital allowances)

"*Daily Mail*" *Income Tax Guide* (Associated Newspapers Ltd, annually) (for a short concise explanation of current taxation matters)

Value Added Tax (HMSO, 1972) (for an explanation of the subject)

15 Capital Structure and Dividend Policy

In the previous chapter we considered the effect of taxation on the wisdom (or otherwise) of a capital investment decision, and studied particularly a long-term decision involving the purchase of capital equipment which produced extra income for a company over a period of years. This chapter deals with two other long-term decisions and questions whether they can affect the capital value of a company. Some companies raise all their capital from shareholders and others raise only a proportion from shareholders and borrow the rest of the capital at a fixed rate of interest. In Chapter 10 we have already seen that this kind of financing could affect the apparent profitability of the company, so that the percentage of return on capital receivable by shareholders is not necessarily the same as its trading profit yield on net relevant assets. In this chapter we shall pursue the subject further and decide whether capital structure, gearing or leverage can optimize the value of a company. Is there, or is there not such a thing as optimal capital structure?

Similarly a company need not find extra capital by going to the public at all, either by raising more share capital or fixed interest loans. Instead, it could raise its capital by ploughing back its existing profits instead of distributing them to shareholders. The same question may be asked in this context. Is there an optimal dividend policy for a company to pursue, or is the value of the company unaffected by the kind of dividend policy which it pursues?

Both of these questions will be examined in the context of economic theory, in the almost unrealistic context of a perfect market for capital and rational behaviour of shareholders. Then we shall turn to the real-life situation in which there is a great deal of imperfection and see whether the same premises can be so firmly applied in the real world. In particular, we shall, as in the previous chapter, consider the effects of taxation, for it appears that however true the theories that there are neither optimal capital structure nor optimal dividend policy may be in the perfect world they are certainly untrue in a world which is dynamic, imperfect, unreasonable—and affected by differences in taxation. We shall consider the conclusions of Modigliani and Miller, the theorists who argued that there was neither optimal capital structure nor optimal dividend policy and how their teachings have to be modified, when applied to the real world.

I. Capital structure

Apart from short-term finance from creditors and banks, companies are usually financed either by long-term loans (debentures) carrying a fixed rate of interest on capital or by ordinary shares carrying membership of the company and dividends at rates which depend upon profits. Preference shares are hybrid, carrying fixed rates of return on capital and dormant membership of the company, for they have no voting rights unless dividends are in arrears. They rank as equity for capital-structure purposes but they will be ignored in this simple treatment of the subject.

(a) The ratio between fixed interest securities and equity Capital structure, gearing or leverage is the ratio between debentur and shares, between debt and equity. It is more often expressed as $D/(D+E)$ rather than D/E, where $D=$ debt and $E=$ ordinary shares. Two extremes illustrate the concept.

ILLUSTRATION

Companies A and B have both raised £10,000 capital. Company A has issued £9,000-worth of ordinary shares and a £1,000 debenture. Company B has issued £1,000-worth of ordinary shares and £9,000 in debenture stock. Both companies pay 10 per cent per annum to their debenture holders and both companies make and distribute £900 profit in year 1 and £2,500 in year 2. Consider the differences in ordinary share dividends paid by the companies.

	Company A			**Company B**		
	Invested	*Income*	*Percentage*	*Invested*	*Income*	*Percentage*
Year 1	£	£		£	£	
Total	10,000	900	9	10,000	900	9
Debentures	1,000	100	10	9,000	900	10
Equity	£9,000	£800	8·9	£1.000	NIL	NIL

Year 2	£	£		£	£	
Total	10,000	2,500	25	10,000	2,500	25
Debentures	1,000	100	10	9,000	900	10
Equity	£9,000	£2,400	26·7	£1,000	£1,600	160

EXPLANATION

Company A is low-geared. Its proportion of debts is low and thus the rate of dividend paid to members differs little from the profit ratio of the company as a whole. Company B is high-geared. Its members do very well when profits are high; they risk losing dividends when profits are low and they would be obliged to pay the £900 per annum due to debenture-holders even if there were losses.

Not all profits are usually distributed. Sometimes reserves are created by issuing bonus shares instead of distributing dividends. Directors may consider it unwise to distribute 160 per cent in the above example, for shareholders may expect this high rate of dividend as a regular feature and share values would be unstable. Each £10 share in company B would be worth £26 cum div, that is, before the distribution of dividend. Instead of creating a general reserve, the directors could create extra "capital" by issuing £1,000 in the form of bonus shares. The holder of a £10 share would receive an extra £10 share in lieu of dividend, the number of shares would be doubled and the value of each share would now be £13 cum div. The directors could now distribute the remaining £600 as a 30 per cent dividend on the nominal value (book value) of its capital (£2,000) or leave the £600 in a general reserve to pay debenture interest at some future time.

(b) Is there optimal capital structure?

(*i*) *The traditional view* But how relevant is capital structure in our general theme of maximizing value or reducing capital costs? Is there an optimal capital structure? It was traditionally held that there was, for if shareholders expected an approximate yield of say 20 per cent from a given class of business and 10 per cent debenture-holders could only expect 10 per cent yield upon outlay, it would seem that debt cheapens the cost of capital and increases the value of a company. Assuming that companies M and N have the same capital structures as companies A and B above, and that both companies' shareholders expected an average dividend of 20 per cent the weighted average cost of capital would differ for companies M and N, thus—

EXAMPLE

	Company M			Company N		
	Invested	*Expected income*	%	*Invested*	*Expected income*	%
Hypothetical year	£	£		£	£	
Shares	9,000	1,800	20	1,000	200	20
Debentures	1,000	100	10	9,000	900	10
Capital	£10,000	£1,900	19	£10,000	£1,100	11
Weighted average cost of capital			19%			11%

Alternative N seems to cheapen cost of capital and so to increase the present value of the company. But, of course, a very highly leveraged company would be unable to borrow further short-term finance. Shareholders would be reluctant to invest because a large number of debentures would claim prior interest payments of 10 per cent, and so banks and creditors would follow suit and be reluctant to allow overdrafts and further credit. The result would be either of the capital rationing situations of Chapter 6.

(*ii*) *The theory propounded by Modigliani and Miller* The doctrine of an optimal capital structure was challenged by Modigliani and Miller in 1958. The argument proceeded like this. Let I be the average expected annual income of a company, given certain trade risks. Let c be its cost of capital and V its value. As I is an average figure the normal valuation model—

$$V = \sum_{j=0}^{\infty} \frac{I}{(1+c)^j}$$

simplifies to—

$$V = \frac{I}{c}$$

For example, M's average expected income I would be £1,900 and its cost of capital 19 per cent so that its value would simply be £1,900/19% = £10,000.

Using S and D for shares and debentures and d and i for dividends and interest respectively, we can evaluate c, the cost of capital—

$$c = \frac{I}{V}$$

but $I = iD + dS$, so that—

$$c = \frac{iD + dS}{V}$$

or

$$c = \frac{iD}{V} + \frac{dS}{V}$$

If, as is legal in the USA, company M borrowed an extra £10 and repurchased one of its shares, V would remain the same, for operating income I would be unaffected. But because of higher leverage risks shareholders would expect a higher rate of dividend. They would expect rate h where—

$$c = \frac{i(D + 1)}{V} + \frac{h(S - 1)}{V}$$

Now let us calculate h, the new rate of dividend which M's shareholders would expect instead of d, the previously expected rate of 20 per cent.

$$h = \frac{I - i(D + 1)}{S - 1} = \frac{1{,}900 - 10\%\,(1{\cdot}010)}{8{,}990}$$

$$= \frac{1{,}799}{8{,}990} = 20{\cdot}01\%$$

So, in theory, M's shareholders will require the additional 0·01 per cent as compensation for the additional leverage risk.

In this country a company may not repurchase its shares, except redeemable preference shares, but the market makes its adjustment. If companies M and N conducted the same class of business and expected the same trading income and risks, the differences of capital cost (19 per cent in M against 11 per cent in N) would be permanently impossible, for a shareholder in N could adjust his personal leverage to that of M but manipulate a better yield.

If he had £100 N shares yielding £20 he could sell them for £100, borrow an additional £800 at 10 per cent interest and invest the whole £900 in M's shares yielding 20 per cent or £180. Leverage would still be 9:1, but eight-ninths would be due to his own personal debt and one-ninth due to the debenture-holders of company M. But now he would be £80 per year better off, for he would receive £180 dividend from M, pay his personal creditors £80 (i.e. 10 per cent of £800 borrowed) and there would be a net yield of £100 instead of the £20 per year which he received before the manipulation. Other shareholders would follow suit and create pressure to reduce the price of Company N's shares, ultimately making their value commensurate with both trade and leverage risks.

(*iii*) *The debate afterwards* There are arguments against Modigliani and Miller's clear conclusions, but they tend to challenge not the arguments but the premises on which they are based. Can an unsecured investor borrow money as easily and at the same rate as a company? Do all shareholders behave as rationally as Modigliani and Miller assume? Is there really a linear relationship between return and uncertainty? Is there a perfect market in shares for both individuals and investing companies? What about minimum costs of manipulations, such as brokerage and stamp duty? Finally, what about tax? Can tax considerations alter leverage policy as they affected a plant purchase decision in the previous chapter? It is easy to challenge all these premises, but we turn to taxation to illustrate the irrelevance of the theory to the "real world".

(c) The effect of taxation The greatest practical argument against the simple logic of Modigliani and Miller is based on tax considerations. Companies pay corporation tax on income after deduction of debenture interest. Consider the following illustration, in which leverage extremes are similar to previous examples.

	Company X			**Company Y**		
Investment	*Invested*	*Return*	*Percentage*	*Invested*	*Return*	*Percentage*
	£	£		£	£	
Capital	10,000	2,000	20	10,000	2,000	
Debentures	1,000	100	10	9,000	900	
Ordinary Shares	£9,000	£1,900	21	£1,000	£1,100	110

Both companies are in the same class of business risk; both have invested capital of £10,000 and both have a trading income of 20%. Debenture-holders will suffer income tax at source and shareholders will receive an imputed three-sevenths credit against their income tax. Even so the net corporation tax position (i.e. the unavoidable tax upon the company even if it distributed all its profits) is based on profits after the payment of debenture interest. Let us examine the position—

	Company X	Company Y
	£	£
Income subject to corporation tax	1,900	1,100
Corporation tax (say 40% for simplicity)	760	440
Net income after tax	1,140	660
Add back: debenture interest	100	900
Trading income net of corporation tax	£1,240	£1,560

If the class of trade risk and income for X is similar to that of Y there is no reason why arbitrage should not, under the Modigliani and Miller assumptions, bring the expected yield on ordinary shares to 21 per cent and 110 per cent respectively and thus gross average cost of capital would still be 20 per cent, yet Company Y now has a higher expected net trading income than Company X and its value must be correspondingly higher.

II. Dividend policy

The previous arguments assumed an expected rate of dividend per share, a perfect capital market, perfect certainty and rational behaviour on the part of investors. The Modigliani–Miller arguments about dividend policy are similar to those about optimal capital structure. They argued that a company can have no optimal dividend policy because share prices do not depend on dividends but on trading income. If P is the present price of a share and Q its price at the end of a period after distributing dividend D, and if shareholders expect a yield of r on their outlay then—

$$P = \frac{D + Q}{(1 + r)}$$

Now suppose that at the end of the period it borrowed £x to increase its dividend to $D + x$, the value of the company would then be—

$$P = \frac{(D + x) + (Q - x)}{(1 + r)}$$

which simplifies to the previous equation since the company's value at the end of the period would be reduced to $Q - x$ net, and the increased dividend has not altered the value of the company.

(a) A closer look at Modigliani and Miller's assumptions The exposition assumed that the company's expected income is approximately constant, that reinvested earnings produce the same yield as shareholders expect to receive on their shares, that there is no variation resulting from risk attitude, that people behave rationally, that there is a perfect market for shares and that the situation is not affected by tax legislation. Let us consider these assumptions carefully.

If, as Modigliani and Miller say, share values do not depend on dividends, but on income, and I represents expected average income and r the expected rate of dividend, the value of company P for n years if j denotes each year is—

$$P = \sum_{j=1}^{n} \frac{I}{(1 + r)^j}$$

and if the company is a perpetuity with indefinite life, this could become—

$$P = \frac{I}{r}$$

This would be true if the company distributed all its income I in each year when it was earned, for then I would represent both income and dividend for each year, or if the company earned the same yield on reinvested income as shareholders would have expected if the income had been distributed to them.

(b) The problem of reinvested income Let us see how this works. Suppose that the company retained and reinvested its year 1 income at rate r, but distributed all income from year 2 onwards. The reinvestment of I in year 1 would increase future years' income to $I(1 + r)$ or $I + rI$ per year and the value of the company would now be—

$$P = \frac{0}{(1 + r)^1} + \sum_{j=2}^{n} \frac{I + rI}{(1 + r)^j}$$

but if we divide throughout by $1 + r$ we return exactly to the previous formula

$$P = \sum_{j=1}^{n} \frac{I}{(1+r)^j}$$

So P is unaffected if reinvestment yield equals that which the shareholders expect on their outlay, if both are r. If you doubt whether this is mathematically correct try working it out algebraically for three, four or five periods or work through the practical exercise at the end of the chapter.

However, if the company's directors expect to earn i on reinvested income and $i > r$, P would increase and shareholders' expectations rise to a new potential yield e, such that—

$$P \equiv \frac{0}{(1+r)^1} + \sum_{j=2}^{n} \frac{I(1+i)}{(1+r)^j} \equiv \sum_{j=1}^{n} \frac{I}{(1+e)^j} \neq \sum_{j=1}^{n} \frac{I}{(1+r)^j}$$

(c) Retention and reinvestment—the fraction reinvested The previous paragraph has shown that, when the yield expected by shareholders differs from that which the company can earn from reinvesting income, dividend policy will change the price of a share. However in practice a company would not retain all its year 1 earnings and distribute all its subsequent earnings. It would probably retain and reinvest a fraction (f) of its earnings each year and distribute the remainder ($1 - f$). The shareholders would tend to discount their expected dividend $(1 - f)\,I$ by the discount rate ($r - if$), that is the expected rate r less the growth rate upon the reinvested fraction (if), so that now—

$$P = \frac{(1-f)\,I}{r - if}$$

If income is £10,000 and the company distributes 75 per cent and reinvests 25 per cent to earn a 20 per cent yield, and if the shareholders expected to earn only a 15 per cent dividend a company's issued share capital would be worth—

$$P = \frac{75\% \times £10{,}000}{15\% - (20\% \times 25\%)} = £\,\frac{7{,}500}{10\%} = £75{,}000$$

Thus, the price per share would be, say, £75 if there were 1,000 issued shares.

In contrast, if the company had not reinvested a fraction of its income the price per share would be calculated as follows—

$$P = \frac{£10,000}{15\%} = £66,667 \text{ for } 1,000 \text{ shares, or } £67 \text{ per share.}$$

(d) Rationality, expectations and uncertainty This simple formula assumes an expected average income for all the years of a company's life and that the reinvested fraction of such income is reasonably constant. This is rarely the case; and r would have different values for each future year because shareholders would probably have higher time-preference rates for periods well into the future. Indeed if all the components of the above equation, I, f, i and r, change from period to period; and if r changes with peoples' expectations from moment to moment the valuation formula becomes far more complex. The discrete formula would even have to be replaced by an integration formula beyond the scope of the mathematics of this book. The very lack of uniformity in annual income, reinvestment rates, rates of time preference, the uncertainties about gearing and new finance and the even greater uncertainty of human behaviour, which is often neither rational nor constitutes a perfect market, all tend to complicate the rather simple model above, but even the simple model illustrates that dividend policy matters and that companies can optimize their dividend distributions.

(e) The effect of taxation Finally, as in the cases of plant investment and capital structure, tax legislation may make a particular dividend policy optimal. A company will do well to distribute dividends if most of its shareholders are retired and do not pay tax at standard rate. A company would do well to retain profits if its shareholders were mostly people of modest incomes who paid tax at basic rate. Such people would not be able to reclaim income tax paid at source on dividends, but would not pay tax on capital gains unless their net capital gains (capital gains less capital losses) exceeded £50 in any particular year.

In reality both growth-orientated and income-orientated classes of people are represented by unit trusts and many large companies have both classes of unit trusts among their shareholders. What is optimal in all such cases is a question of what is best for those who hold the largest number of shares. Because of all uncertainties, particularly with reference to dividend policy and capital structure, some have argued that share prices follow the pattern of a random walk over time, the pattern of the normal probability curve, which will be expounded fully in the following chapter. The very uncertainties of the real world, the uncertainty of perfect competition, of human behaviour and the different classes of risk attached to different businesses now make it essential that we explore the twin topics of risk and uncertainty more fully. We shall do this in the next chapter.

Summary

The chapter has dealt with twin topics, the questions whether there are—

(I) an optimum capital structure; and
(II) an optimum dividend policy.

(I) The effect of leverage, capital structure or gearing was explained. The question to be considered was whether a company could increase the value of its capital by altering its leverage. The arguments of Modigliani and Miller assume—

(*a*) a perfect market;
(*b*) a uniform class of business risk;
(*c*) rationality of behaviour;
(*d*) no differences in borrowing opportunities; and
(*e*) no taxation.

The arguments of Modigliani and Miller were shown to be reasonable, given the above five assumptions. The premises have been questioned rather than the arguments. An illustration followed which showed that they were inapplicable in "real-world" conditions.

(II) Dividend policy was explored in the same way. The conclusions of Modigliani and Miller do not rest merely upon the validity of the above five premises, but the problems of reinvestment opportunities, and the fraction of income undistributed and reinvested, either in the company or elsewhere, must all be considered. Before concluding with another tax discussion we considered the part which expectations play in the matter.

The chapter ended by stressing the need to consider risk and uncertainty, twin topics which will be studied in the following chapter.

Questions

1. Company M has an ordinary share capital of £20,000 and Company N has ordinary shares of £5,000 and has issued debentures of £15,000 at 10 per cent interest. What are the gearing ratios of the two companies?
2. Assume that in year 1 both the above companies earn £1,500 and that in year 2 both companies earn £15,000. If all income is distributed what rates of dividend are paid on the shares of both companies in both years?
3. If company M's shareholders require 20 per cent yield on their shares and company N's shareholders require 25 per cent per annum, what rates of weighted average cost of capital should companies M and N in the above questions use for project evaluation purposes?
4. Demonstrate how home-made leverage and "arbitrage" are instrumental in forcing down the price of a high-geared investment.
5. A company can borrow an additional £10,000 at 8 per cent. Its shareholders expect at least 15 per cent. Corporation tax is 40 per cent. What is the real marginal cost of borrowing an extra £5,000 to finance a project?
6. A company earns £6,000 per annum. It will last four years and be worthless afterwards. Its shareholders expect a yield of 12 per cent per annum. What is its value if it distributes all its income? What is its value if it distributes no income in year 1 but reinvests it to yield 12 per cent per annum, and distributes all subsequent income? What is its value if it distributes no income in year 1 and reinvests it to yield 18 per cent per annum, but distributes all subsequent income?
7. Assume that the above company, whose income was £6,000 per annum and had an expected dividend rate of 12 per cent, could reinvest half its income at 18 per cent and is expected to last indefinitely. It has 1,000 shares. What is the price per share if it (*a*) distributes all its income? (*b*) reinvests half its income?
8. How is a company's dividend policy affected by individual tax circumstances?
9. How are the dividend policy of a company and the value of its shares affected by attitudes to risk?

Bibliography

On Optimal Capital Structure

D. Durand, "Cost of Debt and Equity Funds for Business: Trends and Problems of Measurement", *Conference on Research on Business Finance*, New York, 1952

D. Durand, "The Cost of Capital, Corporation Finance and the Theory of Investment: Comment", *American Economic Review*, 1959

J. Lintner, "The Cost of Capital and Optimal Financing of Corporate Growth", *Journal of Finance*, May 1963

F. Modigliani and M. H. Miller, "The Cost of Capital, Corporation Finance and the Theory of Investment", *American Economic Review*, September 1959

F. Modigliani and M. H. Miller, "Corporate Income Taxes and the Cost of Capital: A Correction", *American Economic Review*, June 1963

A. A. Robichek and S. C. Myers, *Optimal Financing Decisions* (Prentice-Hall, 1963)

On Dividend Policy

F. Modigliani and M. H. Miller, "Dividend Policy, Growth and the Value of Shares", *Journal of Business*, October 1961

J. Linter, "Distribution of Incomes of Corporations among Dividends, Retained Earnings and Taxes", *American Economic Review*, May 1956

Most of the above readings are reprinted in—

S. H. Archer and C. A. D'Ambrosio, *The Theory of Business Finance* (Macmillan, 1967)

16 Risk and Uncertainty

A crucial question remains unanswered. In Chapter 8 it was argued that value was a function, not of cost but of expected future income or benefit and an attempt was made to show how income could be measured accurately in the hope that we could at least plot the trend of expected future income. Chapter 9 approached the problem of income measurement in a different way, by analysing the parameters of expected income, by discovering expected optimum sales, material costs, labour, overheads and other factors which together determine income. But neither the expected trend of Chapter 8 nor the expected analysed feasible optima of Chapter 9 are certain. To say that value is a function of expected future income is to make value a rather subjective thing unless the strength of our expectations and the certainty of their fulfilment can be measured.

In this context strategy, diversification and flexibility are relevant. Chapter 3 stated that a company should be as flexible as possible, that is, that it should spread its risks over projects, over investments and over time: holding a kind of balance between the present and the future and between one project and another. This is an ancient idea. A section of the Biblical text of Ecclesiastes may be freely translated—

Send your supplies over the seas
and after a while you will have a return
But take shares in seven or eight ventures
for you cannot predict the perils on earth! . . .
Sow your seed in the morning of life
and do not give up until sundown
Perhaps this or that venture will prosper
and possibly both will succeed!

Eccles. 11:1, 2 & 6

The quotation is not as obscure as it seems. It is one of the most valid available indications that diversification was widely practised in the ancient world. The writer says, in effect, that there is greater chance of success if one has shares in a number of different trading ventures or projects, but that one must be persistent over a period of time. Such persistence is, in itself, a form of diversification, for it holds the balance between present and future and recognizes that there is greater chance of success at some times than at others. Here mathematicians would substitute "probability" for "chance" and before we study what risks can or cannot be calculated and determined, it is necessary to examine some of the elements of the mathematics of probability. What follows is not an exhaustive treatment of the subject, but an exposition of principles, so that methods of dealing with risk and uncertainty may be understood.

I. The mathematics of probability

(a) Certainty, probability and impossibility Probability is usually measured as a fraction or a decimal between 0 and 1. Certainty is always expressed as 1 and impossibility is expressed as 0. It is certain that people will continue dying, and the probability of this event is therefore expressed as 1. On the other hand, the probability that you will travel outside the solar system in the next ten years is mathematically expressed as 0. Between 0 and 1, between impossibility and absolute certainty, the probability of an expected event is expressed as a decimal. There are two likely outcomes of tossing a coin, and since if the coin is unbiased each of these outcomes, head or tail, is equally likely, the probability of a head is $\frac{1}{2}$ or 0·5, and that of a tail is similarly $\frac{1}{2}$ or 0·5. There are six equally possible outcomes of throwing a die: that is, any number from 1 to 6 may be uppermost. The probability of a "six" being thrown is therefore expressed as $\frac{1}{6}$ or as 0·1667. Although it would be impossible to "prove" these measures of probability with one toss of a coin or one throw of a die, they could be empirically demonstrated. If you tossed a coin 100 times the number of heads would be about 50, and as the number of tosses increases so the number of head outcomes will get progressively nearer half the number of tosses. In the case of dice-throwing, 100 throws will produce about 16 or 17 "sixes", but as the number of throws increases the number of "six" outcomes will get nearer $\frac{1}{6}$ of the number of throws.

(b) The addition rule—"either, or" Examine the second example. The probability of throwing a "six" is $\frac{1}{6}$, and the probability of throwing a "five" is also $\frac{1}{6}$ because there are six equally possible outcomes. To know the probability of throwing either a "five" or a "six" in any one particular throw of one die, one simply adds the two equal probabilities of $\frac{1}{6}$. So $\frac{1}{6} + \frac{1}{6} = \frac{1}{3}$.

(c) The multiplication rule Suppose that, instead of throwing one die and expecting either a "five" or a "six" to appear uppermost we

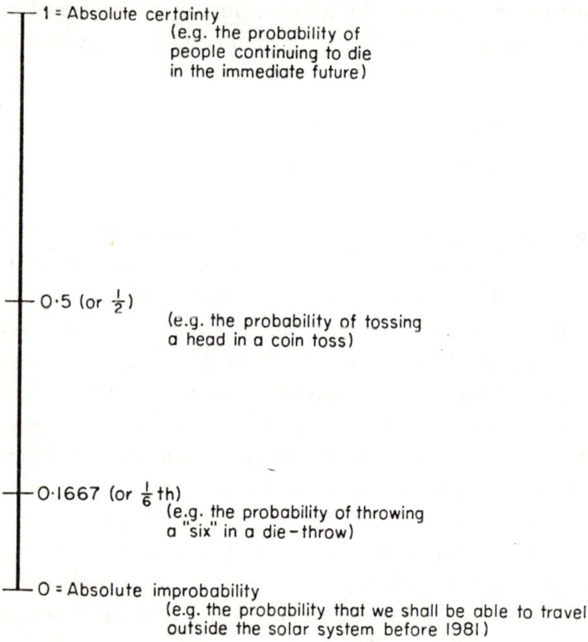

Fig 16.1 Certainty, probability and impossibility

threw two dice and wanted to know the probability of throwing two "sixes" at the same time. Figure 16.3 shows that this is $\frac{1}{6} \times \frac{1}{6} = \frac{1}{36}$. But if we wished to know the probability of a combination "five and six" on one throw of two dice at the same time, we must consider the two different ways in which this could happen. Either die A could exhibit "five" and die B exhibit "six" or die A could show a "six" and die B show "five". The probability of combination "five and six" when throwing two dice at the same time is therefore $\frac{1}{36} + \frac{1}{36} = \frac{1}{18}$. Figures 16.1, 16.2 and 16.3 illustrate the concepts so far.

(d) Application to finance — expected values But how, apart from gambling, can all this be applied to finance? Suppose a firm is faced with two possible events. If it can either acquire plant X by the end of March or acquire market Y by the end of February it will increase net income by £1,000, but if it can acquire plant X by the end of March and acquire market Y by the end of February because of such a favourable combination it will increase its net income by £5,000. There is a

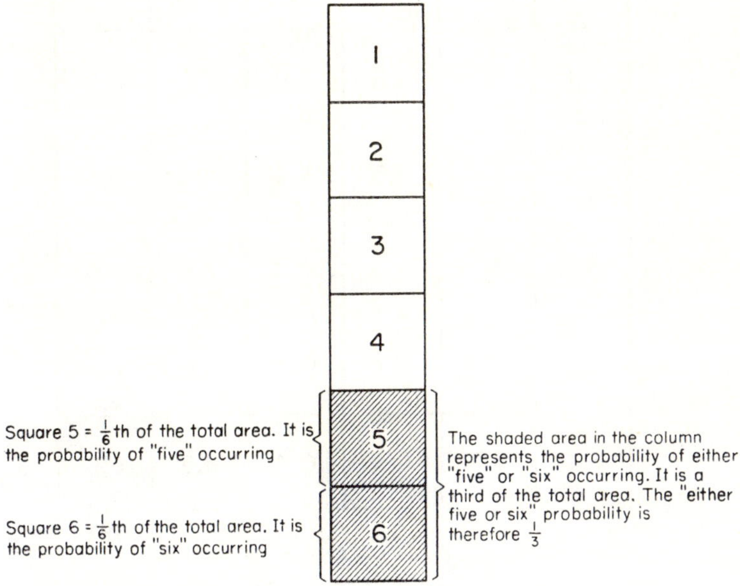

Fig 16.2 The addition rule for "either-or" situations

0·5 chance of plant X being delivered before the end of March and 0·1 chance of market Y being acquired by the end of February. What is the expected value $E(V)$ of the increase in the firm's net income?

ILLUSTRATION

		£
Expected value of probability of both events happening $= (0{\cdot}5 \times 0{\cdot}1 \times £5{,}000) = (0{\cdot}05 \times £5{,}000)$	=	250
Expected value of probability of either event happening $= (0{\cdot}5 \times 0{\cdot}9) + (0{\cdot}5 \times 0{\cdot}1) \times £1{,}000 = (0{\cdot}45 + 0{\cdot}05) \times £1{,}000$	=	500
Total expected value of the increase in the firm's net income	=	£750

This technique is a valuable tool to measure expected increases of value if various combinations of events happen. The problem as we shall see later is that of estimating the various measures of probability. Figure

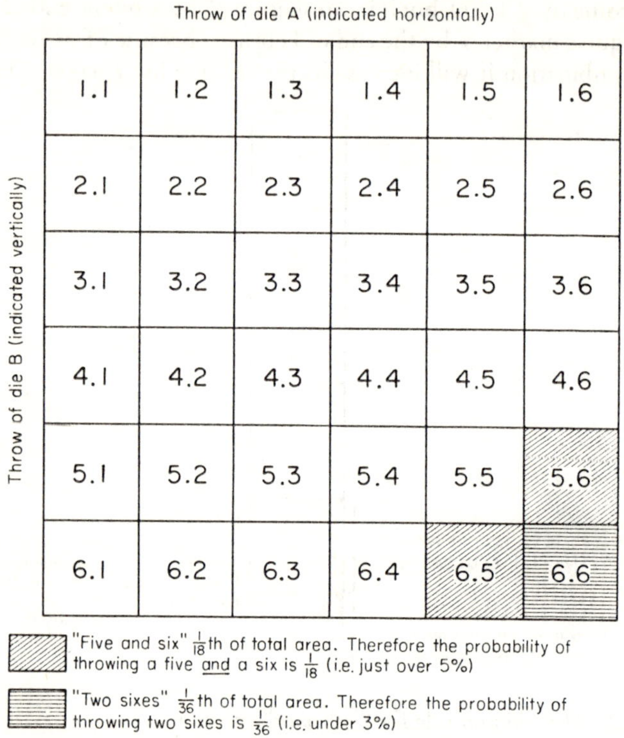

Fig 16.3 The multiplication rule

16.4 illustrates the financial problem of the preceding paragraph diagrammatically.

(e) **Standard deviation as a measure of risk** If we invest £4,000 in 6 per cent debentures or in a savings account bearing interest at 6 per cent it is certain that the expected value of a year's income will be £240. But suppose we invest £4,000 in a type of machine. The profitability of this investment is difficult to measure because only 15 of this type of machine have been sold. They manufacture units which sell at a profit of £50 each so that annual income must be expressed in

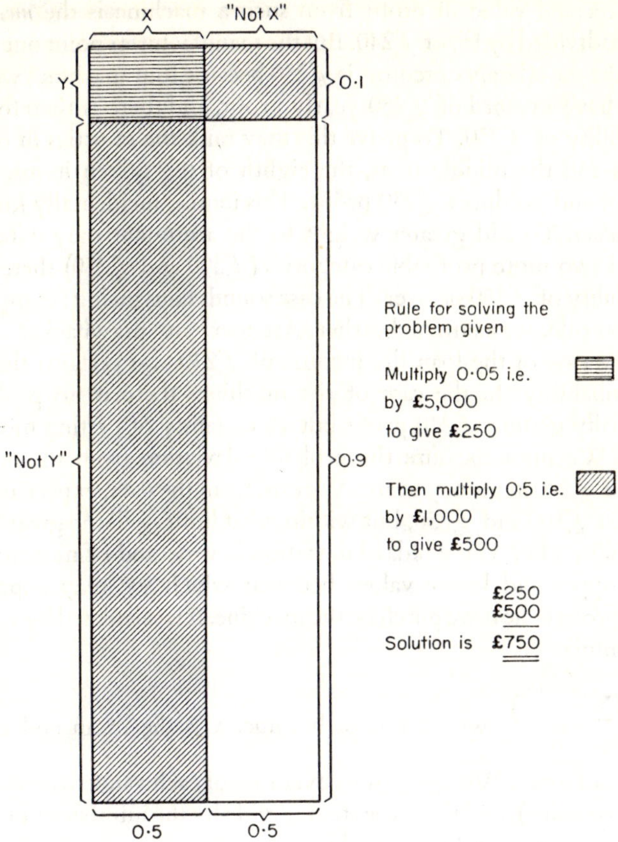

Fig 16.4 Application of addition and multiplication rules to finance

multiples of £50. The manufacturers assure us that we can make at least £240 per year profit by buying one, and present us with the following table of results—

No. of machines	*Profit* £	*Product* £
1	100	100
2	150	300
3	200	600
4	250	1,000
3	300	900
2	350	700
15		£3,600

The expected value of profit from such a machine is the *mean*. It is £3,600 divided by 15, or £240. But the manufacturers point out that the *mode*, the most likely outcome, is £250 because four machines were sold which have a record of £250 yearly profit, and there is therefore a $\frac{4}{15}$ probability of £250. To prove this they rank the statistics in order of success and the middle item, the eighth of the fifteen items, falls in group 4 and produces £250 profit. This item is incidentally known as the *median*. To add greater weight to the argument they state that if we add two more profitable categories (£300 and £350) there is a $\frac{9}{15}$ probability of £250 or over. The case sounds convincing: it applies the addition rule, we examined earlier. Are there any drawbacks?

In the case of the loan the income of £240 was certain: there was 1·0 probability. In the case of the machines there is no probability of actually getting £240 profit but $\frac{9}{15}$ certainty of getting more than £240. We must measure the probable deviation from the expected value of £240 in money terms. We can, from the data, expect anything between £100 and £350, but within what limits will the great bulk of probabilities lie? The standard deviation is a method of measuring the likely upper and lower values between which we may expect our future profit to lie if we purchase the machine. It is calculated by applying the formula—

$s = \sqrt{\frac{\Sigma(x - \bar{x})^2}{n}}$ where x is each value, $\bar{x}$ is the mean and n is the number of items. We square the deviations of each value from the mean (expected value), add them together, divide by the number of items and find the square root. Let us do this.

No. of machines	*Deviation from £240 (mean)*	*Deviation squared*	*Product*
	£	£	£
1	140	19,600	19,600
2	90	8,100	16,200
3	40	1,600	4,800
4	10	100	400
3	60	3,600	10,800
2	110	12,100	24,200
15			£76,000

It remains to divide £76,000 by 15 and find the square root. The square root of £5,067 is £71 to the nearest £. Thus the bulk of the values lie between £169 (that is, £240 − £71) and £311 (that is, £240 + £71). The table shows this is so, for ten of the values fall in this range, and there is a $\frac{10}{15}$ or $\frac{2}{3}$ probability of our income being between £169 and £311.

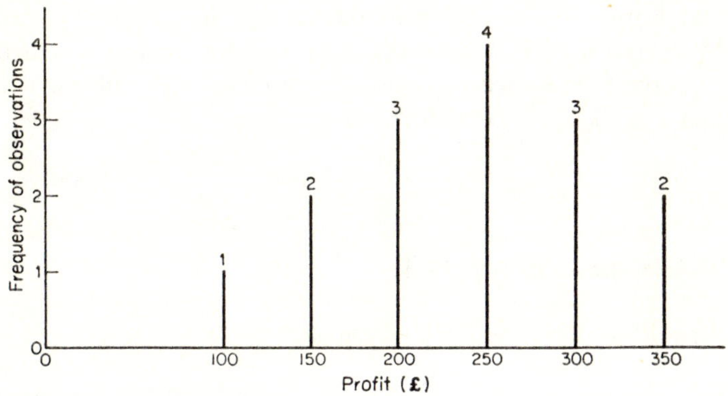

Fig 16.5 The example given—15 machines

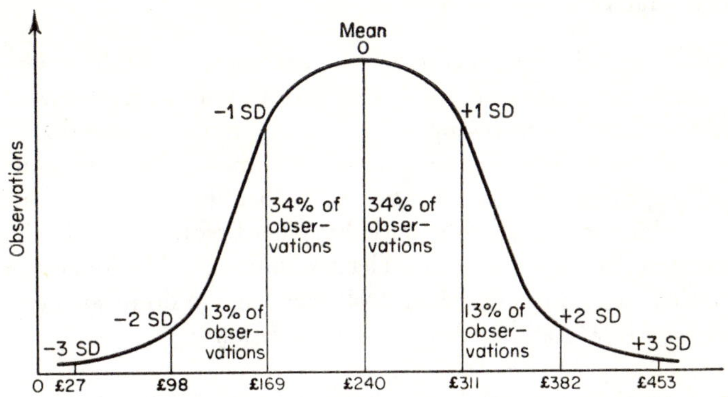

Fig 16.6 Normal distribution—a large number of observations

This is a better estimate of *likely* profit than the manufacturer's unqualified (yet true!) statement that $\frac{9}{15}$ of likely profit figures lie above £240.

This is not an example of normal distribution because (*a*) it is slightly skewed for there is no item of 1 machine at £800 as an upper limit, (*b*) profit is in lumps of £50 and (*c*) there are only 15 items, from which it is not possible to derive the bell-shaped curve of normal distribution. In normal distribution 68 per cent (almost our two-thirds) values lie within one standard deviation each side of the mean, 95 per cent lie within two standard deviations each side of the mean and nearly all values lie within three standard deviations of the mean. In a perfectly normal distribution of a large number of machines whose "incomes" could be measured in very small units, the distribution would be a curve of the type shown in Figure 16.6 as contrasted with the manufacturer's example in Figure 16.5.

II. The mathematics applied

Modern theory distinguishes between—

(*a*) *risk*, which can be measured using the standard deviation (or variance) approach used in the above section; and
(*b*) *uncertainty*, which is so complicated and unpredictable that it cannot be accurately measured.

In fact, both risk and uncertainty are extreme ends of the same spectrum and most classes of business risk come somewhere between the two. The "risk" of throwing a "six" can be easily measured as 0·167. The only reason why the uncertainty of human behaviour cannot be so easily predicted in a measurable way is because of the multitude of factors which determine human behaviour. Before we deal with the "uncertainty" end of the spectrum let us assume a world with measurable risk. What would the investment planner have to do in such circumstances and how could he deal with the situation?

A. A world with risk but no uncertainty Let us remember that his task is to close the gap between ends and means, that is, to marry the uncertainty attitudes of his investors with the uncertainty situations of his own investment opportunities. The "ends" are the uncertainty objectives (or risk attitudes) of the investors and the "means" are the projects, ventures or investment opportunities in which the company can itself invest. What can be done to narrow the gap between the two?

We may—

(i) ignore the problem completely;
(ii) adjust the discount rate;
(iii) evaluate risk utilities; or
(iv) use an indifference curve approach.

These are only four of the methods suggested. Let us examine them in detail.

(i) Ignoring the risk completely This attitude assumes that it is not the function of the management of a company to discover the risk-attitudes of its investing public. Our study of the views of Modigliani and Miller has assumed a different class of risk for different types of business, for example, a different class of risk for gold-mining and Arctic fishing from that for more stable commonplace industries. Investors are assumed to know the risks of each class of investment, and, provided that management diversifies sufficiently, it may, for capital budgeting and other planning purposes, ignore the fact that some of its projects will not work out as planned. The great disadvantage of this alternative is that some projects are, *de facto*, more risky than others, and, if risk is ignored, the company treats them all alike and so makes false comparisons.

(ii) Adjusting the discount rate The logic of this approach is based on ideas similar to those of Chapter 15. If capital costs more because of the risks of leverage, then why should not a risk-premium be added to the cost of capital in capital budgeting calculations to account for (or, at least, to adjust) the risks involved. However, a small mathematical illustration will uncover one of the fallacies of this approach.

ILLUSTRATION

Assume a two-year period.

Let a_n be the benefit, cash flow or income receivable;
c_n be the certainty equivalent factor;
r be the rate of discount normally used; and
i be the inflated rate needed for risk adjustment.

$$\frac{a_1 c_1}{(1+r)} = \frac{a_1}{(1+i)} \text{ so that } c_1 = \frac{(1+r)}{(1+i)}$$

However, in the following year—

$$\frac{a_2c_2}{(1+r)^2} = \frac{a_2}{(1+i)^2} \text{ so that } c_2 = \frac{(1+r)^2}{(1+i)^2} = \left(\frac{1+r}{1+i}\right)^2$$

so, by substitution, $c_2 = c_1^2$

This implies that risk varies in relationship to time, that projects in the distant future are more risky. It also implies that there is no risk attached to the immediate future, but we know this to be untrue. A run on the stock market can occur as easily tomorrow as in ten years' time. So we may dismiss the inflated discount rate suggestion.

(*iii*) *Evaluation of risk utilities* A third approach is to evaluate risk attitudes or utilities, the values which people are said to assign to various probable future outcomes. There have been complicated expositions of utility. Graphs have been drawn of two-outcome situations and investors' indifference curves plotted, but they are omitted from this simple exposition because of the advanced mathematics and economics required to understand them. A simple treatment of risk aversion and risk preference is the Friedman–Savage type curve of Figure 16.7, where segment *AC* is a risk-aversion curve and the segment *CE* is a risk-preference curve.

Our treatment of expected values and probability would indicate that there should be no difference between, say, receiving a sure return of *OX* and a return which has a 50 per cent probability of *OA* and a 50 per cent probability of *OC* (the business equivalent of a lottery ticket with an equal chance of getting *OA* or *OC*) since *AX* = *XC*. But risk-attitude is not the straight line *AXC*; it is the curve *ABC*. The shareholder is indifferent between certainly receiving *OB* and an equal chance of either *OA* or *OC*. *BX* is thus the insurance premium which the shareholder is prepared to forgo for the sure return *OB*. At a higher level the same shareholder may be a risk-lover, hence the segment *CDE*. Here, although the shareholder would have the same expected value from either a sure return of *OY* or a lottery ticket with an equal chance of *OC* or *OE*, since *CY* = *YE*, at this stage he likes the risk and is indifferent between the gamble of 50 per cent *OC* plus 50 per cent *OE* and the certainty of receiving *OD*, for at this level he can afford to lose and his attitude to risk is less conservative.

Utility measurement seems a more logical way of treating risk than either ignoring it or using a crude inflated discount rate, but how can it be applied to project assessment? It means that instead of discounting, say the income of year 3, it is necessary to look at all the probable incomes of year 3 and instead of computing their expected value as we did in Chapter 2, we should compute a figure which in sure terms would have the same utility as the spread of probable incomes for year 3. So

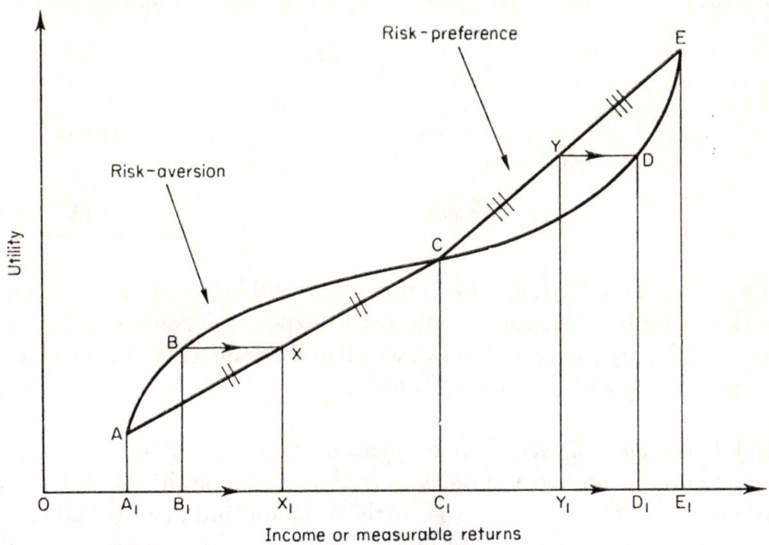

Fig 16.7 Utility-measurement in risk attitudes

the discounted expected income of year 3, which has an equal chance of a present equivalent of £0 or £5,000, is not necessarily £2,500. It depends on the utilities which investors attach to either outcome.

For example, a project requires a £10,000 investment. There is a 0·9 probability of £9,000 return and 0·1 probability of £100,000. If one applied the simple technique of calculating expected values, evaluation would be—

Expectation		*Probability*	£
£100,000	×	0·1	10,000
£9,000	×	0·9	8,100
Gross present value			18,100
Initial outlay			10,000
Net present value			£8,100

This project seems worth while but shareholders know that they are most likely to lose £1,000. What would they prefer? They may be indifferent between a gamble involving 0·1 chance of £100,000 and 0·9 chance of £9,000 and a sure return of £1,190, because they have the following utility preferences—

Probability	*Utility*	*Weighting*	*Expected amount*	*Certainty equivalent*
			£	£
0·1	1·2	0·12	100,000	12,000
0·9	−0·1	−0·09	9,000	−810
	Gross present value			11,190
	Initial outlay			10,000
	Net present value			£1,190

Each project can be dealt with in this way. Possible income figures for a series of future years can be adjusted to expected income utilities by multiplying by a weighted factor, which in each case will be the product of probability and shareholders' utility.

(*iv*) *Using an indifference curve approach* Some investors, however, would not be interested in one expected figure but in the whole range of possible outcomes. In such a case the technique must be to obtain by diversification of projects and investments a set of investments with a risk-probability distribution pattern which matches the probability curve measuring the risk attitudes of shareholders. As Figure 16.6 illustrates it is always possible to draw a normal probability curve if the mean and the standard deviation are known. Risk averters would like a tower-shaped probability curve, so to speak, one which has a small standard deviation, while risk lovers would like a flatter, shallower curve, using the same scales of measurement. The problem is one of finding a set of projects or investments with an expected mean income and possible standard deviation such as to satisfy the risk attitude of investors, and to match the mean income and the standard deviation of risk which they require. This all assumes, for the sake of simplicity, that distribution is normal in both cases.

Figure 16.8 illustrates the position. *OAB* is the efficient frontier of a portfolio of investments, and U_1, U_2, U_3 is a series of indifference curves between risk (standard deviation) and income (average expected return). The bulk of investments are above the line *OAB* and the higher ones are more risky and less satisfying than those on the efficient frontier. By diversification or by altering a portfolio of investments one can travel along the efficient frontier *OAB* and the point of optimality for any given indifference pattern can be reached. For shareholders whose indifference pattern is represented by the curves U_1, U_2, etc., optimality is reached at *A*, but if their risk attitude changed to an indifference pattern represented by the curves I_1, I_2, etc., the optimal portfolio would

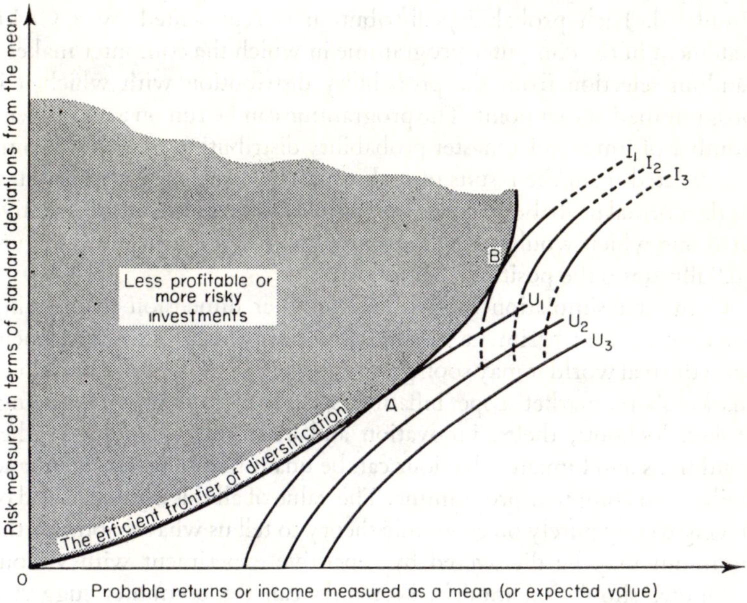

Fig 16.8 The mean-variability approach to diversification

be at *B* and it would be necessary to travel along the efficient frontier from *A* to *B* by changing the mix of projects and investments. Much of this is purely academic for we cannot tell each shareholder's indifference pattern between risk and income, and would not get precise answers even if each shareholder were questioned, because of the complexity of human behaviour. Figure 16.8 applies to the Markowitz type of diversification, the selection of a portfolio of different investments, but it could equally well be applied to the Ansoff type of diversification, the selection of a series of dissimilar projects.

B. Moving from risk to real uncertainty In both the above cases normal probability distributions have been assumed for the incomes from both projects and investments. David Hertz in the *Harvard Business Review* (1964) suggested that one could obtain a sharper probability distribution of a company's income by carefully estimating the probabilities of various features—market size, selling prices, market growth rate, share of market, purchase costs, labour, overheads, etc.—and by building all such carefully estimated probability distributions into a large computer programme in which the whole of a company's activities are simulated. Each probability distribution is represented by a CALL statement in the computer programme in which the computer makes a random selection from the probability distribution with which it is programmed at that point. The programme can be run on a computer a number of times and a master probability distribution of likely income constructed from the results of each run. The resulting curve may not be the normal probability curve but will at least be a little more objective than one which would have been purely a management guess. Figure 16.9 illustrates the position.

Computer simulation models lend another dimension to planning for they make experiment possible. If a company tries to experiment with the real world it may soon go out of business, but market reactions, market share, market scope, inflation, specific price changes, rationing, strikes, lockouts, thefts, innovation and even staff sickness, weather conditions and human behaviour can be quantified to some extent and built into a computer programme. The value of all this is that, instead of having to rely purely on economic theory to tell us what is optimal, the optimum may be discovered by repetitive experiment with various computer simulation models. Not only can the computer suggest a diversification programme to match the risk-distribution of projects and investments with the risk attitudes of shareholders. It can lead us ultimately to produce optimal budgets and standards, taking into account both the economic theory of the earlier chapters and some of the quantitative aspects of human behaviour.

Summary

From earliest times diversification has been practised as a hedge against uncertainty. It may involve spreading risks over time, over projects

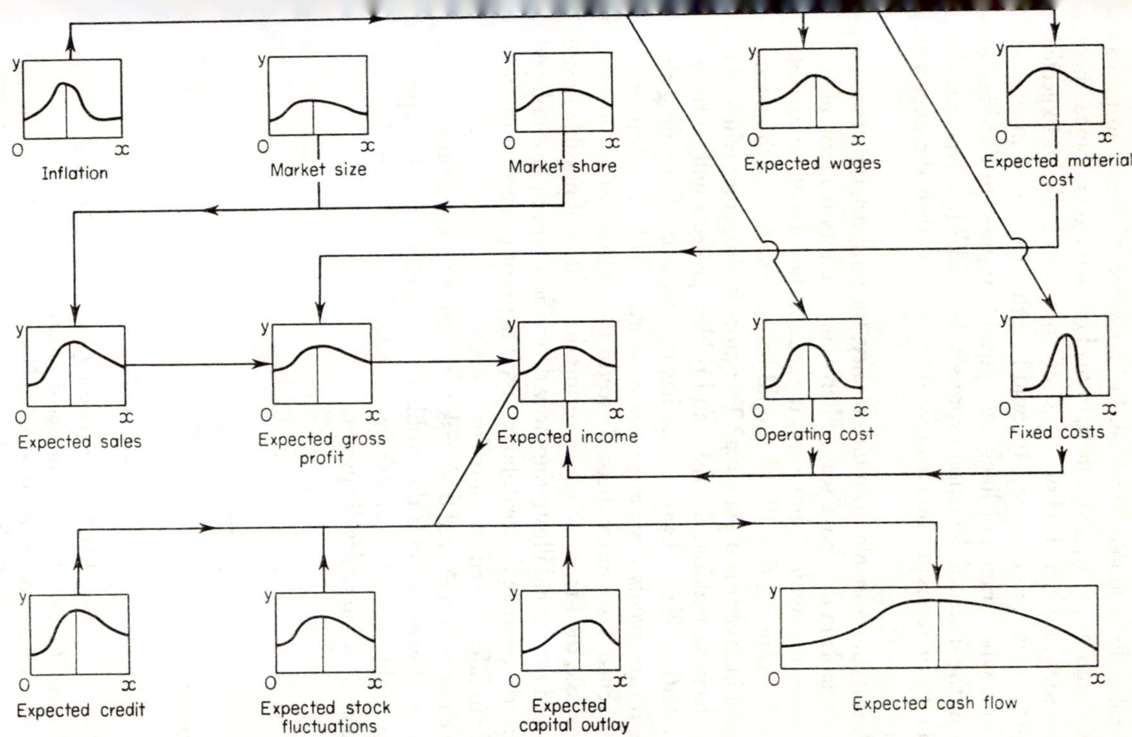

Fig 16.9 Simulated probability curve for project/investment
Note. (1) The final master curve would be derived by computer simulation over a large number of runs in the manner shown. (2) *oy*, chances of achievement; *ox*, range of values

and over investments (portfolio). A mathematical antecedent is necessary. One must study the mathematics of probability before studying the subject in depth. A probability is a fraction (between 0 and 1) which expresses the likelihood of an event happening. In "either-or" situations probabilities should be added. In "both-event" situations probabilities should be multiplied. Often, instead of such circumstances there are situations in which a whole range of outcomes is likely. Expected income falls into this category. It could be either the mean, median or mode of a whole range of likely and possible figures. In this kind of situation, the standard deviation expresses the "risk" involved, i.e. the probability of receiving much more or much less than the expected figure.

Risk is distinguishable from uncertainty, for pure risk is mathematically calculable in the above way, whereas uncertainty is a term used to depict a situation which is not easily measurable because of the variables involved. Assuming that all risks could be measured, how should risk be treated in investment planning? To ignore it altogether will lead to wrong decision-making, for risky and riskless projects will be treated alike. Inflation of the discount rate has the demerit of assuming that distant future events have a greater measure of risk than immediate future events. Two other methods study the attitude of the investor towards risk, the first method measuring the utilities of possible future events and the second illustrating how diversification can be employed to adjust the company's portfolio of investments or projects to the risk-attitude indifference curves of its investors.

The chapter then moved from risk to uncertainty. Computer models can be employed to tackle the problem of complexity, to incorporate all the variables and produce a sharper probability curve to indicate the particular situation under discussion.

Questions

1. 4 firms each earn £10,000 profit, 3 earn £12,000 each, 2 earn £9,000 and one earns £11,000. Calculate the standard deviation.
2. A firm has 3 projects A, B and C. The probability that A will earn over £10,000 is 0·8, the probability that B will earn over £10,000 is

0·75 and the probability that C will earn over £10,000 is 0·5. What is the probability that

(i) They will all earn over £10,000?
(ii) At least one project will earn over £10,000?
(iii) Only one project will earn over £10,000?

3. Distinguish between risk and uncertainty. Do future expectations usually come purely into either category?
4. What is wrong with ignoring risk completely in decision-making?
5. Demonstrate mathematically the unsoundness of using an inflated discount rate.
6. Calculate the expected value of income from Project X given the following probabilities, expectations and utilities—

Probability	*Utility*	*Expected amount* £
0·1	1·8	5,000
0·2	1·5	2,500
0·4	1·0	2,000
0·15	4·0	−1,500
0·15	3·0	−1,000

Note. As the disutilities are negative in this question they have been given positive utility weightings.

7. Construct indifference curves to show how shareholders can be indifferent between risk and expected income, and illustrate how diversification can be employed to adjust portfolios to the risk attitudes of shareholders.
8. How can computer simulation models be used in planning for risk and for optimal budgeting?

Bibliography

J. E. Freund & F. J. Williams, *Modern Business Statistics* (Pitman, 1970).

M. Friedman & L. J. Savage, "The Utility Analysis of Choices involving Risk", *Journal of Political Economy*, 1948

C. J. Grayson, "Decisions under Uncertainty" (Boston: Harvard University Graduate School of Business Administration, 1960).

D. B. Hertz, "Risk Analysis in Capital Investment", *Harvard Business Review*, January 1964

F. S. Hillier, "The Derivation of Probabilistic Information for the Evaluation of Risky Investments", *Management Science*, 1963.

J. Hirshleifer, "Investment Decision under Uncertainty: Choice-theoretic Approaches", *Quarterly Journal of Economics*, November 1965.

J. Hirshleifer, "Risk, the Discount Rate and Investment Decisions", *American Economic Review*, May 1961.

P. H. Carmel & M. Polasek, *Applied Statistics for Economics* (Pitman, 1970)

J. G. Kemeny *et al.*, *Finite Mathematics with Business Applications* (Prentice-Hall, 1962)

M. J. Moroney, *Facts from Figures* (Penguin Books, 1955)

N. R. Paine, "Uncertainty and Capital Budgeting", *Accounting Review*, April 1964

J. S. Porterfield, *Investment Decisions and Capital Costs* (Prentice-Hall, 1965) (the chapter on risk and uncertainty).

H. Thomas, *Decision Theory and the Manager* (Pitman, 1972)

Some of the above readings are reprinted in—

S. H. Archer & C. A. D'Ambrosio, *The Theory of Business Finance* (Macmillan, 1967)

Appendix 1

Answers to Quantitative Test Questions

CHAPTER 4

	£
1. (*a*) The value of £5,000 at present is	5,000
(*b*) £500 rent for 14 years + £500 at present =	
$(a_{14} \times £500) + £500$	4,183
(*c*) Present value of £7,000 in 3 years' time = $v_3 \times £7,000$	5,259

Alternative (*c*) is preferable as it has the highest present value.

2. Calculation of present value of Howard's income

Year	*Income*	*9% present value*	*Present value*
	£		£
1	400	0·917	366·80
2	260	0·842	218·92
3	540	0·772	416·88
4	635	0·708	449·58
	Present value of income		£1,452·18

3. Marsh is wrong on two counts. If the whole £600 had been invested for six years at 5 per cent interest, the total interest would have been £180. On the other hand £100 invested at the outset would have earned £30 interest in six years. In this particular case, a sinking fund of £100 per year is created, which, invested at 5 per cent would accumulate to £680·20 at the end of six years. This is certainly enough to pay for the car.

4. £422 (see tables).

CHAPTER 5

1. Maximize $5M + 3N$

subject to

$$7M + 1N \leqslant 700$$
$$1M + 3N \leqslant 300$$
$$M, N \geqslant 0$$

2. The optimum product mix is—

$M = 90$
$N = 70$

Total profit = £660

3. The dual programme is—

$$\begin{aligned} \text{Minimize} \quad & 700x + 300y \\ \text{subject to} \quad & 7x + y \geqslant 5 \\ & x + 3y \geqslant 3 \\ & x, y \geqslant 0 \end{aligned}$$

4. x (the price per material unit) = 60p
y (the price per labour hour) = 80p

CHAPTER 6

10.

	Project A	*Project B*
Payback period	4 years	9 years
Internal rate of return	8%	9%
Net present value at 5 per cent capital cost	£420	£896
Net present value at 10 per cent capital cost	−£255	−£166

Both projects are comparatively unprofitable if funds can be guaranteed to earn 10 per cent per annum throughout the 10 year period.

11. (i) The alternative use of funds yielding 11 per cent is obviously preferable.
(ii) Project B should be chosen.

12. Assuming that cash flows could be reinvested at the rates of capital cost given, project A would now be preferable for its cash flows could be reinvested much earlier at the increasing rate of interest.

CHAPTER 7

16. Cost of Production = £(15 + 20 + 4 + 6) million
= £45,000,000

17. Cost of Sales =

	£m
Opening Stock	8
Cost of Production	45
	53
Closing Stock	13
	£40m

18. Gross Profit = £60m − £40m = £20,000,000
expressed as (*a*) 50% of cost of sales.
(*b*) $33\frac{1}{3}$% of sales.

19. Net Profit = £5,000,000.

23. BALANCE SHEET OF APRIL LTD ON 31 MARCH 1972

Fixed Assets			£
Freehold Land and Buildings			60,000
Machinery & Equipment			40,000
Motor Vehicles			10,000
Office Equipment			2,000
			112,000
Current Assets less Current Liabilities		£	
Stock-in-trade		15,000	
Trade Debtors		9,000	
		24,000	
Trade Creditors	3,000		
Bank Overdraft	6,000	9,000	
			15,000
			£127,000

Represented by—	
Share Capital	£
100,000 ordinary shares of £1 each authorized & issued	100,000
Profit and Loss Account—profit for year	27,000
	£127,000

24. If £15,000 of the difference between issued capital and net worth had resulted from an appreciation in the value of land and buildings it would be correct to regard only £12,000 (i.e. the remainder) as trading (net) profit.

CHAPTER 8

8. (i)	*December 1971 stock*	*Charged in 1971*
	£	£
FIFO figures	52,000	8,000
LIFO figures	7,000	53,000
	£45,000	£45,000

Income appears to be £45,000 less if LIFO is used unless a cost-plus pricing system is employed and selling prices are correspondingly raised.

(ii) If stocks are priced realistically at "average" or standard prices—

	£
8,000 units charged to production at £20 per unit	160,000
Add: 7,000 units in stock at £25 per unit	175,000
	335,000
Less: Cost of 15,000 units above	60,000
Holding gain on stock during period	£275,000

If selling prices are cost-determined, the additional "cost" of the 8,000 units charged to production (£107,000 more than LIFO and £152,000 more than FIFO) would be added to costs and so would affect the cost-plus determined selling price. If selling prices are market determined, 1971 operating income will appear to fall by these amounts.

9. Accounts converted into December 1971 pounds for comparative purposes.

Balance Sheets	31. 12. 70	31. 12. 71	*Profit and Loss Accounts*	1970	1971
	£	£		£	£
Fixed Assets (net)	50,000	45,000	Sales	96,000	40,000
Stocks	4,000	4,000	Cost of Sales	67,200	31,200
Debtors	5,000	1,000			
Cash	9,000	2,000	Gross Profit	28,800	8,800
	68,000	52,000	Expenses	20,000	5,067
Creditors	18,000	6,000	Depreciation	5,000	5,000
Equity	£50,000	£46,000	Net Profit/loss	£3,800	−£1,267

Notes

Expenses 1970 are $\frac{500}{125} \times$ (£6,000 − £1,000) = £20,000

Expenses 1971 are $\frac{500}{375} \times$ (£4,800 − £1,000) = £5,067

The Balance Sheet at 1 January 1970 is presumed to have been—

	£
Fixed Assets (Plant)	11,000
Less Creditors (for plant?)	1,000
Issued Share Capital	£10,000

CHAPTER 9

4. *Loser Ltd: Traditional Variance Analysis*

	£	£	£
Sales Quantity Variance	8,000		
Sales Price Variance	5,000		
Sales Revenue Variance			3,000
Materials Price Variance	2,500		
Materials Quantity Variance	2,500		
Materials Cost Variance		5,000	
Wage Rate Variance	5,000		
Labour Efficiency Variance	1,000		
Labour Cost Variance		4,000	
Overhead Absorption Variance	1,250		
Overhead Volume Variance	1,500		
	2,750		
Overhead Efficiency Variance	3,750		
Overhead Cost Variance		1,000	
Total Cost Variance			10,000
Profit Variance			−£7,000

5. Fixed Cost = £1,500.
   Variable Cost = £67 per 100 units.

CHAPTER 10

1. Current Ratio = 2:1
   Acid-Test Ratio = 10:55 or 0·18
   Although the working capital position of the company appears to be good its acid-test ratio is poor and it would not be able to pay its commitments in a quick liquidation if its stock were not easily realizable.

2. Freelance Salesman: Balance Sheets

	1 January		31 December	
Fixed Assets		£		£
Warehouse & Fixtures		2,765		2,936
Motor Car		880		660
		3,645		3,596
Current Assets (less liabilities)				
Stocks	432		382	
Trade Debtors	736		867	
Bank Account	79		93	
	1,247		1,342	
Trade Creditors	95		69	
		1,152		1,273
Capital		£4,797		£4,869

Computation of Profit for 1971		£
Capital at 31 December 1971	4,869	
Less Capital at 1 January 1971	4,797	
	72	
Add back drawings during the year	1,632	
	1,704	
Deduct investment during the year	25	
Therefore profit during the year (1971) =	£1,679	

3. The £25 addition can be regarded as immaterial. The profitability can be taken as $\frac{1,679}{4,797} = 35\%$

4. If the opportunity cost of the proprietor's salary is estimated as £2,000 the business has made an effective loss of £321.

   This produces a "loss" ratio of $-\frac{321}{4,797} = -6{\cdot}7\%$

5. If £1,000 had been borrowed at 20 per cent interest there would have been need to provide for £200 interest out of profit leaving £1,479 return on the remaining £3,797.

   This is $\frac{1,479}{3,797} = 39\%$

6. *Statement of sources and disposition of funds*

		£
Net Profit for 1971		1,679
Add back depreciation on motor vehicle		220
		1,899
Deduct drawings		1,632
		267
Capital movements—	£	
Purchase of fixtures	171	
Less capital invested	25	
		146
(*a*) Increase of working capital (£1,273—£1,152)		121
Adjust Increase of debtors	131	
Decrease of creditors	26	
	157	
Decrease of stock	50	
		107
(*b*) Increase of bank balance (£93—£79)		£14

7. (*a*) The conventional ratios cannot be used to assess stock and credit positions because no figure of sales is given, but the reduction of creditors and increase of debtors would normally be regarded as reasonably healthy from a liquidity standpoint.

(*b*) Liquidity is exhibited by—

Current Ratios $\frac{1{,}247}{95}$ (= 13) to $\frac{1{,}342}{69}$ (= 19)

While indicating very favourable liquidity, the ratios may mean that the business is over-liquid. It may pay to realize some of the debtors and invest the money somewhere.

Acid-test ratios $\frac{815}{95}$ (= 8·6) to $\frac{960}{69}$ (= 14).

The same fault is indicated—over-liquidity.

9. Stock turnover ratio is $\frac{3{,}000}{750} = 4$

Chapter 11

3. (*a*) 3,000 units
   (*b*) between 3,000 units and 6,000 units
   (*c*) £6,000
   (*d*) 3,333 units
   (*e*) 2,333 units

7. Decisive Ltd

(*a*) *Annual Cost Computations*

	(*i*) *Current Situation*	(*ii*) *Install New Machinery*	(*iii*) *Close Department*
	£	£	£
Materials/components*	10,000	15,000	40,000
Labour	18,500	8,500	—
Relevant Overheads	8,000	8,000	—
	£36,500	£31,500	£40,000

(*b*) *Present cost comparison*	£	£	£
Present cost of 10% annuity for 5 years of totals (× 3·791)	138,371	119,416	151,640
less relevant present cost of 3,000 finished units in stock (included in * above)	3,000	4,500	12,000
	135,371	114,916	139,640
Add: New Machinery	—	37,000	—
	135,371	151,916	139,640
Less: Scrap Values—			
Machine £1,000; Materials £800	—	1,800	1,800
	£135,371	£150,116	£137,840

Neither of the changes is advisable. The company should continue its present operations.

Chapter 12

4. £8, £18 and £25 respectively.
5. (*a*) The transfer price of the product of division A would now be £10, so transfer prices would be £10, £20 and £27 respectively.
   (*b*) Transfer price of product of division C would be £26 but other prices would remain at £8 and £18 as in 4 (above).

Chapter 13

4. Maximize $2A + 6B + 5C$

subject to

$$\begin{aligned} 4A + 3B + 1C &\leqslant 18{,}000 \\ 1A + 2B + 3C &\leqslant 40{,}000 \\ 100A + 150B + 400C &\leqslant 4{,}000 \\ 3A + 6B + 4C &\leqslant 2{,}500 \\ A, B, C &\geqslant 0 \end{aligned}$$

Chapter 14

1. The relevant rate would be 75 per cent only if the additional £500 income did not carry the tax payer into a higher rate of tax.
2. The pensioner should not cash his local authority loan unless he pays the tax at standard rate.

Chapter 15

1. Company M: 0; Company N: 0·25.

2.

	Company M	*Company N*
Year 1	7½%	NIL
Year 2	75%	270%

3. Company M: 20%; Company N: 13¾%
5. Effectively 8% despite corporation tax
6. (*a*) £18,223; (*b*) £18,223; (*c*) $\sum_{j=}^{4} \frac{7{,}080}{(1{\cdot}12)^j} + \frac{6{,}000}{(1{\cdot}12)^4}$

$= £15{,}180 + £3{,}813 = £18{,}993$

7. (*a*) £50; (*b*) £100.

Chapter 16

1. Standard deviation is £1,120
2. (i) 0·3
   (ii) 0·975
   (iii) 0·2
6. £1,100

Appendix 2

A new cumulative arrangement of compound interest factors

Misuse of compound interest tables is a common cause of error. Annuity tables are often mistaken for sinking fund tables, and single exponential values are sometimes mistaken for cumulative values. The following arrangement helps to avoid uncertainty, for values are presented in pairs, and the reader can easily check whether he is using sinking fund or annuity values by glancing at the next upper or next lower value, and by seeing whether the value is a sub-total of the two previous values in the same column.

Interest rates normally fall between 2½ and 10 per cent, so that this is the most common range of percentages for discounting purposes. In this range each "box" contains a set of four values—

v^n	S_n
a_n	$(1 + r)^n$

But because of inflation effective cost of capital can frequently be as high as 18 per cent, so that in the 11 to 18 per cent range pairs of single and cumulative present value factors are exhibited—

v^n
a_n

The other two values can easily be calculated. Divide $1/v^n$ to find $(1 + r)^n$. To find S_n from $(1 + r)^n$, simply deduct 1 and divide the difference by r.

EXAMPLE

$$
\begin{aligned}
&\text{Find } S_4 \text{ at } 14\% \text{ if } (1{\cdot}14)^4 &&= 1{\cdot}689 \\
&\quad 1{\cdot}689 - 1 &&= 0{\cdot}689 \\
&\quad (0{\cdot}689 \times 100) \div 14 &&= 4{\cdot}92 \\
&\quad S_4 &&= 4{\cdot}92
\end{aligned}
$$

Year	2½%		3%		3½%		4%		5%	
1	0·976 0·976	1·000 1·025	0·971 0·971	1·000 1·030	0·966 0·966	1·000 1·035	0·962 0·962	1·000 1·040	0·952 0·952	1·000 1·050
2	0·952 1·927	2·025 1·051	0·942 1·913	2·030 1·061	0·934 1·900	2·035 1·071	0·925 1·886	2·040 1·082	0·907 1·859	2·050 1·103
3	0·929 2·856	3·076 1·077	0·915 2·829	3·091 1·093	0·902 2·802	3·106 1·109	0·889 2·775	3·122 1·125	0·864 2·723	3·153 1·158
4	0·906 3·762	4·153 1·104	0·888 3·717	4·184 1·126	0·871 3·673	4·215 1·148	0·855 3·630	4·246 1·170	0·823 3·546	4·310 1·216
5	0·884 4·646	5·256 1·131	0·863 4·580	5·309 1·159	0·842 4·515	5·362 1·188	0·822 4·452	5·416 1·217	0·783 4·329	5·526 1·276
6	0·862 5·508	6·388 1·160	0·837 5·417	6·468 1·194	0·814 5·329	6·550 1·230	0·790 5·242	6·633 1·265	0·746 5·076	6·802 1·340
7	0·841 6·349	7·547 1·190	0·813 6·230	7·662 1·230	0·786 6·116	7·779 1·272	0·760 6·002	7·898 1·316	0·711 5·786	8·142 1·407
8	0·821 7·170	8·736 1·218	0·789 7·020	8·892 1·267	0·759 6·874	9·052 1·317	0·731 6·733	9·214 1·369	0·677 6·463	9·549 1·478
9	0·801 7·971	9·955 1·249	0·766 7·786	10·159 1·305	0·734 7·608	10·368 1·363	0·703 7·435	10·583 1·423	0·645 7·108	11·027 1·551
10	0·781 8·752	11·203 1·280	0·744 8·530	11·464 1·344	0·709 8·317	11·731 1·411	0·676 8·111	12·006 1·480	0·614 7·722	12·578 1·629

11	0·762	12·483	0·722	12·808	0·685	13·142	0·650	13·486	0·585	14·207
	9·514	1·312	9·253	1·384	9·002	1·460	8·760	1·540	8·306	1·710
12	0·744	13·796	0·701	14·192	0·662	14·602	0·625	15·026	0·557	15·917
	10·258	1·345	9·954	1·426	9·663	1·511	9·385	1·601	8·863	1·796
13	0·725	15·140	0·681	15·618	0·639	16·113	0·601	16·627	0·530	17·713
	10·983	1·379	10·635	1·469	10·303	1·564	9·986	1·665	9·394	1·886
14	0·708	16·519	0·661	17·086	0·618	17·677	0·578	18·292	0·505	19·599
	11·691	1·413	11·296	1·513	10·921	1·619	10·563	1·732	9·899	1·980
15	0·691	17·932	0·642	18·599	0·597	19·296	0·555	20·024	0·481	21·579
	12·381	1·448	11·938	1·558	11·517	1·675	11·118	1·801	10·380	2·079
16	0·674	19·380	0·623	20·157	0·577	20·971	0·534	21·825	0·458	23·657
	13·055	1·485	12·561	1·605	12·094	1·734	11·652	1·873	10·838	2·183
17	0·657	20·865	0·605	21·762	0·557	22·705	0·513	23·698	0·436	25·840
	13·712	1·522	13·166	1·653	12·651	1·795	12·166	1·948	11·274	2·292
18	0·641	22·386	0·587	23·414	0·538	24·500	0·494	25·645	0·415	28·132
	14·353	1·560	13·754	1·702	13·190	1·858	12·659	2·026	11·690	2·407
19	0·626	23·946	0·570	25·117	0·520	26·357	0·475	27·671	0·396	30·539
	14·979	1·599	14·324	1·754	13·710	1·923	13·134	2·107	12·085	2·527
20	0·610	25·545	0·554	26·870	0·503	28·280	0·456	29·778	0·377	33·066
	15·589	1·639	14·877	1·806	14·212	1·990	13·590	2·191	12·462	2·653

Year	6%		7%		8%		9%		10%	
1	0·943	1·000	0·935	1·000	0·926	1·000	0·917	1·000	0·909	1·000
	0·943	1·060	0·935	1·070	0·926	1·080	0·917	1·090	0·909	1·100
2	0·890	2·060	0·873	2·070	0·857	2·080	0·842	2·090	0·826	2·100
	1·833	1·124	1·808	1·145	1·783	1·166	1·759	1·188	1·736	1·210
3	0·840	3·184	0·816	3·215	0·794	3·246	0·772	3·278	0·751	3·310
	2·673	1·191	2·624	1·225	2·577	1·260	2·531	1·296	2·487	1·331
4	0·792	4·375	0·763	4·440	0·735	4·506	0·708	4·573	0·683	4·641
	3·465	1·263	3·387	1·311	3·312	1·361	3·240	1·412	3·170	1·464
5	0·747	5·637	0·713	5·751	0·681	5·867	0·650	5·985	0·621	6·105
	4·212	1·338	4·100	1·403	3·993	1·470	3·890	1·539	3·791	1·611
6	0·705	6·975	0·666	7·153	0·630	7·336	0·596	7·523	0·564	7·716
	4·917	1·419	4·767	1·501	4·623	1·587	4·486	1·677	4·355	1·772
7	0·665	8·394	0·623	8·654	0·583	8·923	0·547	9·200	0·513	9·487
	5·582	1·504	5·389	1·606	5·206	1·714	5·033	1·828	4·868	1·949
8	0·627	9·897	0·582	10·260	0·540	10·637	0·502	11·028	0·467	11·436
	6·210	1·594	5·971	1·718	5·747	1·851	5·535	1·993	5·335	2·144
9	0·592	11·491	0·544	11·978	0·500	12·488	0·460	13·021	0·424	13·579
	6·802	1·690	6·515	1·839	6·247	1·999	5·995	2·172	5·759	2·358
10	0·558	13·181	0·508	13·816	0·463	14·487	0·422	15·193	0·386	15·937
	7·360	1·791	7·024	1·967	6·710	2·159	6·418	2·367	6·145	2·594

11	0·527 7·887	14·972 1·898	0·475 7·499	15·784 2·105	0·429 7·139	16·645 2·332	0·383 6·805	17·560 2·580	0·350 6·495	18·531 2·853
12	0·497 8·384	16·870 2·012	0·444 7·943	17·888 2·252	0·397 7·536	18·977 2·518	0·356 7·161	20·141 2·813	0·319 6·814	21·384 3·138
13	0·469 8·853	18·882 2·133	0·415 8·358	20·141 2·410	0·368 7·904	21·495 2·720	0·326 7·487	22·953 3·066	0·290 7·103	24·523 3·452
14	0·442 9·295	21·015 2·261	0·388 8·745	22·550 2·579	0·340 8·244	24·215 2·937	0·299 7·786	26·019 3·342	0·263 7·367	27·975 3·798
15	0·417 9·712	23·276 2·397	0·362 9·108	25·129 2·759	0·315 8·559	27·152 3·172	0·275 8·061	29·361 3·642	0·239 7·606	31·772 4·177
16	0·394 10·106	25·673 2·541	0·339 9·447	27·888 2·952	0·292 8·851	30·324 3·426	0·252 8·313	33·003 3·970	0·218 7·824	35·950 4·595
17	0·371 10·477	28·213 2·693	0·317 9·763	30·840 3·159	0·270 9·122	33·750 3·700	0·231 8·544	36·974 4·328	0·198 8·022	40·545 5·055
18	0·350 10·828	30·906 2·854	0·296 10·059	33·999 3·380	0·250 9·372	37·450 3·996	0·212 8·756	41·301 4·717	0·180 8·201	45·599 5·560
19	0·331 11·158	33·760 3·026	0·277 10·336	37·379 3·617	0·232 9·604	41·446 4·316	0·194 8·950	46·018 5·142	0·164 8·365	51·159 6·116
20	0·312 11·470	36·786 3·207	0·258 10·594	40·995 3·870	0·215 9·818	45·762 4·661	0·178 9·129	51·160 5·604	0·149 8·514	57·275 6·728

(Present Value Factors Only)

Year	11%	12%	13%	14%	15%	16%	17%	18%
1	0·901	0·893	0·885	0·877	0·870	0·862	0·855	0·847
	0·901	0·893	0·885	0·877	0·870	0·862	0·855	0·847
2	0·812	0·797	0·783	0·769	0·756	0·743	0·731	0·718
	1·713	1·690	1·668	1·647	1·626	1·605	1·585	1·566
3	0·731	0·712	0·693	0·675	0·658	0·641	0·624	0·609
	2·444	2·402	2·361	2·322	2·283	2·246	2·210	2·174
4	0·659	0·636	0·613	0·592	0·572	0·552	0·534	0·516
	3·102	3·037	2·974	2·914	2·855	2·798	2·743	2·690
5	0·593	0·567	0·543	0·519	0·497	0·476	0·456	0·437
	3·696	3·605	3·517	3·433	3·352	3·274	3·199	3·127
6	0·535	0·507	0·480	0·456	0·432	0·410	0·390	0·370
	4·231	4·111	3·998	3·889	3·784	3·685	3·589	3·498
7	0·482	0·452	0·425	0·400	0·376	0·354	0·333	0·314
	4·712	4·564	4·423	4·288	4·160	4·039	3·922	3·812
8	0·434	0·404	0·376	0·351	0·327	0·305	0·285	0·266
	5·146	4·968	4·799	4·639	4·487	4·344	4·207	4·078
9	0·391	0·361	0·333	0·308	0·284	0·263	0·243	0·225
	5·537	5·328	5·132	4·946	4·772	4·607	4·451	4·303
10	0·352	0·322	0·295	0·270	0·247	0·227	0·208	0·191
	5·889	5·650	5·426	5·216	5·019	4·833	4·659	4·494

11	0·317	0·287	0·261	0·237	0·215	0·195	0·178	0·162
	6·207	5·938	5·687	5·453	5·234	5·029	4·836	4·656
12	0·286	0·257	0·231	0·208	0·187	0·168	0·152	0·137
	6·492	6·194	5·918	5·660	5·421	5·197	4·938	4·793
13	0·253	0·229	0·204	0·182	0·163	0·145	0·130	0·116
	6·750	6·424	6·122	5·842	5·583	5·342	5·118	4·910
14	0·232	0·205	0·181	0·160	0·141	0·125	0·111	0·099
	6·982	6·628	6·302	6·002	5·724	5·468	5·229	5·008
15	0·209	0·183	0·160	0·140	0·123	0·108	0·095	0·084
	7·191	6·811	6·462	6·142	5·847	5·575	5·324	5·092
16	0·188	0·163	0·141	0·123	0·107	0·093	0·081	0·071
	7·379	6·974	6·604	6·265	5·954	5·669	5·405	5·162
17	0·170	0·146	0·125	0·108	0·093	0·080	0·070	0·060
	7·549	7·120	6·729	6·373	6·047	5·749	5·475	5·222
18	0·153	0·130	0·111	0·095	0·081	0·069	0·059	0·051
	7·702	7·250	6·840	6·467	6·128	5·818	5·534	5·273
19	0·138	0·116	0·098	0·083	0·070	0·060	0·051	0·043
	7·839	7·366	6·938	6·550	6·198	5·877	5·584	5·316
20	0·124	0·104	0·087	0·073	0·061	0·051	0·043	0·037
	7·963	7·469	7·025	6·623	6·259	5·929	5·628	5·353

Bibliography

R. Ackoff, *A Concept of Corporate Planning* (Wiley, 1970)

M. Alexis and C. Z. Wilson (eds.), *Organizational Decision Making* (Prentice-Hall, 1967) (particularly articles by C. T. Horngren, A. C. Stedry, H. A. Simon and H. I. Ansoff)

L. R. Amey, *The Efficiency of Business Enterprises* (Allen & Unwin, 1969)

H. I. Ansoff, *Corporate Strategy* (McGraw-Hill, 1965)

H. I. Ansoff (ed.), *Business Strategy* (Penguin, 1969)

H. R. Anton and P. A. Firmin, *Contemporary Issues in Cost Accountancy* (Houghton, 1966)

S. H. Archer and C. A. D'Ambrosio (eds.), *The Theory of Business Finance* (Macmillan, 1967) (all articles, but particularly the Modigliani–Miller debate and Markowitz article)

K. J. Arrow, "Optimization, Decentralization and Internal Pricing in Business Firms", *Contributions to Scientific Management*, Stanford, 1955

J. Batty (ed.), *Developments in Management Accountancy* (Heinemann/ICMA, 1968)

W. J. Baumol, *Economic Theory and Operations Analysis* (Prentice-Hall, 1965)

W. T. Baxter, *Depreciation* (Sweet & Maxwell, 1971)

W. T. Baxter and S. Davidson (eds.), *Studies in Accounting Theory* (Sweet & Maxwell, 1962)

H. Bierman, *Financial and Managerial Accounting* (Collier-Macmillan, 1963)

H. Bierman, *Financial Accounting Theory* (Collier-Macmillan, 1965)

H. Bierman, *Topics in Cost Accounting and Decisions* (McGraw-Hill, 1963)

H. Bierman and A. R. Drebin, *Managerial Accounting: An Introduction* (Collier-Macmillan, 1968)

H. Bierman and S. Smidt, *The Capital Budgeting Decision* (Collier-Macmillan, 1968)

C. P. Bonini (ed.), *Management Controls: New Directions in Basic Research* (McGraw-Hill, 1964) (particularly articles by K. J. Arrow, C. P. Bonini, M. J. Gordon and G. Shillinglaw)

M. Bromwich, "Standard Costing for Planning and Control", *Accountant*, April/May, 1969

W. J. Bruns and D. T. DeCoster, *Accounting and Its Behavioural Implications* (McGraw-Hill, 1969)

R. J. Bull, *Accounting in Business* (Butterworths, 1969)

B. V. Carsberg, *An Introduction to Mathematical Programming for Accountants* (Allen & Unwin, 1969)

B. V. Carsberg, "On the Linear Programming Approach to Asset Valuation", *Journal of Accounting Research*, 1969

B. V. Carsberg and H. C. Edey (eds.), *Modern Financial Management* (Penguin, 1969)
G. P. E. Clarkson (ed.), *Managerial Economics* (Penguin, 1969)
R. M. Cyert and J. G. March, *A Behavioral Theory of the Firm* (Prentice-Hall, 1963)
S. Davidson (ed.), *An Income Approach to Accounting Theory* (Prentice-Hall, 1964)
J. Dean, *Managerial Economics* (Prentice-Hall, 1951)
J. Dearden, "New System for Divisional Control", *Harvard Business Review*, 1966
H. Demski (*see under* D. Solomons (ed.))
H. C. Edey, *Business Budgets and Accounts* (Hutchinson, 1959)
H. C. Edey, *Introduction to Accounting* (Hutchinson, 1963)
E. O. Edwards and P. W. Bell, *The Theory and Measurement of Business Income* (California U. P., Cambridge U. P., 1961)
F. E. Emery (ed.), *Systems Thinking* (Penguin, 1969)
D. W. Ewing, *The Practice of Planning* (Harper & Row, 1968)
D. W. Ewing (ed.), *Long Range Planning for Management* (Harper & Row, 1964)
I. Fisher, *The Theory of Interest* (New York, 1930)
J. W. Forrester, *Industrial Dynamics* (M. I. T. Press, 1965) (for an exposition of simulation model building)
J. E. Freund and F. J. Williams, *Modern Business Statistics* (Pitman, 1970)
D. Garbutt, *A Simple Introduction to Capital Expenditure Decisions* (Pitman, 1967)
M. J. Gordon, *The Investment, Financing and Valuation of the Corporation* (Homewood: Irwin, 1962)
A. J. Grant, *Accounting Made Simple* (W. H. Allen, 1970)
R. W. Gynther, *Accounting for Price-level Changes—Theory and Procedures* (Pergamon, 1966)
E. S. Hendriksen, *Accounting Theory* (Homewood: Irwin, 1965)
J. R. Hicks, *Value and Capital* (Clarendon Press, 1962)
C. T. Horngren, *Cost Accounting: A Managerial Emphasis* (Prentice-Hall, 1967)
Y. Ijiri, *The Foundations of Accounting Measurement* (Prentice-Hall, 1967)
Y. Ijiri, *Management Goals and Accounting for Control* (North Holland, 1965)
R. K. Jaedicke and R. T. Sprouse, *Accounting Flows: Income, Funds and Cash* (Prentice-Hall, 1965)
J. Johnson, *Statistical Cost Analysis* (McGraw-Hill, 1960)
R. A. Johnson *et al.*, *The Theory and Management of Systems* (McGraw-Hill, 1963)
E. R. Jones, *Finance for the Non-Financial Manager* (Pitman, 1972)
J. G. Kemeny *et al.*, *Finite Mathematics with Business Applications* (Prentice-Hall, 1962)
F. P. Langley, *Introduction to Accounting for Business Studies* (Butterworths, 1970)
J. H. Lorie and L. J. Savage, "Three Problems in Capital Rationing", *Journal of Business*, Vol. 28, 1955
F. Lutz and V. Lutz, *The Theory of Investment of the Firm* (O. U. P., 1951)
R. N. McKean, *Efficiency in Government through Systems Analysis* (New York: Wiley; London: Chapman & Hall, 1958)

J. G. March and H. A. Simon, *Organizations* (New York: Wiley; London: Chapman & Hall, 1958)
H. Markowitz (*see under* S. Archer and C. A. D'Ambrosio (eds.))
A. J. Merrett and A. Sykes, *Capital Budgeting and Company Finance* (Longmans, 1966)
F. Modigliani and M. Miller (*see under* S. Archer and C. A. D'Ambrosio (eds.))
C. Moore and R. K. Jaedicke, *Managerial Accounting* (Cincinnati: S. W. Publishing, 1963; London: Edward Arnold, 1965)
A. R. Oxenfeldt, *Industrial Pricing and Market Practices* (Prentice-Hall, 1951)
F. W. Paish, *Benham's Economics* (Pitman, 1967)
F. W. Paish, *Business Finance* (Pitman, 1968)
J. T. S. Porterfield, *Investment Decisions and Capital Costs* (Prentice-Hall, 1965)
C. D. Querin, *The Capital Expenditure Decision* (Homewood: Irwin)
D. D. Ray, *Accounting and Business Fluctuations* (University of Florida Press, 1960)
A. A. Robichek (ed.), *Financial Research and Management Decisions* (Prentice-Hall, 1965)
A. A. Robichek and S. C. Myers, *Optimal Financing Decisions* (Prentice-Hall, 1965)
H. Ross, *Financial Statements: A Crusade for Current Values* (Pitman, 1969)
P. A. Samuelson, *The Foundations of Economic Analysis* (O. U. P., 1947)
R. Sidebotham, *Introduction to the Theory and Context of Accounting* (Pergamon, 1966)
H. A. Simon, *The New Science of Management Decision* (New York: Harper, 1960; London: Hamish Hamilton, 1961)
J. Sizer, *An Insight into Management Accounting* (Penguin, 1970)
E. Solomon, "The Arithmetic of Capital Budgeting Decisions", *Journal of Business*, Vol. 29, 1956
E. Solomon, *The Management of Corporate Capital* (Collier-Macmillan, 1959)
E. Solomon, *The Theory of Financial Management* (Columbia U. P., 1963)
D. Solomons, *Divisional Performance Measurement and Control* (Homewood: Irwin, 1965)
D. Solomons (ed.), *Studies in Cost Analysis* (Sweet & Maxwell, 1968) (particularly for article by Demski mentioned in the text)
G. J. Stigler, *The Theory of Price* (Macmillan, 1952)
H. Thomas, *Decision Theory and the Manager* (Pitman, 1972)
S. A. Tucker, *Successful Managerial Control by Ratio-Analysis* (McGraw-Hill, 1961)
S. Vajda (ed.), *Readings in Linear Programming* (Pitman, 1958)
H. M. Weingartner, *Mathematical Programming and the Analysis of Capital Budgeting Problems* (Prentice-Hall, 1963)
J. F. Weston, *The Scope and Methodology of Finance* (Prentice-Hall, 1966)
J. F. Weston and E. F. Brigham, *Essentials of Managerial Finance* (Holt, Rinehart & Winston, 1968)

Index